Resurrecting the Death of God

Resurrecting the

Death
of God

THE ORIGINS, INFLUENCE, AND RETURN
OF RADICAL THEOLOGY

edited by

DANIEL J. PETERSON
and G. MICHAEL ZBARASCHUK

with an afterword by Thomas J. J. Altizer

Published by
STATE UNIVERSITY OF NEW YORK PRESS
Albany

© 2014 State University of New York

For information, contact
State University of New York Press
www.sunypress.edu

Production, Laurie Searl
Marketing, Michael Campochiaro

Library of Congress Cataloging-in-Publication Data

Resurrecting the death of God: the origins, influence, and
   return of radical theology / edited by Daniel J. Peterson and
   G. Michael Zbaraschuk ; afterword by Thomas J. J. Altizer.
      pages cm.
   Includes bibliographical references and index.
   ISBN 978-1-4384-5045-2 (hc : alk. paper) 978-1-4384-5046-9 (pb : alk. paper)
   1. Death of God theology.   I. Peterson, Daniel J., 1972–, editor of
compilation.
   BT83.5.R47 2014
   230'.046—dc23   2013017502

10 9 8 7 6 5 4 3 2 1

And so I ask God to rid me of God.

— Meister Eckhart

Contents

Editors' Acknowledgments

The desire to "resurrect" death of God theology began as a conversation between the editors of this volume in a coffeehouse on the edge of Pacific Lutheran University in Tacoma, Washington, where they were, at the time, colleagues in the Department of Religion. Books lined the walls of the coffeehouse, including some that were donated by retired professors of the university. One of those books was *Radical Theology and the Death of God*, published in 1966 by William Hamilton and Thomas J. J. Altizer, which one of the editors picked up on a whim and read. This text contributed greatly to the theological controversy over God's death that briefly swept the nation in the middle of the 1960s thanks, in large part, to *Time* magazine. Upon discussing *Radical Theology and the Death of God* it became evident to both editors that the topic, though theologians and philosophers were still discussing it "underground," had to be raised up for broader consideration.

Since then, great effort has gone into the production of this volume. We, the editors, would like to thank the following accordingly: first, all of our contributing authors for their historical perspective (in the case of our incredibly generous and encouraging veteran scholars who looked back to the origins of radical theology and assessed its significance) as well as their innovative efforts to take radical theology in new directions (as evident in our contributors more recent to the conversation). We are especially grateful to Thomas J. J. Altizer, who not only contributed to the volume by writing its afterword but also provided invaluable suggestions with regard to the volume's content.

Beyond those who contributed to the volume directly, we would like to thank Patricia Killen, formerly of Pacific Lutheran University, for her critical suggestions at the outset of this project as well as Catherine Keller of Drew University for her referrals with regard to potential contributors to our collection. We are also grateful for the encouragement we have received from our colleagues at our respective academic institutions (Pacific Lutheran University and Seattle University/Matteo Ricci College) as well as the various Lutheran congregations in the Seattle-Tacoma, who entertained presentations by the editors (Daniel Peterson in particular) on reconsidering radical theology as an option for contemporary faith, especially Hope Lutheran Church and Pastor Dan Wilson of Enumclaw along with Agnus Dei Lutheran Church and member Donald Heinz of Gig Harbor.

A word of gratitude, finally, goes to the State University of New York Press and senior acquisitions editor Nancy Ellegate for giving us the opportunity to make this volume available. We would also like to thank our families for their support throughout this process, especially (for Michael Zbaraschuk) Lisa, Ana, and Elizabeth Zbaraschuk and (for Daniel Peterson) his parents, Jim and Olga Peterson, and brother, Brian Peterson.

Resurrecting the Death of God

DANIEL J. PETERSON

> Now that it has been agreed that the first American coming of the
> death of God in [the twentieth] century was either a media event or
> a mildly useful emetic, it is now time—in these apocalyptic days—to
> examine [its] second coming.
>
> —William Hamilton, *Reading Moby-Dick and Other Essays*

Nineteen sixty-six was a difficult year for God. A small group of young
theologians, Thomas Altizer and William Hamilton prominent among them,
had arrived at a conclusion about God's existence that would incite enormous
controversy across America. God was dead, they told John Elson of *Time*
magazine, and in scorching red letters cast across the dark cover of what
would become one of its best-selling issues, *Time* shared the prospect with the
country.[1] The response was fierce. Altizer received death threats and nearly
lost his position at Emory University. Hamilton was less fortunate. Colgate
Rochester Divinity School mysteriously "removed" his chair of theology.[2]
Other theologians, perhaps afraid of the backlash, denied their affiliation
with the "movement" that Altizer and Hamilton had spearheaded. By the
end of the decade, both theologians found themselves teaching not only at
other universities but also in a different field entirely. The controversy they
started was apparently over. The death of God was dead.

Many commentators have no doubt characterized the death of God
or radical theology as little more than a creation of the media, a fad of its
time, or a blip on the radar screen of twentieth-century theology.[3] In 1969,
only three years after the uproar began, *Time* magazine was already asking,

"Whatever became of the death of God?" Some, including the theologian Langdon Gilkey, acknowledged that as a "catch phrase" the phenomenon had come and gone even though its constructive value had lasting implications. Others more hostile to the idea of God's death, or *theothanatology*, were quick, as Doris Donnelly reported, "to dismiss the movement as both irreverent and irrelevant."[4] By 1976, just ten years after *Time* had brought radical theology to the nation's attention, one journalist for the *Richmond Times Dispatch* concluded that "for millions of Americans in the pews, God never died."[5] Most people were still attending church. Conservative Christianity, the reporter added, was actually experiencing a revival. Today this way of reading death of God theology and its impact continues: "God is back!" we hear. The secularization thesis was wrong. The news of "God's demise was premature."[6] Reports of the Almighty's death, various keepers of the American sanctuary insist, have been grossly exaggerated.

Careful observers of contemporary culture would have to concur: the first decade of the new millennium was witness to an almost unprecedented resurgence of religion, at least in its fundamentalist forms.[7] Megachurches thrive. Christian radio bombards America with preaching that calls for the "personal acceptance" of Jesus Christ, and popular ministers ranging from Joel Osteen to Rick Warren reach millions of people through television, the internet, and other forms of media. Even the appearance of the new atheism and with it a plea to reject faith in the name of reason presupposes the ubiquity of belief. To say, then, that "religion is making a comeback" as the *New York Times* did in 1997, would now be passé.[8] Religion at the dawn of the third millennium has arrived, and it is big business. As John Micklethwait and Adrian Wooldridge confirm, "The world of megachurches, 'pastorpreneurs,' and house churches is booming at home and abroad."[9]

Of course, the success of "pastorpreneurs" and house churches, much less the noisy gong and clanging cymbal of the modern megachurch, tells us nothing about the existence or nonexistence of God. What it does illustrate is that sociocultural circumstances have changed significantly in the span of merely four or five decades. Today the death of God is no longer the "cultural fact" it ostensibly was for some Americans just after the middle of the twentieth century. Times are different. Western evangelical faith in God, the kind that sanctions preemptive war and American nationalism, the kind that Hamilton foresaw as "too male, too dangerous, [and] too violent to be allowed to live," has become the norm in our churches, in our military, and among our politicians.[10] Radical theology, were it to speak to our situation, would accordingly do so not by confirming the widespread loss of faith in a secular society that has "come of age." Instead, it would challenge a culture that now largely sees itself as religious. Against the grain of popular American piety, it would shift from pronouncing the death of God in terms of unbelief to putting a spoke in the wheel of belief itself. Its task, in short, would be deicide—its vocation, the murder of God.

The question is whether the return of religion demands the return of radical theology. We, the editors of the present volume, believe it does. Fundamentalist religion—particularly in its now-dominant evangelical Christian form—has become a destructive and alienating force in our culture, one that sanctifies "the unjust power of oppressors,"[11] validates amassing personal wealth at the expense of others, and more than ever presents a "providential God incompatible with scientific explanation."[12] Radical theology may have been crucified and abandoned by popular culture shortly after its inception, but its return today is absolutely imperative. With great necessity and prophetic urgency, therefore, we declare the need to speak against a culture of misguided faith by resurrecting the death of God for public reconsideration. We invite the reader—religious or otherwise—to contemplate an updated and revised version of radical theology for our time, one that *actively seeks* to eradicate the gods of fundamentalist Christianity insofar as they threaten our civil liberties, our capacity to think critically, the progress of science, and finally the democratic principles that inform our government itself. Behind this new version of theothanatology lies a single conviction: if silence or indifference is no longer an option, then perhaps the best alternative is nothing less than a *radical* one.

Radical Theology Never Died

One can easily imagine a first response to resurrecting the death of God: radical theology never died. Altizer's work, for example, would reach its creative and most groundbreaking expression nearly ten years after the fad he helped inspire had vanished from the scene.[13] His retrieval of a fully Hegelian Christianity, one in which God the Father empties Himself (Greek, *kénōsis*) and dies by becoming incarnate in Christ followed "by Christ's complete and irreversible self-emptying into the Holy Spirit, conceived as the bond of the religious community," would directly influence the postmodern thought of Mark C. Taylor and, more recently, the political philosophy of Slavoj Žižek.[14] Hamilton likewise continued to proclaim the death of God long after the media lost interest. By 1989 he already knew that "the frightening silence of God" identified two decades prior was being replaced by "the more frightening danger of God—not silent or dead at all, but very much alive, murderous and needing to be killed."[15] The emphasis may have changed, but Hamilton persevered. God's death occupied him with a quiet passion long after the "movement" he helped initiate had evaporated.

Is there any truth, then, in the claim that radical theology was a "theology of the month" that disappeared as quickly as it came? The answer is yes and no: Gilkey was indeed correct to note the existence of two radical theologies. The first was the sensation created by the media. In this form radical theology "fizzled only after a few years in the limelight," reflecting perhaps what Nathan Schneider of *The Guardian* (October 4, 2009) has called a "last gasp of the liberal Protestant theology that was quickly losing ground in American culture and politics to a more literalistic evangelical tide." The version that prompted Altizer and Hamilton to continue, however, did not die and go under like the one created by the media—it went *underground*. There, as Lloyd Steffen wrote in 1989, "death of God theology has not disappeared at all; it has simply been transformed. It has entered, or is in the process of entering, mainstream theology."[16] Radical theology's burial, in short, was not the last word; it would rise again sporadically in new and surprising ways even though *a full and more sustained recovery has not yet occurred*.

Finding glimmers of radical theology's occasional reappearance or detecting tremors of what Hamilton called its second coming can be difficult. Close inspection nonetheless reveals traces of its activity along two primary fault lines or trajectories over the past few decades. The first trajectory is implicit. Theologians in this line appear indifferent to questions concerning the reality of God. For them, talk about God serves a pragmatic purpose, one that provides a means for producing a desired effect typically in sociopolitical terms. This, the Hamiltonian trajectory of theothanatology, tacitly informs any "metaphorical theology" that accepts the position that language for God does not actually correspond or point to divine reality; instead, the importance of theology lies entirely in its *function* to inform certain practices or behaviors and not in its alleged capacity to describe the nature or existence of God.

The second trajectory is more explicit. Its point of departure is the work of Altizer, and its initial resurgence appeared in the deconstructive "hermeneutics of the death of God" initiated by Taylor in *Deconstructing Theology* (1982) and then *Erring* (1984). Since then, several other major thinkers have criticized, appropriated, and transformed the Altizerian form of kenotic death of God theology, making the label of "deconstruction" too restrictive. In fact, as Cyril O'Regan observes, kenosis as either a story or an event that occasions the death and sometimes "self-saving" of God has been "refigured" three times since Altizer: first by Taylor and then by Gianni Vattimo and Žižek.[17] Obviously the Altizerian form of radical theology with its emphasis on the death of God in Christ differs greatly from its Hamiltonian sibling. Their founding conviction nevertheless remains the same: we must "clear aside" the God of conventional theism. *That* God is dead.

Tracing the Two Trajectories

Paul Tillich, an early influence on both Altizer and Hamilton, provides the most famous modern example of "clearing aside" the God of ordinary theism in *The Courage to Be*, published in 1952.[18] Ordinary or objectified theism, he says, conceives of God as a being or object "out there" who is subject by implication to the broader structures and polarities of reality. This God is not God. The true God transcends the greater totality of space and time; "he" is not merely a being among beings but the depth, foundation, and power of being-itself. This means, in the language of Søren Kierkegaard, that God is the power that continuously generates or "establishes" each human being along with all other finite realities. Everything that exists derives its being from the power of being, that is, by participating in being-itself as its ground and source. Tillich calls God understood as the power of being or being-itself the "God beyond God" who appears after the God of ordinary/conventional theism has fallen away. In this respect, though critical of the radical theology that emerged toward the end of his lifetime, Tillich anticipated the movement by pronouncing the death of a *misconception* of God even though a more plausible conception of God (as being-itself) remains.

Many today would challenge Tillich's "ontotheological" understanding of God. His primary legacy, however, lies not in the content of his theology but in the transition he invokes and endorses from God to the God beyond God.[19] While early admirers of Tillich's theology would, as in the case of Bishop John Robinson, simply reiterate his move from God to the God above God in more accessible terms, others would accept the transition and then depart from it significantly. Hamilton is the best example. Once we have cleared away the God of ordinary theism, he says, we must acknowledge and live with the void left in God's place. Robinson may therefore be "perfectly right to reject objectified theism," Hamilton argues in 1966, "but he is wrong to think that his non-objectified theism is any more satisfactory."[20] The God above God, in other words, is not being-itself. The God above God is dead, and there is nothing we can substitute in God's absence.

What happens, then, when the God above God about whom Tillich spoke fails to appear? Does it truly mean that God is dead, and if so what are we to do? How should we respond? Hamilton suggests two possibilities. The first is to wait. Perhaps new forms of discourse for God will emerge after we take "God" out of the dictionary. The second option is more radical: we follow Jesus! When Jesus speaks, for example, of casting fire upon the earth (Luke 12: 49), Hamilton explains that "[w]e are to *be* this fire, to bring warmth and comfort where needed, to bring light to someone's darkness, beauty to ugliness, justice and healing to injustice and suffering."[21] Talk about God is useless, but Jesus can still be the way, a "model for radical living" or a "place to be." He becomes, as R. C. Sproul explains Hamilton's view, "a kind of symbol for authentic action."[22] Following Jesus *without* God for the sake of justice and love in the world is ultimately what matters. This way of being, one that finds as its inspiration the later writings of Dietrich Bonhoeffer, is the ethic of Hamiltonian Christian atheism.

Few theologians since Hamilton have spoken explicitly of Christian discipleship without God.[23] A significant number, however, have at least moved in the same direction.[24] One way this becomes evident occurs when theologians refrain from using realist language for God, insisting that when a person talks about God, she or he is not truly referring to any sort of reality outside of a mental or cultural construction. The work of Sallie McFague provides a perfect example. She utilizes nonrealist God-language exclusively for the sake of addressing practical problems like environmental degradation. Statements such as "the kind of theology advanced here is what I call metaphorical or heuristic theology, that is, it experiments with metaphors and models, and the claims it makes are small" illustrate her nonrealist orientation. Indeed, when McFague observes that "what can be said with certainty about the Christian faith is very little" and that "theology, at any rate my theology . . . is mostly fiction," she confirms the Hamiltonian death of God. The focus of theology, she implies, needs to be on finding models for God that improve the world,—not on pointless speculation about the metaphysical reality that supposedly grounds or establishes it.

Like Hamilton and McFague, Altizer also makes the world his focus even though he does so with a vastly different conviction in mind. For him, the world is a stage, not for the Bard's "poor player" who "struts and frets his hour" but for what Altizer depicts as the ongoing self-annihilation of God brought about by divine kenosis or sacrifice.[26] The sacrifice occurs when God, taken by Altizer to mean otherworldly transcendence or "every preincarnate form of Spirit," negates itself as entirely different from the world to become manifest in, through, and as world history.[27] This "metamorphosis" of God from one mode of being to another informs what Altizer has called the gospel of Christian atheism: the death or self-emptying of God in Christ and creation frees us from God understood as "a Father and Judge infinitely distant from the world" to live fully *in* the here and now.[28] The incarnation and crucifixion accordingly reenact and illustrate a "transition within God by which the transcendent God became immanent," one where "the God-above-us had to die in order to become the God-with-us."[29]

Altizer's version of theothanatology has a rich conceptual history that reaches back through Hegel, Milton, Boehme, and Blake to Martin Luther, who claimed in 1520 that God became human in Christ to fulfill the testament that God would one day die.[30] Over the past forty-five years Altizer has refined his thought considerably, moving from his early proclamation of the gospel of Christian atheism to a comprehensive treatment of the Divine Spirit's forward-moving descent into "the full actuality of the body of the world," one that "enacts genesis, exodus, judgment, incarnation, and apocalypse as an integral series of self-embodying transfigurations of the Godhead itself."[31] Here "Godhead" refers to a cumulative process or unfolding of divine being *in time* rather than a motionless divine entity that hovers *above time*. At the beginning of the cosmos as well as each moment thereafter the preactualized abundance of undifferentiated being (God or Being-Itself) empties and depletes itself sacrificially to bring forth the actual being of the world. This amounts to a "death" or outpouring of divine being for the sake of our existence, an existence into which divine reality then submerges itself through the process (as noted) of a dialectical unfolding.

Perhaps the most astounding feature of Altizer's work has appeared in his more recent reflections on a major implication of God's self-annihilation and subsequent descent into flesh. In *Godhead and the Nothing* (2003), the radical theologian addresses a problem especially acute for those who believe in God: "If there is a God, from where does the nothingness and death that is the annihilating ground of our infinite universe and our fleeting human life come?"[32] To answer this question, Altizer begins by observing that since the Middle Ages Western literary figures, philosophers, and theologians have become increasingly conscious of the abyss of nothingness and death that pervades and mercilessly swallows up human existence. By the nineteenth century Nietzsche stared into this abyss and boldly proclaimed the death of God—a death that signaled the absence of meaning in life. Like Nietzsche, many in the twentieth and now twenty-first centuries have become aware at some level of the "consuming Nihil that is the grim reaper of everything,"[33] a dark void that makes us mute (like Job) when we finally acknowledge and confront its inevitability and with it the horror of our own inexplicable end.

Where, then, does this void originate and what is its nature? Not surprisingly, orthodox theologians have refused to grant the "consuming Nihil" about which Altizer speaks any reality of its own. For them, death, nonbeing, and evil constitute a privation or absence of the good lacking any substance or self-sufficiency; were evil to exist then it would condition God (assuming God is good) and God would not be "all in all." Altizer offers an alternative explanation: the forward-moving descent of the Divine Spirit into flesh gradually generates its own antitype, a "fallen Godhead" or Nothing (*Nihil*) that is the cause or "ground" of the pervasive nihilism we experience in our world today. The *Nihil* or void (i.e., that reality that consumes being and life) is, in other words, a part of divine reality! It is an aspect of the Godhead we encounter when we experience meaninglessness, death, and destruction. The erosion of meaning in our lives, the vacuity of contemporary consumerist culture, the terror of death, or the dark abyss beneath our precarious existence that Kierkegaard once described as seventy thousand fathoms deep are *all ways of encountering the negative pole of the Godhead generated by God's initial self-annihilation.*

Altizer's controversial claim regarding darkness as part of the Godhead (versus a separate reality inimical to God or entirely unreal) brings with it an enormous responsibility: we are to name the terror of the abysmal Godhead instead of avoiding it. Naming the darkness—as with naming a condition of poor health or identifying a disease—leads potentially to its resolution or transfiguration. Hope in the metamorphosis of divine darkness into divine light accordingly constitutes the basis of a truly radical, apocalyptic faith. Here "apocalyptic" refers to an absolutely new and salvific reality in history, one in our case that has evil or the darkness of the Godhead as its precondition.[34] Having named the darkness of God, we look forward with apocalyptic joy to a new revelation or self-disclosure of the divine, one where the light of day (i.e., a new epiphany of the Godhead) breaks the darkness of God that has enveloped our world. This shows that the fate of divine reality and the world go together: the redemption of the "fallen Godhead" has implications not just for itself but also for us. The "self-saving of God" and the healing of life (if not our planet) are inextricable.

Contrary to radical faith or genuine apocalyptic hope, Altizer sees "bad faith" as a desperate reaction against the pervasive nihilism that shrouds our contemporary experience. Instead of looking forward to a new disclosure of God *in the world* out of absolute nothingness, "bad faith" (as evident in Christian fundamentalism) denies the sacrificial self-emptying of God by focusing on what is now a shattered or vacated transcendence—just as orthodox Christianity has done over the course of nearly two thousand years. Unable to face the terrifying abyss of the Godhead, fundamentalist Christians avert their eyes out of fear and look up to an imaginary God in a heaven of their own making. Unfortunately, says Altizer, that heaven is empty: the God who resides there (the immutable, sovereign God of traditional theism) no longer exists. Here we can see that while Hamilton provides us with an example of what it means to fight fundamentalism from a radical Christian perspective, Altizer gives us a framework for understanding it.

Altizer, of course, does more than explain the origin of fundamentalism along with what he has more recently identified as "our new conservative political world or worlds." He also provides a constructive alternative in two ways: first, we can celebrate with him the self-annihilation of God as an event that liberates us from an alien or heavenly "other" to live completely in the world. Secondly, we can share with him in the hope of a new disclosure of the Godhead to appear out of the present abyss, darkness, or pervasive nihilism so evident in our time. Both of these possibilities illustrate that the death of God is not an occasion for sadness or despair but a release from bondage to an otherworldly transcendence as well as a profound hope in and for the future of our world. Obviously, the depth and complexity of Altizer's vision may overwhelm any newcomer to his description of radical faith and hope; divine kenosis nevertheless remains the linchpin of all his work. Whenever we find hints or talk of kenosis in conjunction with the death of God we have in our proximity the Altizerian trajectory of radical theology, the earliest retrieval of which appears in the work of Mark C. Taylor.

Taylor's appropriation and critique of Altizer's perspective as a "metaphysics of presence" have long been a topic of theological conversation and need not concern us in the present discussion. His mature work, by contrast, merits brief attention. In *After God* Taylor follows Altizer by emphasizing the importance of temporal reality and the immanence of divine presence: God subsists not in metaphysical skies above being and time but *down here* "in" emergent networks of creativity as "the network of networks," one that provides the condition for the possibility of "life to take shape" while remaining open to future possibilities of being.[35] These networks illustrate, as Jeffrey Robbins observes, that "after the death of God a world of stable meaning and fixed structures has given way to radical indeterminacy and fluidity."[36] This indeterminacy is precisely where Taylor locates the divine, totally incarnate in the flux and flow of time, giving life on earth infinite worth and value.[37]

Where, then, does kenosis appear in Taylor's *After God?* The answer is "nowhere," at least directly. Instead, it informs the entire discussion as the "controlling event." This "controlling event," as Caputo explains, "derives from the death of God story . . . where the Wholly Other empties himself into the world and resurfaces in the Spirit."[38] The Spirit, in turn, "takes the form of our informational network culture," which places the onus for its detection on the perceptive theologian of culture who "sees" the divine hidden in the midst of the ostensibly secular or, to use more traditional terminology, who finds God in the midst of what appears to be godlessness. The transition from the otherworldly to the immanent confirms Taylor's debt to radical theology. He focuses entirely on the presence of what he calls the "divine milieu" within the secular. The secular may now be a postmodern flurry of networks and God may now be the "network of networks," but the shift is all the same. "God-above-us" has become "God-with-us." The divine Spirit is fully present in the "eternal restlessness of becoming," granting form to ever-changing constellations of being as a configuration wholly within the temporal process. Nothing lies beyond our world.

Like Taylor, Gianni Vattimo also employs and refigures kenosis. The difference is that he does so ultimately for pragmatic reasons: the self-emptying of God through the incarnation becomes a "model" for affirming secularization, one that encourages the Christian to *empty herself* of absolutist truth claims for the sake of charitable or loving coexistence with others. "In kenotic Christianity," as Thomas Guarino explains, "religion finds its actual vocation, the weakening of strong metaphysical claims in service to the greater flourishing of [postmodern] interpretation."[39] The death of "God-above-us" by way of kenosis provides the basis, in other words, for denying all metaphysically robust or ontotheological talk about God as the cause of being, the source of being, the ground of being, or the absolute structure of being. Practically speaking, a strong claim in the metaphysical sense is problematic because it suffocates multiple voices in the name of a singular, hegemonic perspective. Weak thought, the alternative Vattimo suggests, empties itself of the absolutist view and selflessly affirms "the other" based upon the Christian practice of love or *caritas*.

Vattimo's recovery of kenosis illustrates a second tremor along the Altizerian trajectory of radical theology but with a Hamiltonian twist. By avoiding any realist language for God and interpreting God's relinquishment of power in Christ as a model for how Christians should follow suit in the company of others who hold alternative points of view, the self-emptying of God serves the exclusive purpose of endorsing as well as explaining the arrival of secularization in the West. It is a story, not an "objective" event or referential truth. This means that Vattimo finally *empties kenosis itself* of its metaphysical content: there was no actual moment in time where God emptied Godself in Christ. Nevertheless, since the death of God through the incarnation is real as an idea influential *on* history (even though it never happened *in* history) we can draw upon it to serve the practical purpose of promoting postmodern secularization. Here the Altizerian and Hamiltonian trajectories converge. Kenosis has pragmatic value, but its content—as McFague would say—is "mostly [if not entirely] fiction." God-above-us *and* God-among-us are effectively dead. Only interpretation and *caritas* remain.

Beyond the Trajectories

Up to this point we have seen evidence for two basic and sometimes intertwining trajectories along which tremors of radical theology have occurred—refigured and transformed—since the "death of the death of God" in the late sixties. Now a new question appears before us: what would it be like to imagine and construct a more sustained and comprehensive retrieval of radical theology, heralding its resurrection or second coming both for the present and the future? What direction(s) would it take beyond the perspectives already surveyed? How might it understand and incorporate the Altizerian and Hamiltonian trajectories as well as other tributaries from the early movement, including the work of Richard Rubenstein, Paul van Buren, or Gabriel Vahanian? What, finally, would it offer as an explanation of our moment in history and how could it challenge the fundamentalisms of a new millennium that present a God "very much alive" who, again to cite Hamilton, is at the same time "murderous and needing to be killed"?

The essays in the following collection explore and respond to questions about radical theology, its origins, its contemporary influence, and its possible second coming. They are divided into two sections. The first section aims at introducing radical theology to a new generation of readers largely unfamiliar with its claims. Rosemary Radford Ruether begins the discussion. After summarizing and situating the work of the most significant radical theologians of the sixties, she identifies the relevance of their thought for the liberation and feminist forms of theology that arose thereafter, including her own. What emerges is an important distinction: feminist theology, she says, "does not declare that all ideas of the divine are 'dead' but rather seeks to define a more just and life-giving understanding of divinity." The *spirit* of radical theology may have inspired a generation of feminist theologians, in other words, but most have not adhered to the *letter*. With Hamilton especially they denounce the "idols of death" even though they still affirm a God(dess) beyond the patriarchal God.

After Ruether, John Roth helps readers new to death of God theology by contextualizing it as an "aftereffect and aftershock" of the Holocaust. He examines major responses to the Holocaust on the part of one Christian and three Jewish intellectuals, each of whom, in accordance with radical theology, insist "that talk about God [after the Holocaust] did not—indeed could not—mean what it apparently had meant in the past." Things changed. Belief in a providential God and the meaningfulness of suffering were no longer credible theological options. So deep, in fact, was the crater in human history left by the death camps of Nazism that the questions they provoked about God and God's existence have persisted into the third millennium. Ongoing conversation about the Holocaust, including its repercussions concerning the possible death of God, illustrates that "its place, its presence is still in the making." It would be "lamentable," Roth concludes, if the discussion did not continue.

In chapters 3 and 4 we shift from broader treatments of radical theology's originating context and influence to an introductory focus on Altizer and Hamilton. Here John Cobb reflects on the work of Altizer as a longtime friend and sympathizer, calling him the greatest theologian of the second half of the twentieth century even though the profundity of Altizer's perspective has rarely been understood or truly appreciated. Chapter 4 by Michael Zbaraschuk presents the work and legacy of Hamilton, distinguishing his views from other radical theologians and making the case for a retrieval of Hamilton on his own terms. Indeed, Zbaraschuk says, Hamilton was unique among radical theologians not only with regard to his prophetic orientation but also for his keen emphasis upon imagination as a way to express his view concerning the death of God. Why Hamilton's explicit influence waned remains largely a mystery.

Sarah Pinnock completes the introductory section to radical theology by examining how it spread across the Atlantic and became visible in the work of the German theologian Dorothee Soelle. As a bridge to the second section of the present volume and an example of a feminist theology that stresses the embodied nature of all theological thinking, Pinnock also includes an account of how Soelle has informed her own perspective. For Pinnock, the failure of theodicy adequately to address modern atrocities like the Holocaust amounts to "the death of [the] God of philosophical theism and orthodox Christianity," both of which have endorsed "an authoritarian God of patriarchy and colonialism, the providential God incompatible with scientific explanation, and the omnipotent God who usurps human freedom." Soelle, says Pinnock, provides an alternative for our time by detailing a "mystical response to evil" that expresses solidarity with those who suffer and embodies an "openness to God" that is "transformative even despite God's death or absence." This openness constitutes *radical* faith, the kind that "ventures forth" as Kierkegaard would say—not by fabricating a new concept of God but by a "mystical seeking of divine presence hidden in human experience and suffering itself."

Having looked at the history of death of God theology for readers new to the discussion, we turn in chapter 6 to its constructive implications for political, theological, and ontological reflection. Jeffrey Robbins opens the discussion with a fascinating thesis: "in order both to understand and to more fully embrace the politics of democracy, we must first be prepared to profess the theology of the death of God." Robbins makes his case by analyzing the work of Tocqueville, who came to the conclusion that the American democratic revolution occasioned the death of God by transferring the kind of "divine sovereign power" that establishes the rule of a monarch *over* the people *to* the people. Democracy, in other words, empties God of God's power sociologically by distributing it to a body of citizens who now govern for themselves. The kenotic annihilation of God as the Lord of the universe, one that we recall as central to the Altizerian strain of radical theology, accordingly lies at the root of American democracy! This discovery was for Tocqueville an unpleasant one. For Robbins, on the other hand, it is good news. The death of "God above" *as a construct* frees us to realize that the world—political, religious, or otherwise—is what we make of it.

Christopher Rodkey turns our attention in chapter 7 from the state to the church. His driving question is one that few radical theologians have seriously considered: what kind of church would remain if a religious community accepted the kenotic death of God? Rodkey, himself a pastor, responds by assembling an "extraordinary ecclesiology" in which the church celebrates the life brought about by the progressive descent of God's Spirit into flesh. Here the incarnational sacrifice, dismemberment, and dispersal of the Godhead into the world undergirds an ecclesiology that affirms the sacramental presence of the divine in everything. Such an ecclesiology boldly "reject[s] the church as we know it" by returning to the world and celebrating "human flesh and thinking itself as the bearers of the Holy, rendering extraordinary the banality of ordinariness." This return to the world reflects as well an implicit return to theological tradition: the classic Ignatian claim that "God is in all things" (or at least in human consciousness) finds new life in an ecclesiology for today that paradoxically proclaims God's death as its basis.

After Rodkey, Clayton Crockett offers a second theological revisioning of radical theology by linking together the death of God and the resurrection in an effort to provide an alternative to biblical fundamentalists who trivialize the resurrection by interpreting it as the resuscitation of Jesus's corpse as well as to Hegel, Altizer, and Žižek, who view the resurrection as "a progressive advance" or stage "beyond the death of God." Drawing upon Gilles Deleuze's reading of Nietzsche, Crockett argues that the German philosopher's concept of eternal recurrence or "the return of the same" does not mean that things as they are will someday come back in the same form; instead, the process of becoming itself recurs, constantly rupturing all identity—self-identity, the world's identity, and even God's identity. God grounds and exemplifies the process, opening up the space for new life and creation by constantly passing away. Here the reader encounters a fascinating synthesis of two modern theological schools: divine reality generates life and being by what process thinkers will recognize as *its own perpetual perishing.* The continuous death of divine being, in other words, is not an end but a beginning, a resurrection—of every single moment in history.

Like Crockett, Andrew Hass makes becoming his focus in chapter 9. He starts by noting a surprising consistency among an otherwise disparate group of thinkers: every Western form of the death of God amounts to a rejection of transcendence in favor of "radical and absolute immanence." Nietzsche, Adorno, Altizer, Hegel, Hamilton, Harris, Hitchens—each of these authors share the conviction that "[t]his world, *post Dei,* is . . . *all* we have." The trouble with such thinking is the binary it assumes of transcendence and immanence. Hass accordingly raises a crucial question: Can we think the death of God apart from this polarity or "will the vacillation between the two poles . . . go on indefinitely?" Weaving through the work of Hegel, Nietzsche, Heidegger, and Whitehead, Hass answers his question by forging a third way, one that isolates "the beyond inherent within becoming and its potentiality, the beyond involved in the connection between two disparate elements (not yet/will be) in the process of creation" as the locus or place of divine reality. This move, one that shrugs off the categories of "above" and "below," provides for what Hass takes as the possibility of a return to God after the death of God.

Lissa McCullough concludes our collection of radical theology and its constructive reappraisals by looking at the possibility of a radical return to the world after the Western flight of transcendence has run its course and the soul has stopped "beating [its] wings against eternal walls." She paints in broad strokes: the contemporary death of God marks the end of a long chapter in history that began during the Axial Age (800–200 BCE), when religion, in an attempt to bring freedom from the various deities and divine powers of this world, looked beyond to a God that theology has since understood as "wholly other," a God totally distinct from the world. Now that this God has "evaporated," the prospect of a full return to the earth appears in its place. This return, barring the "bad faith" of fundamentalists who resist it, enjoins us to exist "presently in the immediate and local and real particularity of actual life in the world, where our deepest challenges still await us." To heaven and back constitutes, in short, the death of God that *could be* for McCullough. Whether we have the courage to follow suit remains to be seen.

Deicide into the Third Millennium

Nineteen sixty-six, we recall, was a difficult year for God. The fact is, however, that theologians had been discussing deicide in subtle ways prior to the arrival of radical theology. Alongside Tillich and his talk of a God beyond God at midcentury, H. Richard Niebuhr likewise spoke in 1957 of a "radical monotheism" in which "the One God [lies] hidden in the death of all gods as the object of true faith."[40] Today, as feminist and liberation theologians have attested, the lesser gods about whom Niebuhr wrote abound. These gods (those of Christian fundamentalism specifically) are more dangerous than Niebuhr could have imagined. Those in our culture who speak on behalf of such gods demand the sacrifice of free and critical thinking. They call their listeners to deny the claims of science, to turn a deaf ear to climate change, and to ignore people of the third world (as evident in the prosperity gospel) who suffer so that their audiences can heap up mounds of material wealth in their god's name for themselves.

Many justify violence and war, and they do so—without flinching—in the name of God, Family Values, and Jesus Christ. Resurrecting the death of God marks one way to challenge the idols of our age.

Of course, the reconsideration of radical theology goes well beyond the need simply to challenge fundamentalist forms of contemporary religiosity. It calls us to think more deeply about how we understand ourselves and our experience in relation to whatever it is we deem ultimate. Do the older, more traditional modes of belief in a transcendent God, for example, actually make this a better world, meet us where we are, or help us explain religious or spiritual experience? What in particular do we do with the harrowing silence we come across in prayer or the void we face in tragedy? Is it simply the case that the God of Abraham, Isaac, and Jacob has mysteriously decided to refrain from speaking (whatever that means)? Or must we find more adequate ways to make sense of what the Jesuit theologian Karl Rahner called our "encounters with silence"? If so, might the death of God theologies be an alternative insofar as they take seriously the experience of "Holy Saturday" and with it what Altizer calls the nihilism or emptiness of our contemporary world?

Naturally, other frameworks for interpreting the experience of "Holy Saturday" or challenging fundamentalist forms of religion exist. Prophetically, for instance, the new atheists (Harris, Hitchens, and Dawkins) have taken it upon themselves to counter the destructive capacity of religion. They have also challenged people to accept their place in the universe for what they think it is: we are alone and the silence we experience in prayer merely confirms the absence of any "God" beyond this world. That said, one wonders what new atheism can do to explain the *depth* of this silence. Could it be that such silence marks the consequence of a kenosis on the part of God, a complete self-emptying whereby God sacrifices God's otherworldly form so as to infuse the world with the divine presence, giving the silence a profundity we can only name as sacred? And what about the prophetic critique of religion? Some of the most significant detractors of the Christian faith—Luther, Kierkegaard, Bonhoeffer, Tillich, and Altizer—were Christians who realized in light of Scripture and theological tradition what faith could be over and against the distortions of faith that had taken its place. They criticized faith as an act of faith, and they did so typically without assuming the conventional theism of their opponents.

Radical theology, in short, could move us well beyond more superficial alternatives like new atheism. From the beginning it has taken for granted the claim that new atheists have only more recently begun to discover: any understanding of God as a "supreme being" who exists "out there" in the universe, interfering at whim and will with scientific laws and natural processes, is either dead or should be killed.[41] While some of the radical theologians may have been given to sensationalism or hubris early in the story, the majority had the courage, as Luther puts it, to "call a thing what it is." They named the darkness, the feeling of loss, the sense of divine absence that perhaps many continue to feel—or fail to acknowledge—in our time. They also developed tools for working out a new kind of "God/less" talk that takes the otherwise overwhelming silence of God into account as the starting point for theological reflection. A reintroduction and reconsideration of radical theology thus has value today. In the pages that follow the reader will encounter various forms and interpretations of radical theology and what its second coming does or might entail. Whether the reader agrees with any of these authors will obviously be a matter of personal judgment. One thing, however, remains clear: ours is a time ripe for the reexamination of radical theology. Ours is a time for resurrecting the death of God.

Notes

1. Discussion concerning the death of God in American theological circles actually occurred shortly before the story that made the front cover of *Time* in April of 1966. The *New York Times* and *Time* both ran articles on the topic in October of 1965. See Lissa McCullough, "Historical Introduction," in *Thinking through the Death of God: A Critical Companion to Thomas J. J. Altizer*, ed. Lissa McCullough and Brian Schroeder (Albany: State University of New York Press, 2004), xxvii.

2. Lloyd Steffen, "The Dangerous God: A Profile of William Hamilton," *Christian Century* 106, 27 (September 1989): 844.

3. R. C. Sproul in "Twenty Years After the Death of God Movement" (*Christianity Today* 29, 9 [June 14, 1985]: 19) provides the following preliminary definition of "radical theology" as it was initially conceived in the sixties: "Radical theology takes its name from the Latin word *radix*: root. It seeks to grapple with root issues in times of crises. The crises it addresses [had] several facets, at once cultural, ethical, ecclesiastical, political, historical, and religious. The root problem is that modern man lives in an environment where many human beings experience a profound sense of the absence of God."

4. Doris Donnelly, "The Requiem for God," *Religious Education* 62, 4 (July–August 1967): 316.

5. Ed Briggs, "For Millions of Americans in the Pews, God Never 'Died,'" *Richmond Times Dispatch* (June 26, 1976).

6. William Lane Craig, "God Is Not Dead Yet," *Christianity Today* 52, 7 (July 2008): 22.

7. Mark C. Taylor makes the same point in *After God*: "Since the early 1970s, we have been in the midst of what might be called a Fourth Great Awakening, which was unanticipated by virtually all of the most sophisticated cultural critics. This religious revival is not limited to the United States but is a *global* phenomenon whose causes and implications have yet to be adequately understood" ([Chicago: University of Chicago Press, 2007], 131; emphasis in original). Here we should be clear that *fundamentalist* religion in particular is on the rise—not religion as such.

It is the rise of *Christian* fundamentalism in America that concerns us (the editors of this volume) specifically.

8. Jeffrey Robbins, "Introduction: After the Death of God," *After the Death of God*, ed. Jeffrey Robbins (New York: Columbia University Press, 2007), 11.

9. Austen Ivereigh, "God Makes a Comeback: An Interview with *The Economist's* John Micklethwait," *America* 201, 8 (October 5, 2009): 12.

10. William Hamilton, *Reading Moby-Dick and Other Essays* (New York: Peter Lang, 1989), 177–178.

11. See Rosemary Radford Ruether, "The Death of God Revisited: Implications for Today," chapter 1 in this work.

12. See Sarah K. Pinnock, "Holocaust, Mysticism, and Liberation after the Death of God: The Significance of Dorothee Soelle," chapter 5 in this work.

13. McCullough, "Historical Introduction," xxiii.

14. Adam Kotsko, "Žižek and Theology," *International Journal of Systematic Theology* 12, 3 (July 2010): 142.

15. Hamilton, *Reading Moby-Dick*, 177.

16. Steffen, "The Dangerous God," 845.

17. Cyril O'Regan, "Žižek and Milbank and the Hegelian Death of God," *Modern Theology* 26, 2 (April 2010): 286. Since O'Regan provides a thorough overview of Žižek's "repetition of Altizer's gloss on Hegel's kenotic interpretation of the incarnation" (281), the present introduction confines itself to an analysis of how Taylor and Vattimo have appropriated and "refigured" Altizer's theology.

18. The method of clearing aside names or concepts for God is an old one. Pseudo-Dionysius (c. 500 CE), drawing upon an image first used by Proclus (a Neoplatonic philosopher), employs the language of "clearing aside" (*aphaeresis*) as central to the *via negativa* in *The Mystical Theology* (see *Pseudo-Dionysius: The Complete Works*, trans. Colm Luibhéid [New York: Paulist Press, 1987], 138).

19. One need only consider the influence Tillich would have here on feminist theologians like Mary Daly or Rosemary Radford Ruether who desired to clear away patriarchal conceptions of God the Father in favor of an egalitarian "God/ess above God." For a more recent invocation of Tillich's gesture to a God above God—with a simultaneous critique of Tillich's "ontologism"—see John D. Caputo, "Spectral Hermeneutics," in *After the Death of God*, 185–186 n. 13.

20. William Hamilton and Thomas J. J. Altizer, *Radical Theology and the Death of God* (Indianapolis: Bobbs-Merrill, 1966), 24.

21. Hamilton, *Reading Moby-Dick*, 174.

22. Sproul, "Twenty Years," 19.

23. An important example of a theologian who approximates following Jesus in the absence of God would be Dorothee Soelle. Like Hamilton, she was indebted to Bonhoeffer, who wrote from a prison cell in Nazi Germany about being Christian in a godless world and the importance of being there "for others" as Jesus was during his lifetime. See chapter 5 in this work for a fuller treatment of Soelle's perspective.

24. A tribute to Hamilton by Nancy Haught in *USA Today* (January 5, 2008) credits him—presumably after Tillich—with "paving the way for other radical theologians: feminists, who dropped patriarchal descriptions of God; and liberationists, who saw God in poverty and suffering."

25. Sallie McFague, *Models of God* (Minneapolis: Fortress Press, 1987), xi–xii.

26. McCullough, "Historical Introduction," xxiv.

27. Thomas J. J. Altizer, *The Gospel of Christian Atheism* (Philadelphia: Westminster Press, 1966), 111, 109.

28. Many have since commented upon Altizer's version of the gospel, sometimes to the point of caricature. Caputo serves as a recent example: "In Altizer the death of God primarily meant that the absolute center had shifted its residence from transcendence to immanence by means of a metaphysics of *kenosis*, by which the full presence of a transcendent God was transported to the plane of immanence. Altizer merrily danced in the street over the metaphysics of immanent presence, nay, 'total presence,' brought about as the dialectical offspring of 'total absence' or negation" ("Spectral Hermeneutics," 68). A critique like this may well apply to the early work of Altizer, particularly as Taylor read and deconstructed his "metaphysics of presence" in *Erring*. Whether it applies to the more mature work of Altizer, especially his affirmation of the *coincidentia oppositorum*, appears less likely. After all, Altizer affirms the embodiment of the *Nihil* or an actual Nothing in the world as a consequence of kenosis. How can one say (as Caputo does) that the presence of God in the world is "full" according to Altizer when it coincides with an embodied absence?

29. Sproul, "Twenty Years," 19.

30. Martin Luther, *Martin Luther's Basic Theological Writings*, second edition, ed. Timothy Lull and William Russell (Minneapolis: Fortress Press, 2005), 227.

31. McCullough, "Historical Introduction," xxiii. For Altizer's own reflections on the challenges he has faced over the course of developing his type of radical theology, see Thomas J. J. Altizer, *Living the Death of God: A Theological Memoir* (Albany: State University of New York Press, 2006).

32. Lissa McCullough, "Godhead and the Nothing," *Journal of Religion* 86, 2 (April 2006): 335.

33. Ibid.

34. Thomas J. J. Altizer, *Godhead and the Nothing* (Albany: State University of New York Press, 2003), 32, 73, 93.

35. John D. Caputo, "After God," *Journal of the American Academy of Religion* 77, 1 (March 2009): 165.

36. Jeffrey W. Robbins, "After God," *Journal of Religion* 90, 1 (January 2010): 91.

37. Taylor, *After God*, 377.

38. Caputo, "After God," 165.

39. Thomas Guardino, *Vattimo and Theology* (New York: T & T Clark International, 2009), 27.

40. Grant Stanaway, "Faith in God When All Gods Have Died," unpublished essay, 8.

41. John Haught makes a similar point, albeit perhaps too dismissively, in *God and the New Atheism* (Louisville: Westminster John Knox Press, 2008) when he observes that "the new atheism is so theologically unchallenging. Its engagement with theology lies at about the same level of reflection on faith that one can find in contemporary creationist and fundamentalist literature" (xi). Likewise, Nathan Schneider (*The Guardian*, October 4, 2009) writes, "Unlike some of the prominent

atheists of today, these thinkers [the original death of God theologians] knew inti-
mately the theology they were attacking. Life after God, they believed, could not
move forward without understanding the debt it owed to the religious culture that
had gone before. Consequently the movement went far beyond the simplistic, sci-
entistic concept of God common to both contemporary atheists and many of their
critics: a cartoonish hypothesis, some kind of all-powerful alien. Altizer spoke of the
God of direct experience; van Buren, the God conjured in language; and Cox, the
God that arises in the life of societies. These are incisive approaches that, lately,
have too often been forgotten in exchange for the caricature."

I.

The Modern Death of God

Origins and Influence

The Death of God Revisited

. ·◆· ———— ·◆· .

Implications for Today

Rosemary Radford Ruether

Forty-five years ago, as noted in the introduction, in the mid-sixties a major challenge to Christian theology arose in American theological circles called the "death of God." A *Time* magazine article featured the major theologians involved in using this phrase in their theology. Outcry and even death threats were hurled at the leading figures in this controversy, one of whom lost his job and turned to teaching literature rather than theology. After a few years the issue seemed to disappear from popular discussion. It seemed that "the death of God has died." As one of the major "death of God" theologians, William Hamilton, put it, it was in some ways a media event and "any event the media can create they can uncreate."[1]

In this essay I will revisit the meaning given to the term "death of God" by several of the leading writers of the period and reflect on the implications of these views for theological developments in subsequent years. Has the pursuit of this idea proven to be a dead end that has been rightly rejected? Has it been absorbed into theological thought so it is no longer particularly controversial? Was the announcement of the death of God killed culturally, so the churches and seminaries could continue to do business as usual, refusing to acknowledge the huge empty hole in the center of society where God used to be? Were there radical edges to death of God theology that were hushed up because the Christian culture of churches and seminaries were not ready to deal with them but that need to be revisited today?

The term "death of God" was used in quite different ways by different writers, so much so that one might question whether this was actually a "school" of theological thought at all. In this chapter I first review the different ways that three theologians employing the term "death of God" used this term. These are William Hamilton, Thomas J. J. Altizer, and Gabriel Vahanian. I also refer briefly to the Jewish writer Richard Rubenstein, often associated with this movement, who did not use the term but claimed that the traditional God of Judaism could no longer be believed in "after Auschwitz."

I then turn to two major theological trends of the late sixties to today, feminist theology and Latin American liberation theology. Neither speak of the "death of God," but both are engaged in denunciation of certain dominant ideas about God. For these two movements the "gods" they denounce are not dead, culturally, but deserve to die or be killed, because they mediate injustice, violence, and death. These thinkers are engaged in invalidating these ideas of "god," which they deplore as all too much "alive" in the various cultures. Neither wants to announce that there is no God but rather to proclaim a better or truer God deserving of faith. What kind of God do they want to affirm and how do they believe He or She can be affirmed?

I then assess the problems of a certain kind of "God" current in recent American political rhetoric, particularly from the 1980s to 2008 during the presidencies of Ronald Reagan to George W. Bush. I will ask why, despite the fact that no reputable theologian or church leader has any faith in this American God, no church or theologian felt it was necessary to denounce this God. I conclude by asking where we are in American theology on the usefulness of the term "death of God" for a theological ethics mediating authentic ways of living today.

The Death of God Theologians of the 1960s

William Hamilton was born in 1924 and grew up in liberal churches. In his own words, "I had the worst possible preparation for becoming a theologian. I grew up in a very bland, very liberal . . . Baptist, suburban, middle class parish that bored me silly. And I left it."[2] But before leaving it he got a first rate theological education. He studied at Union Theological Seminary in the days when Reinhold Niebuhr and Paul Tillich reigned there. He earned a doctorate at St. Andrew's University in Scotland under Donald M. Baille and was appointed to the faculty of Colgate Rochester Divinity School, assuming the chair of historical theology in the early sixties.

Yet Hamilton since boyhood had been troubled by questions of reconciling the existence of God with violence and injustice in the world. At fourteen two of his young friends were killed in an accident and he wondered how a good God could allow this to happen.[3] He began to write essays exploring the theme of the death or absence of God in contemporary consciousness, in journals such as *Theology Today*. In 1966 he and Thomas J. J. Altizer published a volume of their essays entitled *Radical Theology and the Death of God*,[4] which quickly gained notoriety. After *Time* magazine publicized this "scandalous" discussion in theological circles, featuring Hamilton among others, his theological chair at Colgate Rochester was taken away. Hamilton himself turned to exploring issues of the death of God primarily through the writings of Herman Melville. He moved to teach in secular schools, first in Sarasota, Florida and then in 1970 at Portland State University in Portland, Oregon, from which he retired in the mid-eighties.

Hamilton spoke of the death of God primarily as an experience, an experience of God's absence in contemporary culture. In an article published originally in 1964 in *Theology Today*, "Thursday's Child," he speaks poignantly about how a theologian going about the routines of teaching at a theological seminary increasingly finds the debates and issues about God empty and meaningless. At a certain point he finds it necessary for his own integrity to end the hypocrisy and openly state his disbelief.

> He knows that his rebellion and unbelief is both deeper and uglier than his bland worldly mask suggests, and he knows also (a bit less assuredly?) that his devout mask is too vapid. To be a man of two masks is, he knows, to be less than honest. Thus he has to come out in the open about his faithlessness even though he may suspect and hope that beneath it is a passion and a genuine waiting for something that may, one day, get transformed into a kind of faith even better than the one he has willed to leave.[5]

Even though he felt it necessary to leave God behind, Hamilton in his own view never ceased to be a Christian, in the sense of abandoning a relation to Jesus. Jesus continued to be, for him, the companion on the journey that gives him a "place to stand." That place to stand was not in the church, or in theological access to God, much less in a personal piety of redemption from sin, but in the streets alongside those who suffer injustice.

> . . . there is one nonnegotiable absolute, and it is not a principle, it's not a moral value; it's an answer to the problem of where you look, where you belong, where you put your body in this world. Not at the altar, and not in the private realms, but out there in the world at the service of human beings. That's where you are. That is what Christianity drives you to, and that for me is the element and the content of the Western religious traditions which I use to attack the temptations to privatism in myself, in my kids and in my students.[6]

In later years Hamilton revised his view that God is simply absent in modern consciousness and culture. Rather, he concluded that God is all too alive and active, but it is a violent and unjust God. It is a God of religious leaders, politicians, and generals who should not be worshiped, who deserves to be killed. He saw feminists as taking the lead in the critique of this violent God.

Thomas J. J. Altizer was born in 1927 in Charleston, West Virginia and received his BA, MA, and PhD at the University of Chicago. His doctoral thesis was on Carl Jung's understanding of religion. He taught English at Emory University from 1956 to 1968 and then in Religious Studies at the State University of New York at Stony Brook. He has continued to be an active writer in radical theology, producing such volumes as *Genesis and Apocalypse: A Theological Voyage toward Authentic Christianity* (1990), *Genesis of God: A Theological Genealogy* (1993), and *Godhead and the Nothing* (2003). A more recent publication tells his own story of the development of his death of God theology: *Living the Death of God: A Theological Memoir* (2006).

Altizer has sometimes been called a mystic, but he is radically opposed to what is generally understood as forms of mysticism, such as Gnosticism, Neoplatonism, or Hinduism. For him these types of mysticism are characterized by hostility to the body and material existence and seek a return to primordial Being by dissolving one's finite existence. He rejects all forms of religion based on the movement of "return" to either original transcendent Being or to some normative ideal of the past.

For Altizer what is distinctive about Christianity is its radical incarnationalism—that God not only embraces but dissolves God's self into the flesh. Altizer interprets the Christian doctrine of incarnation through a Hegelian metaphysic. Whereas traditional Christianity sees Jesus as the unique incarnation of the divine logos of God who continues to reign in the heavens, for Altizer there is no God or Son of God who remains in heaven, but rather God creates the world by a total self-alienation into temporal existence. While this death of God can be spoken of as a cultural event in modern secular consciousness, for Altizer the death of God happens with the appearance of the world and temporary existence itself. It is not a once and for all event either in creation or in Jesus, but it is a continual process. Every new moment in temporal existence is a new incarnation of God. There is no ideal moment of incarnation in the past but only continual forward movement into new futures. This process of new incarnations will culminate only in an apocalyptic fullness of the synthesis of the sacred and the profane in what Altizer continually refers to as a "coincidence of opposites," using the Latin term *coincidentia oppositorum*.

This vision of cosmological-historical process is summed up in the conclusion of Altizer's essay "The Sacred and the Profane":

By a kenotic negation of its primordial reality, the sacred becomes incarnate in the profane. Yet this movement of the sacred into the profane is inseparable from a parallel movement of the profane into the sacred. Indeed the very movement of repetition and renewal—precisely because it is an actual and concrete movement—testifies to the ever more fully dawning power of the reality of the profane. Consequently, a consistently Christian dialectical understanding of the sacred must finally look forward to the resurrection of the profane in a transfigured and thus finally sacred form.[7]

While Altizer considers himself post-Christendom in the sense of being beyond every past expression of Christianity, he does not see himself as "post-Christian" but as radically Christian, expounding the radical nature of the Christian doctrines of incarnation, resurrection, and the coming apocalyptic fullness in the Kingdom of God. Far from being a denial of Christian faith, the announcement of the death of God is the revelation of its deepest meaning that can only now be fully understood:

Now that we have reached a point where it is manifest that history itself has moved through the death of God we must celebrate the death of God as an epiphany of the eschatological Christ. . . . Yet if the Christ of faith is an eschatological Word, he cannot be fully present in the dark and hidden crevices of a turbulent present nor can he be fully at hand in the broken body of a suffering humanity. He must instead be present in the *fullness* of history before us. The time is now past when the theologian can be silent in the presence of the moment before him. He must speak to be Christian, and he must speak the Word that is present in our flesh.[8]

By contrast to Hamilton and Altizer as American-born, Gabriel Vahanian was French Calvinist, born in Marseilles in 1927, who held a diploma and *Licence* in theology from the Sorbonne. He came to Princeton Theological Seminary as a World Council of Churches scholar where he earned a master's degree and a doctorate. He then taught religion at Syracuse University and concluded his teaching career by returning to France to teach at the Marc Bloch University in Strasburg. He was a prolific author, more recently producing *Anonymous God: An Essay on Not Dreading Words* (2002), *Tillich and the New Religious Paradigm* (2004), and *Praise of the Secular* (2008).

Vahanian translated and wrote the introduction to Karl Barth's *The Faith of the Church*, and his view of God remains strictly orthodox in a Barthian way. His book, *The Death of God: The Culture of Our Post-Christian Era*, was published in 1961,[9] several years before Hamilton and Altizer scandalized the American public culture with their use of the term. He uses this term in a way that is largely opposite to theirs, although not responding to them. Rather, his book was written to critique what he saw as the faithlessness of the claimed renewal of American Protestant Christianity of the 1950s.

For Vahanian God is the Wholly Other, who cannot be fit into any cosmological system in which God is one part of a whole, even if claimed to be a "transcendent" part, in the sense of existing on a higher immaterial plane within an ontological system. Nor can humans as radically fallen and alienated from God ever attain knowledge of God through moving "up" from their existing human capacities. Rather God is known only through a revelation coming from God's side. Humans enter into knowledge and relation to God only through knowing themselves as fallen, totally depraved, and reconciled to God only through God's act of redemption in Christ. In this sense every human being and every human culture is "post-Christian" theologically, standing under a divine judgment in which human efforts to know God for themselves are always apostate and sinful.

But only with the European Enlightenment and the dawn of modern consciousness did the Christian world become post-Christian culturally. By this Vahanian means that the modern secular world, partly midwifed by Christianity itself, has become culturally incapable of understanding the authentic biblical view of God. Even when it claims to be overcoming secularity and to be experiencing a religious "revival," as in the Eisenhower era, what such Christians are really doing is creating a new form of "religiosity" that is banal and apostate from the true God of biblical faith.

For Vahanian the primary problem of the modern world is not secularity but various forms of religiosity by which such pseudo-Christians claim to "find" God as some kind of peace of mind, source of happiness, and means of prosperity. True biblical faith is not opposed to secularity. Properly understood, it allows the secular its proper place as the world created by God. In this sense Christianity itself is a source of the Western development of the secular world, although in a wrongful misunderstanding of secularity as autonomous existence that is no longer based on God but only on itself.

For Vahanian the "death of God" in this cultural sense refers to this loss of capacity to understand the biblical God. It is a radically immanentist view of reality that assumes the autonomous existence of the human, but its deepest apostasy lies in conjuring up various forms of religiosity that mask its godlessness. Here the unfaithful human becomes not simply oblivious to God but actively blasphemous and idolatrous toward God. In Vahanian's closing words in the afterword of his book he writes:

> We live in a post-Christian era because Christianity has sunk into religiosity. No longer can this type of Christianity vitally define

itself in terms of Biblical faith. Instead it acquires the attributes
of moralism, or those of a psychological and emotional welfare-
state . . . faith, hope and love have nothing to do with these
substitutes, no more than God with an idol, or my authentic self
with the masks that I am wearing.[10]

Another writer whose name became associated with death of God
theology but who writes from a different angle, is Jewish religious scholar
Richard Rubenstein. Rubenstein's repudiation of traditional Jewish God-
language springs from the problem of theodicy, or how a good God can
allow evil to happen. This is a radical problem for Rubenstein since he is
dealing with a Jewish God who "elected" the Jewish people to be his people
and then allowed or even willed this people to be exterminated. Rubenstein
explored this dilemma in his 1966 book, *After Auschwitz: Radical Theology
and Contemporary Judaism.*

The classic strategy of Jewish religious thought to explain evils befalling
the Jewish people is to define such evils as punishment for sin, particularly
for infidelity to God. God is chastening his people. When they learn from
this punishment and become wholly obedient, then they will be restored to
an abundant life. For Rubenstein, no such explanation can rationalize the
enormity of unjust suffering of the Holocaust. No possible sins could merit
an attempted genocide aimed indiscriminately at all Jews no matter what
their moral behavior, including small children.

A God who could will the destruction of his own people is no longer
believable. Such a God is a cosmic sadist. One cannot honor such a God
but must recoil from him in horror. The God of traditional Judaism is dead
after Auschwitz. Jews must cease to look beyond history for rationality and
justice to make sense out of senseless evil. There is no divine plan that will
work out for the best in the end. The only deity that exists is not the Lord
of history but the cosmic matrix or void of nothingness from which all things
spring and to which they return, a non-ethical god of natural fertility and
renewal of life. Rubenstein declares that what binds him to Judaism is not
its ethical mandates but its cultic side, the collective rituals of community
solidarity that bring the Jewish people together, not to solve the problem
of evil and ultimate meaninglessness but to share it together and comfort
one another in a common affliction.[11]

Feminist Theology and Disbelief in the Patriarchal God

Another theological movement that arose in the late sixties and continues to
be developed today is feminist theology. Today it is being explored worldwide,
not just in Europe and the United States but also in Africa, Asia, and Latin
America.[12] This movement repudiates the God of patriarchy that makes the

divine in the image of male domination over women, subordinating women and nature. It does not declare that all ideas of the divine are "dead" but rather seeks to define a more just and life-giving understanding of divinity.

My own questioning of such an idea of God goes back early in my life. I cannot say that the idea of God as male king ruling from the skies ever had much appeal to me. But the definitive moment when I realized the nonexistence of such a God and at the same time affirmed a different view of the divine came in my early twenties. I cannot remember the exact date but it must have been around 1960 when I was thinking intensely about whether God existed or not. It took the form of a "waking vision."

In this vision I found myself in the antechamber of a great palace facing huge closed doors. I opened the doors and saw a great stairway leading up a tower. I began to climb these stairs, only to find new closed doors. I opened these doors and found more stairs mounting ever higher up the great tower. After climbing many stairs and opening many doors, I finally found myself before a set of closed doors to what I knew was the throne room of God. Flinging open these doors with great nervousness and anticipation, I saw a great throne with its back to me.

I moved into the room to see who was sitting on the throne and saw that no one was there. With thunderous clarity I knew that the throne of God is empty, indeed has always been empty. There is no God sitting on a throne in a great tower room in the skies. But at the same time I knew that there is a divine reality, but one has to look for it elsewhere, in the life energy that is in and through and under all things. This has been my understanding of the divine ever since.

There are many feminist theologians whose critique of patriarchal god-talk could be analyzed. I will discuss three figures: Mary Daly (1928–2010), Carol Christ, and Carter Heyward (both born in 1945). All three reject the patriarchal concept of God. For Daly and Christ this has also meant leaving Christianity. All reconstruct god-language in slightly different ways.

Mary Daly grew up in a Roman Catholic family in Schenectady, New York, and was educated in Catholic institutions from grammar school through three doctoral degrees. In college she developed a burning desire to study Catholic philosophy and theology but was denied admission to leading programs because of her gender. She finally went to the University of Fribourg, Switzerland, where she earned doctorates in theology and philosophy. She returned from Europe in 1966 and took up a teaching position at Boston College. She soon published her first book, *The Church and the Second Sex*,[13] inspired by reading Simone de Beauvoir's *The Second Sex*, in which Daly detailed the long history of Catholic discrimination against women, both in its practice and in its theology.

This book caused Boston College to give her a terminal one-year teaching contract. But when the students rose in protest, it reversed itself and gave her promotion with tenure. She continued to teach at Boston College into her seventies when she was finally forced to retire by the administration. After her tenure fight Daly turned from being a reformer to a radical, publishing her second book, *Beyond God the Father*, in 1973. She had by then come to the conclusion that Christianity and indeed all patriarchal religions are irreformable for women. It was not that Christianity has been deformed by patriarchy, but rather that it simply is the ideology of patriarchal domination over women. For women to be liberated they need to reject Christianity and all patriarchal ideologies, root and branch. On November 14, 1971, she preached a sermon in Harvard Memorial Chapel in which she called all women and men to exodus from Christianity, signaling this by walking out of the chapel, followed by most of the women and a few men.

For Daly the patriarchal God of Christianity is fundamentally alienating and destructive for all women, as well as for the natural world. She speaks of the "most unholy trinity of rape, genocide and war" as being at the heart of the patriarchal God. Daly draws on a radicalized dualism of true Being and delusory appearance, of Foreground and Background. The ideologies of patriarchal culture are false social constructs designed to suck the life out of true being and imprison women in service to an oppressive world of subordination. Hidden behind this system of lies and oppression is the "Background, the true being of life." Women need to leap out of this deluding world of oppression and identify themselves with an alternative feminist community of true life. This is the original human culture led by women, which has been covered up and suppressed by patriarchy. True divinity is the real "ground of being" that underlies authentic life and that can be seen as more of a "verb" or a process than a "thing."[14]

Carol Christ grew up in a Christian family of mixed denominations and did her graduate work at Yale. There she became increasingly alienated from Christianity, which she saw as both sexist and anti-Semitic. She was drawn to the Goddess spirituality movement and studied with pagan priestess Starhawk, author of *The Spiral Dance: A Rebirth of the Ancient Religion of the Great Goddess*.[15] Christ turned from religious studies to women's studies, working primarily in literature.[16] But she became burned out from the academic rat race and moved to Greece where she has lived since, supporting herself by writing, lecturing, and leading Goddess pilgrimages to ancient sites.

For Christ the Goddess is not just a metaphor for a matrix of being or life process but a living feminine being who underlies the cosmos. She rejects the suggestion of some of her friends, such as Judith Plaskow,[17] that this life process expressed as Goddess is amoral or indifferent to human concerns. She believes the Goddess, as the thrust of cosmic life, is fundamentally good but not omnipotent. In her more recent book, *She Who Changes: Re-imagining the Divine in the World*,[18] influenced by the process theology of Charles Hartshorne, she sees reality as mutable, in a constant process of change in the cycle of birth, growth, decline, death, and new birth. But this changing reality is not one of isolated, fragmented selves but beings living in a texture of interrelationship. All beings, human and nonhuman, live in constant interaction with each other.

Deity or the Goddess is integral to this process of change but not just any kind of change, good or bad. Using process theology language, Christ sees the Goddess as a divine "lure" to good, life-giving relationship. Humans and other beings have freedom to choose alienated, hostile ways of relating to each other, but this is contrary to the thrust of life that is toward positive flourishing in harmony with each other. Finitude, chance, and the choice to deny life and love cause suffering and tragedy. These forces of negativity are deeply embedded in the universe and no all-powerful deity assures us of a good outcome.

But we can and are called by the Goddess to resist these negative forces and to constantly seek to respond to the lure of love and goodness to fashion life-giving relationships as best we can in each particular situation and context. There are abundant sources of life available to us, and each new day is an opportunity to try again. She ends her book by suggesting that we rise each day and salute the sun with the prayer "As this day dawns in beauty, we pledge ourselves to repair the web."[19]

Carter Heyward grew up in an Episcopalian family and community in the hill country of North Carolina. She studied religion and psychiatry at Union Theological Seminary in New York City and received her PhD in 1980. In 1974 she, along with ten other Episcopalian women, were ordained priests in an irregular ceremony led by retired bishops. Her 1976 book, *A Priest Forever*,[20] reflects on the meaning of the priesthood for her. In 1976 she was given a teaching position at the Episcopal Divinity School in Cambridge, Massachusetts, retiring in 2006 to return to North Carolina to live in a community of artists and teachers that she helped develop.

Heyward's doctoral thesis at Union Theological Seminary was on God-language and redemption. This work was developed for publication in her 1982 book on her understanding of God, *The Redemption of God: A Theology of Mutual Relations*.[21] In this book Heyward develops the distinctive understanding of the divine as the power of right relations that would underline all of her subsequent theological and social justice writings. For

Heyward sin is wrong relations, both power over others and disconnection of people from one another. Redemption is conversion into right relations, into justice-making, loving relations that create mutual flourishing.

God is the power that empowers us to transformation into right relations. God is not a separate being over against us, situated in some disembodied space outside the "world," disconnected from reciprocal relations with us. Rather, God is the ground of right relations. There can be no split between loving God and loving ourselves, loving God and loving our neighbor. God is present in the process of mutuality in which we become persons who love our neighbor as ourselves. God empowered us to love one another, and God comes to exist in that process. God is born and grows through our mutual relations. We birth God and God births us. Heyward calls this reciprocal relation between humans and God "godding," becoming God-like and creating God through our loving, justice-making relation to each other.[22]

Heyward credits Mary Daly with inspiring her to think of God as a verb, a process and activity, rather than an entity. As she defines this term:

> Godding is a mutual process of co-creating right-relation in which all Participants—including the relational power and process—are being affected and changing. There is no unchanging deity in or beyond the universe, either patriarchal or feminist, although men have created just such a god, untouched and unmoved, in their own image, and this fabricated god/father forms the basis of patriarchal religion. . . . Godding, we ourselves become agents of transformation in the world and church and, together, bear up the hope of the world.[23]

Latin American Liberation Theology: Idols of Death and the God of Life

Latin American liberation theology, which developed in the 1960s, also has been engaged in denouncing false gods and announcing the true God of liberating life. Latin American theologians in the 1970s and 1980s were wont to say that, unlike Europe, secularism and atheism are not Latin American problems. Their people are believers; affirmation of God is pervasive in the culture.[24] The issue is not atheism or the death of God but concerns the God in which one should believe. In Latin America in the seventies and eighties death squads of the National Security States that dominated most of the Latin American countries tortured catechists and assassinated nuns, priests, and even bishops. At the same time the leaders of such states declared themselves to be Christians and to be defending "Christian civilization" against "godless Communism." Right-wing Christians killed left-wing Christians in the name of God.

The hypocrisy has not gone unnoticed. In the words of Chilean biblical theologian Pablo Richard,

> Throughout the entire history of Latin America, the oppressors of the people have almost always declared themselves to be believers—which is tantamount to an idolatrous perversion of the name of God. The Conquistadors were all Christians, and colonization was carried out in the name of God. Likewise those responsible for slavery were Christians, supported by Christian European nations. As for the church, it endorsed slavery for centuries. Today all of the military dictators and practically all of those responsible for economic, political and ideological oppression are Christian.[25]

The task of theology for Richard is to critique false, alienating concepts of God that sanctify the unjust power of oppressors and counsel the poor to submit passively to impoverishment and subjugation as the "will of God" and the "order of creation," hoping to receive their reward in heaven. Theology needs to denounce this God as an idol and to lift up a liberating God who is with the poor in their struggles for justice.

> The basic theological task in America is not that of establishing the existence of God, but of discerning the true God from false idols. The problem is not to know whether God exists, but to demonstrate in what God we believe. . . . Likewise it is meaningless to declare oneself an atheist; one must specify in what God one does not believe. . . . The basic problem is not the existence but the presence of God, . . . of discovering in the concrete the historical presence of God in the world of the poor and oppressed, . . . to demonstrate that God is with the poor and their liberation in a special way. . . . This discernment, this distinction is usually made not over against revolutionary atheism, but over against the dominant idolatry.[26]

For Richard this means that the enemy of theology is the god-language of National Security States and American imperialism, not the atheism of revolutionary Marxism. Liberation theologians understand Marx's critique of religion as a critique of the alienating use of religion as an ideology of domination that holds out the promise of an illusory happiness and reward in heaven in order to make the poor accept injustice and misery on earth. In Marx's words in his *Contribution to the Critique of Hegel's Philosophy of Right*:

> Religious suffering is, at one and the same time, the expression of real suffering and a protest against real suffering. Religion is the sigh of the oppressed creature, the heart of a heartless world, and the soul of soulless conditions. It is the opium of the people. . . . The abolition of religion as the illusory happiness of the people is the demand for their real happiness. To call on them to give up their illusions about their condition is to call on them to give up conditions that require illusions. The criticism of religion is, therefore, in embryo, the criticism of that vale of tears of which religion is the halo. . . . It is the immediate task of philosophy, which is at the service of history, to unmask self-estrangement in its unholy forms once the holy form of human self-estrangement has been unmasked. Thus the criticism of Heaven turns into the criticism of Earth, the criticism of religion into the criticism of law, and the criticism of theology into the criticism of politics.[27]

What Marx is saying here is that the majority of humans live in a condition of economic exploitation rooted in the alienation of the worker from his labor whose profits are appropriated by the capitalist as the owner of the means of production. The ideologies of economics, philosophy, and politics mask this oppressive system by making it appear natural and good, while religion adds a further level of ideological mystification by claiming that it is the will of God, the acceptance of which will be rewarded by happiness in heaven. Thus the first stage of Marxist criticism is the criticism of the religious forms of ideological mystification, and the second stage is to critique its ideological justifications in legal, economic, and political thought, leading to the final stage, which is the actual overcoming of oppressive socioeconomic structures to create a new relation of workers to the ownership of the means of production.

For liberation theologians this critique of religion leading to critique of society is not a rejection of God, although Marx believed it was, knowing no other kind of religion than the alienated variety. Rather it is a critique of false religion or idolatry. This Marxist critique of religion emerges out of the prophetic faith of the prophets and Jesus who denounce alienating and oppressive religion in order to announce the liberating God. Thus liberation theology affirms the Marxist critique of religion, while claiming faith in the true God of life who does not direct the poor to accept injustice on earth in the name of heaven, but who is with the poor in their struggle to overcome alienating conditions on earth. Christian and Marxist revolutionaries are not enemies but partners in the struggle for liberation. Although differing in the "God" dimension of their future hope, both recognize that the enemy to be overcome is the social structures of oppression, rationalized in social ideologies and sacralized in idolatrous religion.[28]

Liberation theology's critique of idolatrous religion has by no means become passé in the twenty-first century. Rather it became more urgent since the onslaught of the Bush administration's "war against terrorism" and its efforts to secure American imperial dominion around the world. This project of economic and military imperialism under Bush appeared ever more stridently in religious language as a war between "good and evil," of God's elect people against the enemies of God. This justification of American power in religious language has a long history in the United States, rooted in four centuries of claims to be God's elect nation.[29] The Cold War from the 1950s to the demise of the USSR in 1990 also employed strongly religious language as a war against "godless Communism."

Religious claims rose to a new level during the second Bush administration of 2001–2009. Messianic god-language, identified with the American corporate and military empire, was made explicit in the speeches of General William Boykin, the U.S. general charged with the search for al-Qaeda leader Osama bin Laden. In talks to his Christian constituency, Boykin opined that America is an object of hate because it is uniquely "a Christian nation." Boykin went on to say that "our spiritual enemies can only be defeated when we confront them in the name of God." He asserted that Muslims worship an idol, not the true God. God, he said, put George Bush in the White House in the critical moment in world history. "We are an army of God . . . raised for such a time as this."[30]

In 2003, horrified by such blatantly imperialist God-talk from the Bush administration, I wrote an article calling for a new "Barmen Declaration," paralleling the declaration made by German theologians in 1934 to denounce German Christianity in its support for Hitler as a redeemer. Although this call attracted some attention in the United States, and was published in the *National Catholic Reporter* in 2004,[31] no U.S. church body and few American theologians[32] took up this challenge. Apparently American religio-political rhetoric was seen as trivial and did not require any serious critique.

By contrast, global Christian bodies took this challenge more seriously. In 2006 the World Alliance of Reformed Churches issued a document calling Christians and all people to resist U.S. empire as a matter of faith. This document, "An Ecumenical Faith Stance against Global Empire," declared that the U.S. empire, which combines military domination and economic hegemony, victimizes the whole earth and its peoples. Such empires are equivalent to the Pauline characterization of the powers and principalities as principles of evil (Rom. 8: 38–39). They not only threaten all people and the earth with poverty and war but also buttress themselves with an appeal to religious ideology. They are false messianisms, the opposite of true faith in Jesus Christ.

The closing paragraph of the document makes clear that this condemnation of American empire is both a matter of global ethics and a matter of faith. It touches foundational theological principles on which all Christians must take a stand, or what the Reformed tradition calls a *"status confessionis."*

> The global empire with its unprecedented reach represents a massive threat to life. In the face of this pervasive and death-dealing reality of world-wide hegemony, we are inspired by Jesus of Galilee to resist empire and renew communities of life. This new reality has economic, political, social, cultural and spiritual dimensions. It represents life and death challenges to Christians, as the empire uses religion to justify its domination and violence and makes claims that belong to God alone.[33]

Conclusions

In conclusion, what can be said about the relevance of "death of God" theology today? In my view, as I stated at the outset of the present chapter, this term in the 1960s never constituted a coherent theological movement, but rather there were several theologians who used the term in extremely different ways. William Hamilton expressed a sad experience of emptiness in regard to a faith that had become for him meaningless, although he was still committed to social justice in the name of Jesus.

Thomas Altizer seems to me brilliantly manic, an impression confirmed by Mark C. Taylor who writes

> To speak—truly to speak—with Altizer is to encounter a passion the excess of which borders on madness. Madness is not a destiny Altizer avoids: to the contrary, he often seems to solicit madness as if it would testify to the truth of his vision.[34]

Altizer's thought system reaches for a profound synthesis of everything and at the same time portends a dangerous collapse of distinctions in which good and evil, God and Satan become interchangeable, summed up by his constant invocation of a *coincidentia oppositorum*. One wonders what this can mean in a twenty-first-century America deeply sunk in a triviality-masking murderousness that finds it increasingly difficult to distinguish between truth and lies, reality and illusion.[35]

Altizer aside, I am sympathetic to Vahanian's critique of a religiosity of self-fulfillment, although his wholly-other God seems so disconnected to anything that humans can experience that He might as well be dead. My allegiance lies with feminist and liberation theologians who do not deny God but denounce idols of death. For me this continues to be highly relevant and needs to be taken up in the context of American politico-religious god-rhetoric. Feminist theologians not only reject patriarchal gods of all kinds but also affirm an experiential god/goddess of life connected to the ontological foundations of the universe.

Vahanian would reject this move as denying God's radical transcendence. But it is a move that has been made by Christians from the beginning, when biblical God-talk first connected with Greek philosophy. Even St. Paul announced the biblical "unknown" God to the Athenians as the God "in whom we live and move and have our being" (Acts 17: 28). What the divine as "ground of being" means and how it can be affirmed as a source of ethical spiritual transformation, and not just an amoral basis of ongoing existence, is a problem that feminist theologians, like Christian theologians generally, have not resolved.

Yet the function of God-talk both to affirm hope in more just and loving ways of life and to denounce false gods that betray us is vitally important, and I doubt we can do the second without holding on in some way to the first. Here I return to some paragraphs from an article that I wrote forty-three years ago on death of God theology, which still seems to be the best, aside from masculine language, I can say on the subject:

> How do we dare rise to new hope? Has not our sinful world history, and yes, our still more sinful church history so weighed us to the ground that we dare not again raise our eyes to heaven and consecrate our petty striving, loves and hates with the word "God"? Is not the greatest humility and honesty to abandon this word forever? Should we not confine our horizon to the service of this earth and our fellow man (human)? Is not all temptation to put this struggle in a higher context beyond this earth our great madness and self-delusion? Are we not finally wise enough to ourselves, our powers and limitations, to put off this blasphemy? Perhaps the final community beyond the death of all man's idols should be a community mature enough, chastened enough in its self-knowledge, to do without this word "God"?[36]

I responded to these queries by quoting some passages from Martin Buber's reply to an elderly philosopher who challenged his use of the word God because so much evil has been done in the name of God:

> Yes, it is the most heavy-laden of all human words. None has been so soiled, so mutilated. Just for this reason I cannot abandon it. Generations of men have laid the burden of their anxious lives upon this word and weighed it to the ground. It lies in the dust and bears their whole burden. The races of men with their religious factions have torn the word to pieces. They have killed for it and died for it, and it bears their finger-marks and their blood. Where might I find another word like it to describe the Highest? If I took the purest, most sparkling concept from the inner treasure-chamber of the philosophers I could only capture thereby an unbinding product of thought. I could not capture the presence of Him whom the hell-tormented and heaven-storming generations of men mean. Certainly they draw caricatures and write "God" underneath; they murder one another and say "in God's name." But when all madness and delusion fall to the dust, when they stand over against Him in loneliest darkness and no longer say "He, He," but rather sigh "Thou," shout "Thou," all of them the one word, is it not the real God whom they all implore, the one living God. . . . And just for this reason is not the word "God" the word of appeal, the word which has become a *name*, consecrated in all human tongues for all times? . . . We must esteem those who interdict it because they rebel against the injustice and wrong that are so readily referred to "God" for authorization. But we cannot give it up. . . . We cannot cleanse the word "God," and we cannot make it whole; but, defiled and mutilated as it is, we can raise it from the ground and set it over an hour of great care.[37]

Notes

1. Lloyd Steffen, "The Dangerous God: A Profile of William Hamilton," *Christian Century* 106, 27 (September 27, 1989): 844; www.religion-online.org/show-article.asp? Title=892.

2. Ibid., 844.

3. Nancy Haught, "Theologian Who Heralded the Death of God Ponders His Own," *USA Today* (May 1, 2008), http://www.USAtoday.com/new/religion/2008-01-05-god-dead_N.htm.

4. William Hamilton and Thomas Altizer, *Radical Theology and the Death of God* (New York: Bobbs-Merrill, 1966).

5. Ibid., 91.

6. Steffen, "The Dangerous God," page 7 of "religion-online" version of article.

7. Hamilton and Altizer, Radical Theology, 155.

8. Ibid., 139.

9. Gabriel Vahanian, The Death of God: The Culture of Our Post-Christian Era (New York: George Braziller, 1961).

10. Ibid., 228–229.

11. Ibid., 196, 222.

12. For a discussion of leading feminist theologians of Latin America, Africa, and Asia, see Rosemary Radford Ruether, Women and Redemption: A Theological History (Minneapolis: Fortress Press, 1998), 241–272.

13. Mary Daly, The Church and the Second Sex (Boston: Beacon, 1968).

14. See the account of Mary Daly's theology in Ruether, Women and Redemption, 215–221.

15. Starhawk, The Spiral Dance: A Rebirth of the Ancient Religion of the Great Goddess (San Francisco, CA: HarperSanFrancisco, 1979; revised edition, 1989).

16. See Christ's Diving Deep and Surfacing: Women Writers on the Spiritual Quest (Boston: Beacon, 1980).

17. Judith Plaskow, Standing again at Sinai: Judaism from a Feminist Perspective (New York: HarperCollins, 1990).

18. Carol P. Christ, She Who Changes: Re-imagining the Divine in the World (New York: Palgrave, 2003).

19. Ibid., 240. This summary of Christ's thought is taken from Rosemary Radford Ruether, Integrating Ecofeminism: Globalization and World Religions (Lanham, MD: Rowman & Littlefield, 2005), 98–100.

20. I. Carter Heyward, A Priest Forever (New York: Harper and Row, 1976).

21. I. Carter Heyward, The Redemption of God: A Theology of Mutual Relations (Washington, DC: University Press of America, 1982).

22. These remarks are drawn from a larger account of the theology of Carter Heyward in Ruether, Women and Redemption, 224–229.

23. From "Godding," in An A to Z of Feminist Theology, ed. Lisa Isherwood and Dorothea McEwan (Sheffield, UK: Sheffield Academic Press, 1996), 85.

24. Pablo Richard, Victorio Araya G., Joan Casañas, and Hugo Assman, The Idols of Death and the Gods of Life: A Theology (Maryknoll, NY: Orbis Books, 1983), 1.

25. Pablo Richard, "Theology in the Theology of Liberation," in Mysterium Liberationis: Fundamental Concepts of Liberation Theology, ed. Ignacio Ellacuria and Jon Sobrino (Maryknoll, NY: Orbis Books, 1993), 155.

26. Ibid., 155–156.

27. These passages from Marx's Critique of Hegel's Philosophy of Right are found in http://www.angelfire/or/sociologyshop/marxrel.html.

28. For liberation theology's appropriation of Marx's critique of religion, see José Miguez Bonino, Christians and Marxists: The Mutual Challenge to Revolution (Grand Rapids, MI: Eerdmans, 1976) and José Miranda, Marx and the Bible (Maryknoll, NY: Orbis Books, 1974).

29. See Rosemary Radford Ruether, *America, Amerikkka: Elect Nation and Imperial Violence* (London: Equinox Press, 2008).

30. Boykin quoted by Richard Cooper, "General Casts War in Religious Terms," *Los Angeles Times*, October 16, 2003.

31. Rosemary Radford Ruether, "U.S. Churches Must Reject 'Americanist' Christianity," *National Catholic Reporter* (April 23, 2004): 17.

32. An important exception is Catherine Keller: see Catherine Keller, Michael Nauser, and Mayra Rivera, eds., *Postcolonial Theologies: Divinity and Empire* (St. Louis, MO: Chalice Press, 2004).

33. This document is available on the WARC website, http://www.christianto-day.com/article/reformed.theologians.tell.churches.resist.the.global.empire/7405.htm.

34. Mark C. Taylor, "Introduction," in Thomas Altizer, *Living the Death of God: A Theological Memoir* (Albany: State University of New York Press, 2006), xi.

35. See Chris Hedges, *The Empire of Illusion: The End of Literacy and the Triumph of Spectacle* (Toronto: Knopf, 2009).

36. Rosemary Radford Ruether, "Vahanian: The Worldly Church and the Churchly World," *Continuum* 4, 1 (Spring 1966): 61–62.

37. Martin Buber, *Eclipse of God: Studies in the Relation between Religion and Philosophy* (New York: Harper, 1952), preface.

2

Is God Dead?

. ·•· ———— ·•· .

Some Aftereffects and Aftershocks of the Holocaust

JOHN K. ROTH

You will sooner or later be confronted by the enigma of God's action in history.

—Elie Wiesel, *One Generation After*

Religion was not a sufficient condition for the Holocaust, but it was a necessary one. What happened at Auschwitz is inconceivable without beliefs about God first held by Jews and then by Christians. Holocaust and genocide scholars have explored the similarities and differences between the Holocaust and other genocides. Although the field of comparative genocide does not often make the point, one aspect of the Holocaust that is qualitatively different from all other programs of extermination and mass destruction in the modern period can be stated as follows: No example of mass murder other than the Holocaust has raised so directly or so insistently the question of whether it was an expression of *Heilsgeschichte*, that is, God's providential involvement in history. More than any other disaster in modern times, the Holocaust resonates and collides with the religio-mythic traditions of biblical religion, the dominant religious tradition of Western civilization. Unavoidably, the Holocaust raises questions about the "death" of God.

Breaking Silence

Steeped in silence, which it also broke, Elie Wiesel's memoir, *Night*, abridged from the Yiddish version (1956), appeared in French (1958) and then in

English (1960). One of its recollections focuses on the observance of Rosh Hashanah at Auschwitz in 1944. Amid the congregation's sighs and tears, Wiesel (b. 1928) heard the leader's voice, powerful yet broken: "All the earth and the Universe are God's!"[1] As the words came forth, Wiesel recalls that they seemed to choke in the speaker's throat, "as though he lacked the strength to uncover the meaning beneath the text."[2] *Night* does not explain that meaning, silently leaving readers to wonder about it.

Almost thirty years later, another Holocaust survivor, the philosopher Sarah Kofman (1934–1994), wrestled with silence when she spoke about smothered words, knotted words that "stick in your throat and cause you to suffocate, to lose your breath"; they "asphyxiate you, taking away the possibility of even beginning."[3] Expressing the dilemma she felt as a survivor trying to communicate with others, Kofman went on to ask, "How is it possible to speak, when you feel . . . a strange *double bind*: an infinite claim to speak, *a duty to speak infinitely*, imposing itself with irrepressible force, and at the same time, an almost physical impossibility to speak, a *choking* feeling?"[4]

Wiesel and Kofman help to show that *silence*—the word and reality—is fraught with meanings. They can include a lack of interest, even indifference about events and ideas. Silence may reflect ignorance, humility, or shame; it may be a response to awesome beauty or immense destruction. It may signify, with special intensity and emotion, that even when one speaks, it is still possible to be speechless, for one may not know what to say or cannot find words that are appropriate, meaningful, and credible in relation to what is present, remembered, or yet to be faced.

It is one thing to remember that the Holocaust happened, to memorialize that disaster, to find ways to incorporate memory and memorialization into religious ritual, and to do so with reverence and love.[5] It may be something else, however, to deal with the philosophical and religious questions that continue to jar consciousness and conscience as those actions take place. Whatever silence(s)—mythical or otherwise—may have surrounded the Holocaust during and after that disaster, questions about God, justice, evil, and meaning reverberated in that chasm and continue to do so.[6] Theologians and philosophers have a long history of attempts to respond to versions of those dilemmas, but what responses did they make—and when did they make them—as awareness of the Shoah grew? In what ways did their encounters with the Holocaust make theologians and philosophers grapple not with myths of silence but with metaphysical and moral silences that still leave their traditions shattered and even reduced to silence when the Shoah penetrates them deeply? As post-Holocaust theology and philosophy attempt to salvage fragments of meaning from the Holocaust's devastation, the credibility of those efforts depends on reckoning with silence(s) that remain even when they are broken.

Forty years after World War II, the Jewish philosopher and theologian Emil Fackenheim (1916–2003) made an exaggerated but still valid point when he asserted that "philosophers have all but ignored the Holocaust."[7] Fackenheim prominent among them, notable exceptions to that judgment can be found in the relatively early postwar years.[8] Nevertheless, the Holocaust has never attracted as much philosophical and specifically ethical inquiry as might be expected after an event of such devastating proportions. Perhaps philosophy's reluctance to break silence about the Holocaust is an expression of humility, a profound puzzlement about what to say, but a stronger case can be made that much of philosophy in the second half of the twentieth century and on into the twenty-first has simply not attended to history as much as it might have done. In the meantime, while the impact of the Holocaust on religious thought and practice—within Jewish and Christian traditions in particular—was felt to a greater extent, and earlier too, it remains to be seen how deeply the Holocaust's reverberations have penetrated and to what lasting effect.

Especially among Orthodox Jews, whose Eastern European communities were devastated by the Shoah, a great deal of theological reflection took place, as circumstances permitted, in German-occupied areas, ghettos, and camps or in places of refuge to which they had escaped while the Holocaust raged. Many of those who produced these wartime *Responsa* did not survive the Holocaust. According to Gershon Greenberg, a leading scholar on this *Responsa* literature, during the first two postwar decades, the wartime theological reflections, whether their authors survived or not, were "overlooked by the historians, even denied."[9]

In the anguished wartime reflections of those who wrestled with God and the catastrophe engulfing them, one finds versions of the themes and quandaries that remain key parts of post-Holocaust religious thought, except that the wartime *Responsa* are particularly poignant because they were made in the midst of the destruction. Some of the major issues, which can be put in five question-clusters, include the following: 1) How is the traditional covenant between God and the Jewish people to be understood in the light of that people's decimation? Will there be a saving remnant, and, if so, what is its destiny? 2) How, if at all, is God involved in the devastation? Is the destruction part of a redemptive plan? Does it signify the birth pangs of the Messiah? 3) Is something new and unprecedented taking place, or does the destruction fit within traditional interpretations of the tribulations that have befallen the Jewish people in the past? 4) How should God be identified in such crushing circumstances? As omnipotent? Hidden? Suffering? Beyond understanding? 5) What responses to God are appropriate? Rejection? Protest? Faithful waiting? Repentance? Martyrdom? Justification of God's ways—theodicy? Silence?

During and after the Holocaust—whether in the first two decades or those that followed—versions of these issues have remained central in post-Holocaust religious thought. As those efforts explore events and the meanings beneath words and texts, versions of Kofman's "double bind" are detectable. The Holocaust may make one feel a duty to speak, an obligation to state how the Shoah relates to religious traditions, but such work can produce a choking feeling, a sense that too much harm has been done for a good recovery to be made, a suspicion that religious convictions may be overwhelmed by the challenges they face. The bind is double because any attempts to overcome these difficulties remain hopelessly optimistic and naïve unless they grapple with the despair that encounters with the Holocaust are bound to produce. To be touched by that despair, however, scarcely encourages religious commitment and belief. Hasia Diner's study of postwar American Jewish life, for example, shows that the Holocaust produced a resurgence of Jewish identification in the United States, but she aptly cites Albert Gordon, rabbi and anthropologist, whose 1959 study concluded that "while the suburban Jew 'believes that there must be a God who created this world, he cannot understand [God's] continuing association with the Jews or, for that matter, with mankind. He has seen so much misery and wretchedness. . . . The fate that recently overtook six million Jews in Europe has shaken what little faith was left in him."[10] Fifty years later, the relevance of that judgment and its challenges still hold.

Whatever the silence(s) produced by the Holocaust, they were not absolute. In the English-speaking world, important Jewish thinkers such as Martin Buber (1878–1965), Abraham Joshua Heschel (1907–1972), and Chaim Grade (1910–1982) early on raised agonizing questions concerning how traditional beliefs about God could be sustained in a world shadowed by the Holocaust. On the Christian side, the work done before, during, and after the Holocaust by the British scholar James Parkes (1896–1981) forcefully documented the Christian roots of anti-Semitism and persistently made important contributions to postwar Christian-Jewish relations.[11] In the Anglo-American context, however, the most widely discussed and long-term influential theological writings by individual thinkers who focused explicitly and persistently on the Holocaust did not appear primarily in the late 1940s, the 1950s, or even the early 1960s. A longer gestation period seems to have been required, as writers struggled to figure out what most needed to be said and then sought the words to break difficult silences. The results were more challenging than comforting, a point that can be illustrated by attention to four significant thinkers—three Jews and one Christian—who have done much to sustain attention to issues that deserve to remain prominent in post-Holocaust religious thought.

The God of History

In the summer of 1961, a young rabbi named Richard L. Rubenstein (b. 1924) planned to begin a research trip to West Germany on Sunday, August 13. That same day, the East Germans created a major Cold War crisis by hastily building a wall between East and West Berlin. Postponing his trip for two days, Rubenstein arrived in Bonn, the West German capital, and accepted an invitation from his hosts, the *Bundespressamt* (Press and Information Office) of the Federal Republic to fly to Berlin to see the unfolding crisis. In an atmosphere charged with fear that nuclear war might erupt, Rubenstein took the opportunity to interview Heinrich Grüber (1891–1975), a prominent German Christian leader who had resisted the Nazis, rescued Jews, and suffered imprisonment in Sachsenhausen.[12] Earlier in 1961, Grüber had been the only German to testify for the prosecution at the Jerusalem trial of Adolf Eichmann, a leading perpetrator of the Holocaust.

With American tanks rumbling through the streets of Dahlem, the West Berlin suburb where Grüber lived, Rubenstein interviewed him in the late afternoon of August 17. When their conversation turned to the Holocaust, this meeting became a turning point in Rubenstein's personal and intellectual life. Grüber affirmed a biblical faith in the God-who-acts-in-history. More than that, he held that the Jews were God's chosen people; therefore, he believed, nothing could happen to them apart from God's will. When Rubenstein asked Grüber whether God had intended for Hitler to attempt the destruction of the European Jews, Grüber's response was yes—however difficult it might be to understand the reason, he told Rubenstein, the Holocaust was part of God's plan.

Rubenstein was impressed that Grüber took so seriously the belief that God acts providentially in history, a central tenet of Judaism and Christianity. To Grüber, that belief meant specifically that God was ultimately responsible for the Holocaust. Although Grüber's testimony struck him as abhorrent, Rubenstein appreciated the consistency of Grüber's theology, and the American Jewish thinker came away convinced that he must persistently confront the issue of God and the Holocaust. The eventual result was Rubenstein's first and immensely important book, *After Auschwitz: Radical Theology and Contemporary Judaism*, which appeared in 1966. A second edition of *After Auschwitz*, so extensively enlarged and revised as to be virtually a new book, was published in 1992 with a different subtitle: *History, Theology, and Contemporary Judaism*.

After Auschwitz was among the first books to probe systematically the significance of Auschwitz for post-Holocaust religious life. Rubenstein's analysis sparked ongoing debate because it challenged a belief that many people have long held dear. After Auschwitz, Rubenstein contended, belief in a redeeming God—one who is active in history and who will bring a fulfilling end to the upheavals in the human condition—is no longer credible.

In the late 1960s, the stir caused by *After Auschwitz* linked Rubenstein to a group of young American Protestant thinkers—Thomas Altizer (b. 1927), William Hamilton (1924–2012), and Paul van Buren (1924–1998) among them—who were dubbed "death of God" theologians. The popular media picked up the story. *Time* magazine's cover story on April 8, 1966, featured the topic, and the movement ignited public discussion for some time.[13] Although the spotlight eventually moved on, these thinkers' contributions—especially Rubenstein's—did not fade. Their outlooks posed questions and their testimonies raised issues too fundamental to disappear. Yet neither the labeling nor the clustering of these thinkers was entirely apt. None was atheistic in any simple sense. Nor were their perspectives, methods, and moods identical. What they loosely shared was the feeling that talk about God did not—indeed could not—mean what it apparently had meant in the past. In that respect, the term "radical theology" described their work better than the more sensationalistic phrase "death of God." Creating breaks with the past and intensifying discontinuities within traditions, they ventured to talk about experiences that were widely shared even though most people lacked the words or the encouragement to say so in public. Unlike his Protestant brothers, however, Rubenstein put the Holocaust at the center of his contributions to radical theology in the 1960s. *After Auschwitz* provoked Holocaust-related searches that continue to this day.

The 614th Commandment

In 1968, Emil Fackenheim delivered the Charles F. Deems Lectures at New York University, which were published two years later as *God's Presence in History: Jewish Affirmations and Philosophical Reflections*.[14] About one hundred pages in length, this brief and often reprinted book contains one of the most powerful of the relatively early religious responses to the Holocaust. According to Fackenheim—he fled his native Germany in 1939 after imprisonment in the Nazi concentration camp at Sachsenhausen, taught for many years at the University of Toronto, and then immigrated to Israel, where he died in 2003—the Holocaust was the most radically disorienting "epoch making event" in all of Jewish history.[15] In contrast to Rubenstein, Fackenheim argued that the Jewish people must respond to this shattering challenge with a reaffirmation of God's presence in history. Fackenheim acknowledged that it is impossible to affirm God's saving presence at Auschwitz, but he did insist that while no "redeeming Voice" was heard at Auschwitz, a "commanding Voice" was heard and it enunciated a "614th commandment" to supplement the 613 commandments of traditional Judaism. The new commandment was said to be that "the authentic Jew of today is forbidden to hand Hitler yet another, posthumous victory." Fackenheim spelled out the 614th commandment, which he first articulated in 1967, as follows:

> We are, first, commanded to survive as Jews, lest the Jewish people perish. We are commanded, second, to remember in our very guts and bones the martyrs of the Holocaust, lest their memory perish. We are forbidden, thirdly, to deny or despair of God, however much we may have to contend with Him or with belief in Him, lest Judaism perish. We are forbidden, finally, to despair of the world as the place which is to become the kingdom of God, lest we help make it a meaningless place in which God is dead or irrelevant and everything is permitted. To abandon any of these imperatives, in response to Hitler's victory at Auschwitz, would be to hand him yet other, posthumous victories.[16]

Few, if any, post-Holocaust religious statements by a Jewish thinker have become better known.[17] For some time, Fackenheim's 614th commandment struck a deep chord in Jews of every social level and religious commitment. Much, but by no means all, of Fackenheim's writing was on a philosophic and theological level beyond the competence of the ordinary layperson. Not so this passage, which is largely responsible for the fact that Fackenheim's interpretation of the Holocaust arguably became for a time the most influential within the Jewish community. A people that has endured catastrophic defeat is likely to see the survival of its community and its traditions as a supreme imperative. By referring to a divine command, Fackenheim gave potent expression to this aspiration. Instead of questioning whether the traditional Jewish understanding of God could be maintained after Auschwitz, he implied that those who questioned God's presence to Israel, *even in the death camps*, were accomplices of the worst destroyer the Jews have ever known. The passion and the psychological power of this position are undeniable.

Nevertheless, Fackenheim's position could have unfortunate consequences. Not only were those Jews "who denied or despaired" of the scriptural God seemingly cast in the role of accomplices of Hitler, a serious and controversial allegation indeed. In addition, Fackenheim went so far as to suggest that those who did not hear the "commanding Voice" at Auschwitz were *willfully* rejecting God: "In my view," he wrote, "nothing less will do than to say that a commanding Voice speaks from Auschwitz, and that there are Jews who hear it and Jews who *stop their ears*."[18] To stop one's ears is a voluntary act. Fackenheim seems to have either excluded or ignored the possibility that some Jews might honestly be unable to believe that God was in any way present at Auschwitz, no matter how metaphorically the idea was presented. Furthermore, in spite of its power, Fackenheim's position was not without difficulty even for the tradition he sought to defend. Given his conviction that revelation was inseparable from interpretation, it was not clear whether the commanding Voice was to be taken as real or metaphorical. Subsequently there was reason to believe that Fackenheim would reject both alternatives and would hold that the commandment would have been unreal absent an affirmative Jewish response. Taken literally, there does not appear to be any credible evidence that anybody heard the 614th commandment, as indeed Fackenheim's later description of how he came to write the passage indicates. In his 1982 book *To Mend the World*, Fackenheim told his readers that after he had come to the conclusion that the Holocaust was a radical challenge to Jewish faith, "my first response was to formulate a '614th commandment.'"[19] Clearly, as understood in traditional Judaism, one does not formulate a commandment. It derives from a divine source. In any event, whatever the psychological power of the 614th commandment, its status as commandment remains—perhaps unavoidably—ambiguous.

Fackenheim's critics also found considerable difficulty with his assertion that the commanding Voice had enjoined Jews to "survive as Jews." In the case of traditional Jews, no such commandment was necessary. They have always believed that Jewish religious survival was a divine imperative. They had no need of an Auschwitz to receive such an injunction. In the case of secularized Jews, the commandment appeared perhaps to be a case of pedagogic overkill. It hardly seemed likely that even a jealous God would require the annihilation of six million Jews as the occasion for a commandment forbidding Jews to permit the demise of their tradition.

Perhaps the most important aspect of the 614th commandment was the injunction not to deny or despair of God lest Hitler be given "yet other, posthumous victories." Here Fackenheim confronted the fundamental issue of Holocaust-related theology. He told his readers what God has commanded. Does this mean that Fackenheim perpetrated a fiction in order to maintain the theological integrity of his reading of Judaism? Given Fackenheim's faith in some sense of a Divine Presence, it was hardly likely that he could have thought of God as absent from Auschwitz. As Fackenheim came to realize that the real difficulty lay in formulating a view of God that took the Holocaust into account, he understood that one could no longer speak of a *saving* presence at Auschwitz. Yet, utter defeat and annihilation could not be the last word. A way out of the ashes had to be found. The 614th commandment expressed what most religious Jews regard as their sacred obligation in response to the Holocaust. In the language of Jewish faith, that response could most appropriately be communicated in the imagery of the commandments. Fackenheim's 614th commandment is religiously and existentially problematic. That, however, may remain beside the point. It is perhaps best to see Fackenheim's 614th commandment as a cry of the heart, transmuted into the language of the sacred. That would at least help to explain why it has touched so many Jews—and a lot of Christians, too—so deeply.[20]

A Credibility Crisis

Along with interest in Wiesel's *Night* and his early essays and fiction, the writings of Rubenstein and Fackenheim influenced some Christians as well as Jews.[21] One of them was Franklin Littell (1917–2009). On July 23, 1998, his friend, the Holocaust historian Yehuda Bauer, interviewed Littell at Yad Vashem in Jerusalem, where the two scholars frequently led seminars on the Holocaust. The interview provides an overview of Littell's primary concerns and concludes with remarks that succinctly capture his character, outlook, and aspirations. Underscoring that his motivation in writing and teaching about the Holocaust was above all to prevent "premature closure," Littell ended the 1998 interview by declaring his intent "to keep this thing [the memory of the Holocaust] irritating—you know, be the harpoon that the fish can't escape."[22]

Those who knew Littell may hear his voice in those words—a voice that was earthy and earnest, intense and impassioned, edged at times with laughter and humor, but one that cut to the chase as he expressed his conviction that the unredeemable atrocities of the Holocaust and of all genocides must provoke resistance against the injustice and indifference that produce them.

The catalog of the United States Library of Congress contains thirty-four Littell entries. The earliest titles, from the 1950s, suggest that this ordained Methodist minister, who held a doctorate in theology and religious studies, might have had a conventional professorial career. During this early period, he concentrated on church history in the United States, with an emphasis on Protestant Christianity and church-state relationships. However, much more was gestating. A visit to Nazi Germany in 1939 made an indelible impression on Littell—one that was deepened and intensified by his work in postwar Germany, where he served as the chief Protestant advisor for the U.S. occupation forces. These experiences honed the harpoon that Littell would thrust at multiple targets, including, first and foremost, his own Christian tradition.

Two books loom largest in Littell's body of works. Christian scholars James Parkes (1896–1981) and Edward Flannery (1912–1998) preceded Littell in documenting their tradition's culpability for anti-Semitism, but Littell's 1975 monograph *The Crucifixion of the Jews* was nonetheless groundbreaking in that it drove home Christian responsibility for and complicity in the Holocaust. Written in the aftermath of the military attacks on the state of Israel in 1967 and 1973, Littell's book also staunchly defended "the right of the Jewish people to self-identity and self-definition."[23]

Littell often referred to the Holocaust as an "alpine event," his way of identifying its unprecedented, watershed significance. In his view, the Holocaust constituted the most severe "credibility crisis"—one of his favorite terms—to afflict the Christian tradition. That tradition's "teaching of contempt" about Judaism and Jews had contributed mightily to genocide against the Jewish people, he believed. Only profound contrition and reform, including fundamental theological revision that tackled the New Testament's anti-Judaic themes, could restore integrity to post-Holocaust Christianity.

Littell's belief that Christianity faced a monumental credibility crisis was not based solely on his knowledge of the centuries-old history of Christian hostility toward Judaism and Jews. More immediately, his postwar experiences in Germany made him painfully aware that most German churches had embraced Adolf Hitler and Nazism. He recognized the complicity of German churches in the Holocaust, as well as the widespread indifference of the churches outside Germany when it came to the plight of Jews under the swastika. Yet, he understood that some Christians and churches in Germany had resisted Nazism and, at least to some extent, assisted Jews. Thus, even before Littell published *The Crucifixion of the Jews*, his pioneering work resulted in the other entry that looms largest among his works, the 1974 volume *The German Church Struggle and the Holocaust* (coedited with his friend Hubert G. Locke).

Important in its own right—among other things it contains a memorable exchange between Richard Rubenstein and Elie Wiesel—this volume signaled the pivotal role that Littell played as an organizer and leader in both Holocaust studies and Christian-Jewish relations. *The German Church Struggle and the Holocaust* emerged from a conference that Littell and Locke convened at Wayne State University in 1970. Focused on Christians in Nazi Germany, their support for and resistance against Hitler's regime, and that conflict's implications for the future of Christianity and its relationship to Jews and Judaism, the meeting was the first in a series of conferences that would become the Annual Scholars' Conference on the Holocaust and the Churches. This interfaith, interdisciplinary, and international gathering of scholars, educators, clergy, and community leaders remains the longest continuously running initiative of its kind. The conference's work, including many publications, has significantly influenced and advanced the field of

Holocaust and genocide studies and stands as a tribute to Littell's influence and his persistent thrusting of a "harpoon that the fish can't escape."

No More Theodicy

Influential contributions to post-Holocaust religious thought were also made relatively early by the Jewish philosopher Emmanuel Levinas (1906–1995). By the 1960s and 1970s, he was developing an important post-Holocaust ethical perspective, which drew extensively, if not always explicitly, on his Jewish heritage by arguing that previous ethical theory had failed to concentrate on something as obvious and profound as the human face.[24] Close attention to the face of the other person, Levinas affirmed, could produce a reorientation not only of ethics but also of human life itself, for our deepest seeing of the other person's face drives home how closely human beings are connected and how much the existence of the other person confers responsibility upon us.[25]

Levinas did not write explicitly about the Holocaust very often, but traces of that catastrophe do appear, and the overt emphases of his thought make plain that the Shoah is a powerful point of reference between the lines, in the silence—the void even—that shadows his philosophy. On some occasions, however, the Holocaust comes to the fore in Levinas's writing. One example is found in his brief but highly significant essay called "Useless Suffering," which did not appear early but in 1982. In that article, Levinas explicitly states a conviction that permeated his thought early and late. "The Holocaust of the Jewish people under the reign of Hitler," said Levinas, "seems to me the paradigm of gratuitous human suffering, in which evil appears in its diabolical horror."[26]

As a French prisoner of war, Levinas did forced labor under the Nazis, and almost all of his Lithuanian family perished in the Holocaust. It made a profound impact upon him. Calling the twentieth century one of "unutterable suffering," he emphasized that suffering of the kind that the Nazis and their collaborators inflicted on Europe's Jews was and is "for nothing." To try to justify it religiously, ethically, politically—as the Nazis did when they made the practice of useless violence, as Primo Levi (1919–1987) identified it, essential to the German "superiority" that they envisioned—was what Levinas called "the source of all immorality."[27]

When Levinas said that the useless suffering inflicted during the Holocaust was "for nothing," he did not overlook Nazi "logic" and what it meant. To the contrary, he took National Socialism to be about arrogant destruction, its grandiose rhetoric about a thousand-year *Reich* notwithstanding. The chief element in National Socialism's arrogance was that regime's resolve to deface the human face with remorseless determination. The Nazis did this not in some abstract way but by useless suffering visited upon Jewish women, children, and men that made its anti-Semitic prerogatives dominant until overwhelming force stopped them from doing more of their worst.

Levinas thought that the twentieth century was one of "unutterable suffering." The evil in that suffering, and Levinas believed that "all evil relates back to suffering," was not confined to "persistent or obstinate" bodily pain but included "helplessness, abandonment and solitude," an abjection intensified when "a moan, a cry, a groan or a sigh" brought no relief but were swallowed up by silence. Levinas distinguished between "suffering *in the other*" and what he called "suffering *in me*." The latter's uselessness could have meaning insofar as it was "a suffering for the suffering (inexorable though it may be) of someone else." As for the uselessness of the suffering of the other, Levinas thought that striving to relieve it and to resist the forces that created it should be "raised to the level of supreme ethical principle—the only one it is impossible to question—shaping the hopes and commanding the practical discipline of vast human groups."[28]

No sooner did Levinas write those words than he issued a caution about them. In no way should they be construed as a justification for suffering, as a mitigation of suffering's uselessness, because such suffering could become the means to the good and the virtue of relieving it. Observing that its temptations should not be underestimated, Levinas rejected all forms of *theodicy*, the attempt to make suffering "comprehensible," to find "in a suffering that is essentially gratuitous and absurd, and apparently arbitrary, a meaning and an order." Noting that "Nietzsche's saying about the death of God" had taken on "the meaning of a quasi-empirical fact" in the Shoah and that the paradox in Emil Fackenheim's allusion to the commanding voice at Auschwitz, namely, that it entails "revelation from the very God who nevertheless was silent at Auschwitz," Levinas affirmed that Fackenheim saw something of seminal importance not only for Jews but for humanity itself. Levinas put his point in the form of an extended question:

> Must not humanity now, in a faith more difficult than before, in a faith without theodicy, continue to live out Sacred History; a history that now demands even more from the resources of the *I* in each one of us, and from its suffering inspired by the suffering of the other, from its compassion which is a non-useless suffering (or love), which is no longer suffering "for nothing," and immediately has meaning?[29]

Levinas could not answer this question, at least not simply, because the response to it depends on how humanity breaks the silence that follows his asking.

Conclusion

Attempts to maintain traditional understandings of covenant and God's presence in history, analyses denying the credibility of providential divinity, searches that affirm the more-important-than-ever status of ethics and religion in times when traditions are in crisis and in contexts of atrocity and suffering that make every theodicy problematic—all of these perspectives and more emerged during the Holocaust and in its relatively early aftershocks. If it took time for some of these developments to unfold, if it is still taking time for them to find expression, that outcome should not be entirely surprising. What would be lamentable is failure to keep asking and pursuing the questions that the Holocaust raises—sometimes in word(s), sometimes in silence(s).

The Holocaust's place in history was not fixed at the time of its happening or in its short-term aftermath. The philosophical and religious quandaries evoked during and after the Shoah have no easy closure, if they allow closure at all. No one-size-fits-all quality pertains to them. Nor does a response made at one time suffice for all times. Inevitably, the Holocaust's place, its presence, is still in the making, with aftershocks that will continue to require the recognition and reconsideration, the contesting and breaking of silence, particularly with regard to God's death, reality, power, and relationship to history.

Notes

1. Elie Wiesel, *Night*, trans. Marion Wiesel (New York: Hill and Wang, 2006), 67.

2. Ibid. An earlier translation of *Night* nuances this quotation by referring to "the meaning beneath the words." See Elie Wiesel, *Night*, trans. Stella Rodway (New York: Bantam Books, 1982), 64.

3. Sarah Kofman, *Smothered Words*, trans. Madeleine Dobie (Evanston, IL: Northwestern University Press), 39. Kofman's book originally appeared in French in 1987.

4. Ibid., 38–39.

5. Important reflections on and examples of liturgical responses to the Holocaust can be found in Marcia Sachs Littell and Sharon Weissman Gutman, eds., *Liturgies of the Holocaust: An Interfaith Anthology*, new and revised ed. (Valley Forge, PA: Trinity Press International, 1996). The examples of Holocaust liturgies in the volume listed in this endnote come from civic and religious settings. They include texts, ritual acts, and music from the time of Holocaust itself and from the early postwar years, but the editors also make the following observation: "In the early 1970s, Yom HaShoah was observed by only a few dozen congregations in America. During the administration of President Jimmy Carter, observation of the Days of Remembrance grew rapidly and marked a permanent day on the calendar. Every American president since that time has supported this endeavor" (1).

6. See, for example, Dan Cohn-Sherbok, ed., *Holocaust Theology: A Reader* (New York: New York University Press, 2002) and Steven T. Katz, Shlomo Biderman, and Gershon Greenberg, eds., *Wrestling with God: Jewish Theological Responses during and after the Holocaust* (New York: Oxford University Press, 2007).

7. Emil Fackenheim, "The Holocaust and Philosophy," *The Journal of Philosophy* 82, 10 (October 1985): 505.

8. See, for example, Albert Camus, *The Plague* (New York: Modern Library, 1948); Karl Jaspers, *The Question of German Guilt* (New York: Dial Press, 1948); Hannah Arendt, *The Origins of Totalitarianism* (New York: Harcourt, 1951) and *Eichmann in Jerusalem: A Report on the Banality of Evil* (New York: Viking Press, 1963); Abraham Joshua Heschel, *Man Is Not Alone: A Philosophy of Religion* (New York: Farrar, Straus & Young, 1951); Martin Buber, *Eclipse of God: Studies in the Relation between Religion and Philosophy* (New York: Harper, 1952) and *On Judaism* (New York: Schocken Books, 1967); Theodor Adorno, *Prisms* (London: Neville Spearman, 1967) and *Negative Dialectics* (New York: Seabury Press, 1973); Emmanuel Levinas, *Totality and Infinity: An Essay on Exteriority* (Pittsburgh, PA: Duquesne University Press, 1969); Emil Fackenheim, *God's Presence in History: Jewish Affirmations and Philosophical Reflections* (New York: New York University Press, 1970); and Jean Améry, *At the Mind's Limits: Contemplations by a Survivor on Auschwitz and Its Realities* (Bloomington: Indiana University Press, 1980).

9. See Katz, Biderman, and Greenberg, eds., *Wrestling with God*, 11.

10. Hasia R. Diner, *We Remember with Reverence and Love: American Jews and the Myth of Silence after the Holocaust, 1945–1962* (New York: New York University Press, 2009), 327.

11. Lawrence Baron helpfully discusses some of these early developments in "The Holocaust and American Public Memory, 1945–1960," *Holocaust and Genocide Studies* 17, 1 (2003): 62–88.

12. Rubenstein's essay, "The Dean and the Chosen People," depicts these events. See Richard L. Rubenstein, *After Auschwitz: History, Theology, and Contemporary Judaism*, 2nd ed. (Baltimore, MD: Johns Hopkins University Press, 1992), 3–13. See also Richard L. Rubenstein, *Power Struggle* (New York: Scribner, 1974).

13. See Stephen R. Haynes and John K. Roth, eds., *The Death of God Movement and the Holocaust: Radical Theology Encounters the Shoah* (Westport, CT: Greenwood Press, 1999).

14. My discussion of Fackenheim is adapted from Richard L. Rubenstein and John K. Roth, *Approaches to Auschwitz: The Holocaust and Its Legacy*, rev. ed. (Louisville, KY: Westminster John Knox Press, 2003), 348–352.

15. See Emil Fackenheim, *God's Presence in History: Jewish Affirmations and Philosophical Reflections* (Northvale, NJ: Jason Aronson, 1997), 8–14 and *To Mend the World: Foundations of Future Jewish Thought* (New York: Schocken Books, 1982), 9–22.

16. In traditional Judaism, the number of commandments given by God to Israel is said to be 613. The passage originally appeared in *Judaism* 16 (Summer 1967): 272–273. The text of Fackenheim's contribution to that journal's symposium on "Jewish Values in the Post-Holocaust Future" is reprinted in Emil L. Fackenheim,

The Jewish Return into History: Reflections in the Age of Auschwitz and a New Jerusalem (New York: Schocken Books, 1978), 19–24. See also Fackenheim, *God's Presence in History*, 84–98. In the 1997 edition of the latter work, Fackenheim includes a new preface, "No Posthumous Victories for Hitler: After Thirty Years, the '614th Commandment' Reconsidered." Noting that the phrase "'no posthumous victories for Hitler' became a slogan, often poorly understood, and as such liked by some, disliked by others, mocked by a few," Fackenheim added that "what 'no posthumous victories for Hitler' asked of Jews was, of course, not to spite Hitler, but to carry on *in spite of* him" (xii, Fackenheim's emphasis).

17. One of the most noteworthy competitors for that distinction would be Irving Greenberg's "working principle," namely, that "no statement, theological or otherwise, should be made that would not be credible in the presence of the burning children." See Greenberg, "Cloud of Smoke, Pillar of Fire: Judaism, Christianity, and Modernity after the Holocaust," in *Auschwitz: Beginning of a New Era? Reflections on the Holocaust*, ed. Eva Fleischner (New York: Ktav, 1977), 23.

18. Emil L. Fackenheim, *The Jewish Return into History: Reflections in the Age of Auschwitz and a New Jerusalem* (New York: Schocken, 1978), 31; emphasis added.

19. Fackenheim, *To Mend the World*, 10.

20. For further commentary on Fackenheim's thought, see David Patterson, *Emil L. Fackenheim: A Jewish Philosopher's Response to the Holocaust* (Syracuse, NY: Syracuse University Press, 2008).

21. Prominent among them would be: Robert McAfee Brown, Harry James Cargas, A. Roy and Alice Eckardt, Darrell Fasching, Eva Fleischner, David Gushee, Stephen Haynes, Elisabeth Maxwell, Johann Baptist Metz, John T. Pawlikowski, Carol Rittner, Dorothee Soelle, Paul M. van Buren, and Clark Williamson.

22. Bauer's interview with Littell is available online at: http://www1.yadvashem.org/odot_pdf/Microsoft%20Word%20-%203725.pdf.

23. Franklin H. Littell, *The Crucifixion of the Jews* (New York: Harper and Row, 1975), 3.

24. For evidence of Levinas's engagement with Judaism and Jewish tradition, see Emmanuel Levinas, *Difficult Freedom: Essays on Judaism*, trans. Sean Hand (Baltimore: Johns Hopkins University Press, 1990), *Nine Talmudic Readings*, trans. Annette Aronowicz (Bloomington: Indiana University Press, 1990), and *New Talmudic Readings*, trans. Richard Cohen (Pittsburgh, PA: Duquesne University Press, 1999).

25. See Emmanuel Levinas, *Ethics and Infinity* (Pittsburgh, PA: Duquesne University Press, 1985) and *Entre Nous: On Thinking-of-the-Other*, trans. Michael B. Smith and Barbara Harshav (New York: Columbia University Press, 1998).

26. "Useless Suffering" was published originally in the *Giornale di Metatisica* 4 (January–April 1982): 13–26. It is more readily found in Levinas, *Entre Nous*, 91–101. The quoted passage is on page 97.

27. The quotations in this paragraph are from Levinas, "Useless Suffering," in *Entre Nous*, 94, 97, and 99.

28. The quotations in this paragraph are from ibid., 94.

29. The quotations in this paragraph are from ibid., 96–97 and 100.

3

Altizer

· ◆ ———— ◆ ·

The Religious Theologian, Then and Now

JOHN B. COBB JR.

Cobb on Altizer: 1970

In 1970 I made the following observations about Thomas Altizer, the leading death of God theologian of the 1960s. Today I believe that Altizer was not only the most original theologian of his time but possibly the most creative theologian of the twentieth century. I reflect on this claim by way of conclusion to the 1970 essay, abridged and reprinted here.[1]

The late sixties in this country will be remembered in theology chiefly for the remarkable public attention directed to radical theology and especially to the idea of the death of God. Paul van Buren, William Hamilton, Gabriel Vahanian, and others shared the spotlight of national attention, but Thomas J. J. Altizer was the most prominent figure. In these last few years he has been the most widely and most heatedly discussed American theologian.

Not only has Altizer's theology been the most widely discussed, it has also been the most influential. The furor over the "death of God" has altered the theological climate in America irreversibly. As late as the early sixties, some form of biblical theology or neo-orthodoxy was the point of departure for most theological discussion. As the decade closed, these movements appeared to have chiefly historical interest. Even those whose present positions have developed from them—such as Langdon Gilkey, Gordon Kaufman, Dietrich Ritschl, Thomas Oden, and Peter Berger— now address themselves in a quite different way to what they recognize as a quite different situation. Much of this change was already incipiently occurring, of course, or the response to Altizer's challenge would not have been so dramatic. Nevertheless, it required public discussion to bring into dominance the mood of radicalism. For that public discussion, Altizer has major responsibility.

The claim that Altizer has been the most influential American theologian in the past few years would collapse if it meant that he was the most widely followed or even read! Although he has rejoiced to lead in the shattering of the apparent consensus of the past generation, there remains a gulf between his vast influence in negation and the limited response to his constructive solution of theological problems. Many have agreed that in our time honesty requires that we be atheists, but few have had any appreciation for the remarkable form of "atheism" Altizer actually proposes. His influence has encouraged the emergence of an ethical Christian humanism that is poles removed from his own theology.[2]

A third claim is more subjective than the first two but still widely acceptable: Altizer is also the most original and creative American theologian of this period. For this reason the lack of understanding of his constructive theological position is particularly unfortunate. His theological assertions differ so profoundly from the dominant theological radicalism of our time, as well as from the neo-orthodoxy and liberalism of the recent past, that some have tried to write him off as an irresponsible eccentric. But few who have studied him seriously, and even fewer who have known him well, have found it possible to dismiss his thought in this way. Whether one agrees with him or not, one discovers in his writings a coherent vision of great power. In addition, one finds that this vision has been arrived at, not by personal whim, but by an approach to Christian theology in the context of the history of religions, an approach that is widely approved but rarely attempted. Indeed, Altizer is the first major theologian since World War I to think theologically from the perspective of the study of the history of religions conceived on a world scale.

This point needs explanation. Other theologians, of course, have approached the study of the history of religions from a theological point of view, and their theology has been influenced by what they have learned. Some have studied Christianity as one of the world's religions from the point of view of the historian of religions. Others have thought theologically from a perspective shaped by study of the Near Eastern religions of biblical times. But these are quite different matters. Altizer is not *first* a Christian theologian who *then* is affected by studying other religions, and he is not a historian of religions who wants to place Christianity in the total context. He is a theologian whose categories and questions are shaped by profound immersion in the study of the planetary history of religions. Among past theologians, Troeltsch and Otto come closest to this theological method, but today, approximation to their approach leads to quite different results.

Whereas the first three claims for Altizer's importance may be widely admitted, the fourth may appear strange and even perverse. Of all the American theological writing of this period, it is Altizer's that embodies the most vigorous and passionate faith. The widely assumed contrary view has two major causes. First, the initial impact of Altizer has been upsetting to the faith of others. His negations have come across more effectively than his affirmations, and Altizer, convinced that what is being uprooted is in fact already dead, has done little to soften this destructive consequence of his thought. Second, many associate "faith" indissolubly with "God" and hence cannot understand the denial of God as an act of faith.

Nevertheless, a careful and open reading of Altizer will convince one that he [sic] is encountering a profound expression of faith of a sort rare in current theology. Altizer does not understand himself as a man who, because of holding certain traditional values, *still* calls himself a Christian. That point of view is easy to find in our times. It expresses a situation in which a man's fundamental self-definition is ethical, or humanistic, or scholarly, or secular, but in which he secondarily accepts the designation of himself as Christian also. In contrast, Altizer is first and foremost a Christian. Like many passionate Christians before him (Luther and Kierkegaard, to mention just two examples), he is intensely critical of the Christianity he finds about him. But such criticism has no other basis than faith itself.

Furthermore, this faith is not a name arbitrarily given to some aspect of his existence. It is faith in the Word, in Christ, in the Incarnation of God, in the Kingdom of God. True, these terms take on new meanings in Altizer's thought, but they are not unrecognizable meanings. On the contrary, they are traditional meanings taken with such radical seriousness as to transform them. Even the "death of God" is affirmed, not as a concession to modern skepticism, but as the deepest Christian meaning of Incarnation and Crucifixion. Furthermore, Altizer's faith enables him to discern in the present world what other Christians anxiously miss—the real presence of Christ. He is "persuaded that everyone who lives in what we know as history participates at bottom in the life of Christ" and "that the task of theology is to unveil and make manifest the universal presence and reality of Christ."[3]

These statements make clear that Altizer is also the boldest evangelical[4] theologian of our time. While most American theologians seek to provide some justification for Christians to remain Christian, to overcome some misunderstanding of faith, or to guide the church in the responsible direction of its energies, Altizer addresses the "cultured despisers" with the word that they live by participation in Christ. How successful he will be in reaching his public cannot be foretold. It would be idle to suppose that those whom he persuades will hurry to the local church to share in its worship and cultural activities! But the evangelical purpose is clear.[5]

On Faith and Culture

There is little doubt that Christian morale is currently at low ebb. Historic Christian beliefs appear either incredible or irrelevant. Those who are most sensitive and perceptive have abandoned them, sometimes because they *wished* to do so, more often because traditional faith has simply lost the power to shape vision and experience and to guide action. The great artists have developed new categories. Christians are widely perceived as a rear guard composed of those who do not trust reason, experience, and enlightened sensibility.

One response to this situation is to understand Christianity as the creation in history of a new and in some sense final mode of human existence. Elsewhere, I have characterized this Christian existence as self-transcending selfhood expressing itself in concern for the other as an *other*. This mode of being is the fundamental ground of what has been most dynamic, most creative, and most redemptive in Western history and, more recently, in the Westernized history of the entire planet. It has freed men [sic] personally and intellectually to raise radical questions and to develop whole new disciplines of thought.

Ironically, the thinking for which men [sic] have been freed by Christian existence has increasingly undercut the beliefs that are bound up with that existence. Such existence involves effort, tension, the bearing of burdens, and the postponement of rewards. These have been endurable and even enriching in the context of the historic Christian understanding of man [sic] as living from God and for God. But in the absence of some such vision, men [sic] are empty, and Christian existence cannot long endure. It will be destroyed by its own fruits.

The alternative to the disappearance of Christian existence is the emergence of a new vision capable of sustaining intentional communities whose vitality would enable them to revivify part of the remains of the institutional church. A church in which credible and relevant conviction expressed itself in consistent and appropriate disciplined action would not have to be large to be redemptively effective.

This view defines Christian faith in terms of continuity in a mode of existence, while recognizing the constantly new intellectual task of articulating doctrines required and supported by it. It can acknowledge the powerful attraction of competing ideas and visions without therefore accepting them. Thus the Christian differentiates himself and his faith from the dominant cultural currents of his time, not by ignoring them, but by discriminating appraisal, selective appropriation, and constructive reconceptualization.

This response presupposes that Christian faith has its fundamental existence in some isolation from the fundamental movement of history. For Altizer, precisely this isolation from the movement of vision and spirit is faithlessness. We have, in his view, no static essence of Christian faith or existence in terms of which to evaluate other modes of belief and existence. Where authentic creativity is to be found, there is the reality with which faith has to do. Thus true Christianity can and must reverse itself in the most fundamental ways in order to be true to itself. Since all that we have known as Christian existence, or personhood, or even humanity is swept away in the new visions of our time, faith requires that we affirm their death. The Christian is not to plan strategies for salvaging or reviving what is dying but rather to learn to see the new as the dialectical continuation, through transformation, of the old. In the deepest sense, faith is the affirmation of what *will* be rather than the attempt to shape an indeterminate future.

The task of theology is to articulate the teaching of the church only to the extent that the church's teaching grasps and expresses the reality of our historical situation. Altizer understandably judges that this extent is currently very slight. If Christian theology is to escape from the ghetto in which it has imprisoned itself, it must enter the arena in which man's [sic] reality is being creatively discerned and shaped, and today that is far from the church. Yet Altizer enters that arena convinced that the reality in question, however it is now being named, is truly Christ. Indeed, for him the very essence of faith is this conviction, and it is this faith that frees the Christian for total openness to the reality of his time, however dark and empty it may appear.

On Theological Style

An important feature of the style of Altizer's thought is suggested by the word "Totality." Altizer thinks in terms of wholes. He seeks the essence of an idea, a doctrine, a point of view; when he finds it, he discards all the qualifications with which it is surrounded in order to elicit its pure and radical meaning. This is the reason for much of the exasperation sometimes felt by his critics. In the course of time, many doctrines have been hammered out cautiously, replete with qualifications that adjust them to the various difficulties that have been encountered. Altizer ignores everything but what the doctrine in its purest essence communicates in our situation. Obviously the judgment here is somewhat subjective, and those who have been articulating the doctrine resent the neglect of their careful formulations.

At the same time, this is the reason for much of Altizer's power. He avoids involvement in the subtle and sophisticated arguments in which much academic theology bogs down. By going to what he sees as the heart of the matter and capturing it in pure and extreme form, he breaks open the broader question and forces total reconsideration.

His own intellectual development illustrates this violent refusal of qualification and moderate formulation. As late as the early 1960s, Altizer believed Christianity to require of us a total rejection of all that the modern world understands as reality and creativity. Apocalyptic was for him the pure manifestation of biblical faith, and apocalyptic was the rejection of this world in the name of a Kingdom of God that is wholly alien to it. The error of historic Christianity was that it compromised by coming to terms with the world and by affirming its value.

Altizer found that this position put him in an extremely painful situation existentially. He was forced to reject all that he admired most in art, literature, and scholarship. Furthermore, he recognized that although biblical eschatology resembled Oriental [sic] mysticism in its negation of the given reality, it was a different sort of negation, which somehow also affirmed the forward movement of time and history.

Another man might have responded to this situation by cautiously modifying some of the extreme elements in his earlier position, but not Altizer. Instead, he reversed himself totally. Christian eschatology and Incarnation now are seen to mean a total affirmation of the world, a total identification of the sacred with historical reality. Christianity, instead of being at bottom identical with Oriental [sic] religion, is juxtaposed as its opposite. Historic Christianity is condemned for clinging to the symbols of a transcendent other.

The pattern of negation and reversal of which Altizer writes so much is here embodied in his own development.[6] This can also be illustrated in his view of the traditional Christian doctrine of Creation. At one level this doctrine may be seen as a theory of the origin of the universe, but at this level it interests neither Altizer nor his critics. Fundamentally, the doctrine expresses a particular view of the reality and worth of the world and thus of human life. This view has a twofold movement of thought.

First, he [sic] who understands the world and himself [sic] as created perceives both as real and valuable. All being is affirmed as good because it is the product of God's purposeful intention and activity. In spite of all the horrors of suffering and sin, human life and its entire historical and natural context must be affirmed, and one must devote his energies to serving his fellowman in the concreteness of his bodily existence rather than seeking escape from these given conditions. Because the doctrine of Creation is thus an affirmation of the world, the early Altizer rejected it as a perversion of the apocalyptic negation of the world that was for him then the heart of faith.

Second, he [sic] who understands the world and himself [sic] as created perceives nature, history, and his own being as radically contingent, radically dependent upon God, radically subordinate to the Creator in both worth and reality. The meaning of life is not found, finally, in life itself as empirically given. Goodness, value, and meaning are found unqualifiedly, independently, or intrinsically only in God himself [sic]. The meaning of human existence is derivative. Because the doctrine of Creation thus subordinates the world to God, the later Altizer rejects it as a perversion of the incarnational affirmation of the world that is for him now the heart of faith.

In this way Altizer's thought has exemplified something of the coincidence of opposites that is so important to him. There *is* an affinity between total negation and total affirmation that separates them both from all qualified forms of affirmation and negation. Both total affirmation and total negation repudiate any discrimination between degrees or levels of truth and falsity or of good and evil. Both thus exclude the sphere of the ethical, the weighing of particular values against one another. They exclude in a profound sense positive concern for the individual in his separated individuality. They demand a solution of the human problem that is unequivocal, absolute, total. Thus the forward movement of history must be toward an end in which that movement will come to absolute rest or at least to total moments in which all past and future are abolished.

The most thoroughgoing and disturbing result to which Altizer's program has come thus far is to be found in *The Descent into Hell*. Here the totality toward which we are borne is identified insistently with hell and death. Not only has transcendence emptied itself into immanence, and the sacred into the profane, but heaven empties itself into hell, and life now empties itself into death. In this way, Altizer seeks to claim as an epiphany of Christ even the hell and death to which the modern spirit is drawn in fascinated horror.[7]

Altizer's theological convictions show not only passionate faith but incomparable spiritual strength and courage as well. The theological program to which Altizer enjoins us is a task that only a few men [sic] have attempted or accomplished. First, one must unequivocally renounce one's individual selfhood as the center and ground of consciousness and experience. This proposal in itself is exceedingly difficult for modern man [sic] to comprehend, let alone instigate; for, in order to combat the onslaught of modern alienation, modern man [sic] has withdrawn to the refuge of his inner "self." The irony, however, is that once there, he [sic] discovers that he [sic] has only intensified his [sic] alienation.

Second, one must give up completely any hope of heaven or utopia, the womb or the Garden. In essence, one is called to reject all concepts of a primordial homeostasis; for, according to Altizer, all such yearnings contradict the fundamental movement of the sacred and what Blake called the great "Humanity Divine." Again such a demand threatens modern man's [sic] security and his [sic] deepest desires for a lost paradise. One must realize that this applies not only to the most fundamentalistic Christian but also to the most doctrinaire Marxist-Leninist. Perhaps we will come to realize, despite the passionate convictions of a Blake, a Nietzsche, or an Altizer, that only a few men have had the strength or the courage to will the "final and total loss of Heaven"; that most of us will inevitably cling to visions of utopia and will persistently deny the dialectical movement of the sacred and the New Jerusalem that Altizer claims is dawning in our midst and in our flesh.

Cobb on Altizer Today

At some point in the future Thomas Altizer may be recognized as the greatest theologian in the second half of the twentieth century. That judgment would, of course, depend on a changed understanding of the task of theology. As long as theology is connected with the church and its official teaching, Altizer will remain a marginal figure. But if Christian theology comes to be understood as the interpretation of the spiritual life of that part of the world that has been most deeply informed by Christianity, then Altizer's work may be fully recognized and appreciated as authentic theology.

There is no one else whom I can identify so fully as *homo religiosus*. Altizer lives and breathes in the sphere of religion. For that reason he understands the religious meaning of belief and unbelief, of theism and atheism, of history and of the loss of history, of creation and apocalypse, as no one else. I marvel at the religious depth and power of his writing. I am often more than a little jealous.

Altizer's writing has more the function of poetry than of typical academic theology. We look to the poet neither for dogma nor for argument. We do not expect information. We look to the poet for insight and vision. In Altizer's history of theology, those thinkers the church calls theologians play a very little role. He traces the history of authentic theology as much through poetry and fiction as through philosophy. Dante and Blake and Joyce are as important for him as Hegel and Nietzsche. When teaching theology seemed closed to him, he took a position in an English department teaching Blake.

I met Altizer when we were fellow students at the University of Chicago. His gifts were recognized by faculty and fellow students, but he had little respect or appreciation for the intellectual climate there that I found so exhilarating. The discussions at Chicago were about the implications of new developments in science and philosophy for the understanding of human nature, or the phenomenon of religion, or of God. Historical relativity was fully appreciated, since Chicago had been the center of the socio-historical school. We were interested in the religious dimension of culture, especially of our own, but also elsewhere. What we could now believe was to be determined by reason and experience. We were all empiricists, but our empiricism was the radical empiricism of James rather than the sensory empiricism of the British philosophers. Despite our interest in constructing an appropriate Christian theology for our time, our approach was fully secular.

For Altizer this secular study of matters of religious importance was of little interest. To that, he much preferred Barth, although few Barthians would have recognized him as a colleague. In our professor of the history of religions, Joachim Wach, and especially in his successor, Mircea Eliade, he found something of the depth of religious penetration and vision that he sought. But he did not become a disciple. He thought about what was truly happening in the spiritual depths of Western culture. There he saw not only the death of God but of the human as well.

A few years later we were colleagues at Emory University. For a while he had sought to oppose himself to the cultural reality of unbelief, but in the end he decided that instead he must embrace it. Authenticity could be found only at the cutting edge of the Hegelian *Geist*. That meant for him—in the depths of Hell. He could only hope that in the depths of Hell there would be the coincidence of opposites. Only there could the world find salvation, a position that became clear (as I noted in 1970) in the publication of *The Descent into Hell*.

To will oneself into the movement into Hell requires a tremendous act of faith in the Spirit. If *Geist* leads us into Hell, then we must will Hell in order that Hell will become for us salvation. This total authenticity is to me immensely impressive. But lacking Altizer's faith, I have taken an entirely different direction.

I confess that in my own perception, my efforts remain superficial alongside Altizer's plumbing of the depths. But I lack his gifts, and my calling is different. I agree with Altizer that the modern world, at multiple levels, leads to Hell. But that leads me to ask why, and it seems to me that it has made some profound mistakes that might, even now, to some extent be rectified. I have found in the thought of Alfred North Whitehead the basic corrections that modernity needs, and I have sought to ally myself with feminists, ecologists, Buddhists, and postmodernists of other stripes. Altizer rightly notes that among the deeper thinkers of our day there is little resonance to what any of us have to say.

The level at which I am most concerned and involved is not the religious one so profoundly grasped by Altizer but the secular one outlined half a century ago by the Club of Rome and intensified by our newer understanding of the consequences of climate change. I do not want the world to go into that Hell, although it seems all too probable that it is going just there. I can will only to make what pitiably small contributions I can to reducing the coming suffering. The theology that would help in this respect is a fully secular one.

Altizer understands religiously the quest for secular salvation. I often feel he understands me better than I understand myself, even when he pays little attention to the details of my argumentation. The issue for him is not whether an argument is valid but whether an idea, an insight, a hypothesis touches the deeper chords of sensibility in those whose sensitivity is most fully honed to the spiritual reality of the time. In that respect it is obvious to me as well that thus far I have failed. Only in China is the situation somewhat different.

Altizer had his moment as a public figure. For a few years his proclamation of the death of God joined with that of a few others to create a national sensation. Clearly it resonated widely in the culture. Sadly, although Altizer had many opportunities to speak, the depth of his insight was rarely understood. For the most part, the "death of God" was thought of simply as another way to affirm an increasingly widespread atheism, an atheism that understood itself to reject religion as a whole in the process of rejecting God. Altizer continued his journey into the spirituality of the godless depths almost alone, a reality to which his memoir, *Living the Death of God*, testifies.

Altizer has himself been surprised that the death of God has penetrated so far into the thought of the church that, much to my own distress, "God" has become something of an embarrassment in some parts of the liberal or progressive theology. He bemoans the near disappearance of serious theology in the progressive Protestant seminaries—as do I. Altizer's "death of God" never meant that believers should cease to concern themselves with God. It certainly did not mean that the church could dispense with God and then go about our business as usual. To read Altizer is to know that God is of utmost importance, even, perhaps especially, in God's death.

Notes

1. This material is drawn from the introduction to *The Theology of Altizer: Critique and Response*, ed. John B. Cobb Jr. and Nicholas Gier (Philadelphia: Westminster Press, 1970). Used by permission.

2. Eds.: Identifying Altizer's theology as "Christian atheism" was part of what led so many to a misunderstanding of his thought. Altizer was and is not a conventional atheist. As Cobb subsequently explains, Altizer rejects a particular *mode* of divine being or reality—not the divine as such.

3. Personal letter to Cobb, July 7, 1969.

4. Eds.: Altizer is "evangelical" in terms of his focus on the gospel or good news that something decisive and healing for humanity has happened in Christ.

5. Eds.: We omit the section on ontological realism and include the sections on the normative relation of faith to culture and on Altizer's style.

6. Eds.: This "reversal" would be the last in Altizer's theological development. Thereafter, as Lissa McCullough points out, his perspective would deepen by exploring the implications and consequences of the self-annihilation of God in history. See McCullough, Introduction to *Thinking through the Death of God* (Albany: State University of New York Press, 2004).

7. Eds.: We here omit the review of Altizer's work to 1970, and include only the concluding paragraphs of the essay.

4

God Is Still Dead

.·◆·———·◆·.

Retrieving the Lost Legacy of William Hamilton

G. Michael Zbaraschuk

Mention the death of God and several names immediately come to mind. In philosophy, Nietzsche and Hegel enjoy a renaissance (if they were ever in eclipse). In theology, Altizer and Rubenstein continue to draw attention as well. More recently, Žižek offers a new (or old?) incarnation of the Marxist atheist Christian. New volumes continue to offer ways in which the death of God can be considered.[1] And yet, in most discussions of the death of God in the late twentieth and early twenty-first centuries, one of the primary architects of the movement in the 1960s and 1970s typically goes unnoted. William Hamilton, whom Altizer himself called "the most articulate spokesman of the theology of the Death of God," is curiously absent from most discussions. Is it that he did not have the mystical depth of Altizer, the metaphysical grounding of the process theologians, the orientation to liberation of William Jones? Perhaps not. Why has this particular strand of radical theology been invisible? Why has less attention been paid to Hamilton than to other heralds of the death of God?

Many of the articles that come out as he and the other death of God theologians aged were full of laudatory statements about them as people and their "contributions" to academic or personal contexts. I propose to take Hamilton's theological viewpoint seriously, to ascertain why it has been in eclipse, and to resurrect his understanding of the death of God as essential. Especially given the ongoing and pervasive unholy uses of "God"—the word, the concept, and the reality—resurrecting Hamilton's notion of the death of God is almost a moral imperative.

How, then, does the "most articulate spokesman" of radical theology understand the death of God? Hamilton is remarkably consistent by way of response. It is, as he himself acknowledges, a continuation of biblical theology or neo-orthodoxy—"we know what the word 'God' means, and that concept is no longer a reality." Whether in contemporary religiosity, as a function in the lives of believers, or as a "guarantor of some external future,"[2] "God" the concept or word no longer holds the same meaning as "God" did for Calvin or Barth or Bonhoeffer (or, really, for Niebuhr or Tillich). "God" now means not "the God above God" or transcendence as such, or the wholly other, or anything like them. It is now "pure idol without remainder," the reification of desire, or a justification of selfishness or national interest.

Setting this basic consistency in his perspective aside, we can nonetheless split Hamilton's work into three distinct emphases, which (of course) invoke and overlap one another—they are the descriptive, the prophetic, and the creative moments in his theological enterprise. Represented as cultural types, they are the detective, the assassin, and the artist.[3] They are not strictly (although they are partially) chronological. My emphasis here will be to explicate the methodological and metaphorical emphases in Hamilton's body of work, showing how his own understanding and advocacy of the death of God changes and develops over the years into as constructive a work, albeit with different forms, as Altizer's (or, frankly, Vattimo's or Caputo's or Taylor's—all of whom he anticipates and/or betters). Far from being irrelevant, Hamilton's version of the death of God is a vital resource for combating the lesser gods of tribalism and fundamentalism run amok in our contemporary culture.

Detective

The first of these emphases is the descriptive phase, influenced by Nietzsche, Bonhoeffer, and (to a lesser degree) Barthian and biblical theology of the 1940s and 1950s. In this descriptive phase, the metaphor that Hamilton uses is "discovery," the tone is one of wonder, loss, and (at times) resigned surprise, and the primary characters that arise over and over are Nietzsche's madman and Ivan Karamazov.

In this phase, Hamilton looks at the Christian culture that he (as a professor of biblical theology) plays a leading role in and pronounces it a whited sepulcher and a graveyard of God. In this he is not really that different from Vahanian,[4] or perhaps even more correctly, from Kierkegaard who criticized the Danish church of his time for its complacency. Hamilton, however, is not content to stop there and become a critic of the Christian establishment. That's too easy an escape for someone of his honesty and depth. Hamilton then describes the reality, not that God cannot be found in the Christian religious or theological establishment, but that God, in the

Mosaic-Calvinist mode, the Barthian God of revelation, the God whose mighty acts are revealed in history, is dead. God "has lost the power to persuade in our time."[5] We have not "lost touch" with God—God is *dead*. It is not a reiteration of the trope of human sin but a description of the divine demise.

Toward the end of the so-called Death of God controversy, Hamilton invokes van Buren, another of the primary figures who crafted this call for the death of God from the perspective of linguistic philosophy, and names this discovery of the death of God a "language event," noting that he and lots of other people knew what they meant by the word "God" and that they no longer attach any reality to the concept—it no longer has a "life" in religious thought and practice.[6]

Hamilton, in describing this phase of thought and mode of description, calls himself and others "detectives"—those who have come across God's corpse and hunt to tease out and chronicle the events that led up to the dastardly deed. (While Altizer will locate God's death in the incarnation of the ongoing reality of God, Hamilton is more likely to place it somewhere between 1793 and 1958, depending on who's talking). Post World War II, in American Protestant culture, immediately after the so-called Third Great Awakening and the expansion of white American Protestantism that accompanied the wave of suburbanization, Hamilton finds that God is no longer the reality that he (for Hamilton, this God is male) once was and that the power has gone out of him—he has "given up his spirit."

Hamilton is this "detective" on the trail of the death of God in a variety of his works, especially the early ones. His work in journals from the early and mid-1960s exhibits this detective mode of dealing with God's death—nowhere more evident that in the essays collected in *Radical Theology and the Death of God* and his *New Essence of Christianity*. This second little book outlines continuing themes in Hamilton's "discovery" of God's death—the fragmentary style that he uses with such mastery in *On Taking God Out of the Dictionary*, the insistence on the picture of Jesus (regardless of its historical accuracy) as a place to stand, in the traditional language of "Jesus as Lord," in the sense of the one to whom you owe ultimate allegiance with regard to your ethical or moral stance in the world.

In this detective mode, it must be asked why he is simply not another minister (and theologian) who has lost his faith—another tragic figure like Clarence Wilmot in John Updike's *In the Beauty of the Lilies*? Mostly, it is because Hamilton does not concede either his theological vocation (he will insist "I was, and am ordained") or his academic life (he moves, not to a menial job, but to English departments and academic administration). He also maintains his Christianity, following (perhaps) Feuerbach and (certainly) Bonhoeffer in his insistence on the relevance of Jesus as Christ and Lord without the guarantee of God to cash his metaphysical checks. Jesus's eschatological insistence and his ethical stances, as portrayed especially in the Synoptics, are the creative pieces here.

While this "detective" phase and metaphor is invoked in a variety of his works, it is not a phase that Hamilton ever relinquishes. It is an ongoing trope that continues in various forms as the basis of the other phases—the prophetic and creative emphases that are the other two moments in Hamilton's theological legacy. Especially, this continued emphasis in standing with the neighbor evolves into the full-blown ethical emphasis that is the second of the loose groupings of Hamilton's thought that I will explore here.

Assassin

What does it mean to "stand with the neighbor"? The continued emphasis on the Lordship of Jesus the Christ will inspire Hamilton to move beyond the mere "detective" mode, which articulates the death of God as a cultural fact, and into the assassin phase, actively seeking to kill God. Rooted in the earlier characterization of God as a language event (evocation of van Buren), Hamilton notes the changing character of the word "God" in the American situation, and his consistent stance leads him to change his tactics. By *On Taking God Out of the Dictionary*, he claims that we cannot reinterpret the meaning of "God" to fit our own tastes but must reject God entirely. By *On Reading Moby-Dick*, he has moved to an actively murderous agenda.

Hamilton, in several different places, invokes Alice from Carroll's eponymous work, and her insistence that one cannot make words into whatever one wants them to be. The word "God" has an accepted usage for Hamilton, and he sees his own position of denying the reality of the experience as more honest than that of those he variously calls the "revisers" or the "re-definers" or the "do-overs." His basic point here is that it is unfair to say that God is something so radically different than what accepted usage has been that no one would recognize it. Thus the critique of a Cobbian process "God" is that it is not really the God of the tradition of biblical theology at all.[7]

In the move from the 1960s through the 1980s and beyond, Hamilton's attention to the usage of the word "God" in American theological discourse gives him more and more pause and will encourage him to move into the "killer" mode. As he points out, this new "God" is very much alive, functioning as a force for hatred, division, bigotry, racism, and exploitation. This is not even the God of the biblical theology movement who was so useful for resisting the Nazis or other nationalisms—this is the God of the "Jesus Freaks" who reinforces white middle-class culture and who caused a

Black Panther leader to note that if one "scratches them you find a middle-class white supremacist pig."[8]

This insight, that "God" may not be as dead as advertised but has perhaps taken new and demonic form, continues in Hamilton's relatively consistent emphasis on the problematic character of the "maleness" of God—from his early nods to the "women's movement" to his insistence that this activist God is "too male" to be allowed to live. He does not spell out why this is (perhaps he assumes that it is obvious), but he moderates this criticism with his suspicion of feminist theology and the problematic character of redefining "God" as "female" or Goddess. "She can castrate as effectively as God, but with different weapons."[9] All in all, he is consistent in his critique of "re-defining" God and allowing him *or* her to live—he finds it too dangerous.

Prophetic talk of the murdering of God takes on its most eloquent expression in several chapters of Hamilton's *Reading Moby-Dick and Other Essays*. In "The Second Coming of the Death of God" and "To Cast Fire Upon the Earth," Hamilton outlines the constructive task of the second-wave "killer" death of God—the prophetic insistence that "God" has become, instead of "an antidote to idolatry . . . pure idol without remainder."[10] In "The Second Coming," all too short but pithy, the entire essay is memorable phrases strung together, for example: "to have faith in one of the monotheistic Gods is more a moral than an intellectual defect." This is especially clear from the Christian side in the case of Judaism: "Christianity, even when it wraps itself in the language of brotherhood, even when it says the correct things about liberation and Karl Marx, has real trouble in not giving the impression that it is a little richer, wiser, fuller than the world of Jewish faith."[11] This is not just an affirmation of one's own self-complacency, according to Hamilton, but a real ethical danger: "the mirror of self-approval quickly turns into a sword of judgment . . . and [transforms this God's] advocates into self-righteous and dangerous sinners."[12] Far from an "innocent discovery," the murder of this murderer-God is a positive duty: "to protect ourselves, and to protect others from ourselves, we must learn to do without God." And again, "we must learn to divest ourselves of God and to be wary of those who do not." The outcome of this moral attitude may not be clear: ". . . we may or may not become more desolate, more bereft," but the payoff is worth it: "We will become more human, more tentative, more able to live easily with both adversaries and friends."[13]

Next to the negative formulations and prophetic injunctions of "The Second Coming" lies Hamilton's modest positive/constructive project on living with the death of God after we have killed him—"To Cast Fire on the Earth." This little piece, a baccalaureate address to a college in the

1980s, contains the core of Hamilton's construction of what a Christian life might look like after the death of God.

Hamilton begins the essay by rejecting any comfort from a false idea of God and with it any intrinsic meaning in life: "Life itself is an accident, life after death is a lie, and there is no excuse for being here except just being here." Nevertheless, Hamilton calls this "really good news, for it means that you and I have to make our own meaning and sense."[14] He appeals to the metaphor of fire—especially the "fire cast upon the earth" of the title, calling on the students (and readers) to "be this fire to bring worth and comfort where needed, to bring light to someone's darkness, beauty to ugliness, justice and healing to injustice and suffering."[15] He calls on the strength of the great religions of the West: Judaism, Islam, and Christianity to "maintain their teachings of deep strength and power"—that is, "that we are not our own, that we are all not absolutely free to do with our bodies and souls and lives whatever we feel like . . . that we belong in particular places in the world: alongside suffering and loneliness, making humor and love, fighting injustice, making humor and truth and beauty when we can, keeping our natural order intact."[16]

Hamilton explicitly denies a cosmic or meta-cosmic reverence for such acts: "if you make such a decision [to be the fire] in your life, no gratitude can be counted on; your decency may never be acknowledged, you are not likely to make a lot of money, and you may not even have the satisfaction of a hostile audience."[17] Nevertheless, it is to those lives that people are called—without God but with "the neighbor and the enemy." While the ethical mandates of Judaism, Islam, and Christianity mean something to Hamilton, the God supposedly behind them does not. We are to be the fire and light someone's darkness simply because it is right—not because God sanctions it.

Artist

In the third moment of his work on the death of God, Hamilton advocates for the creative imagination, informed by an eschatological faith, as the ideal way to explore the content of the death of God. From his early work in the *New Essence of Christianity*, Hamilton consistently orients himself to imaginative and creative strands, reserving his greatest praise for poets (like Dickinson) and novelists (like Melville) who explore this experience of the absence of God. This is a consistent emphasis in Hamilton's work, all the way from the *New Essence* to the *Post-Historical Jesus*. In *Radical Theology and the Death of God*, he invokes Dostoyevsky, Lionel Trilling, and the Beatles. In *On Taking God Out of the Dictionary*, besides the title borrowed from Melville, Hamilton has an extended section on Norman Mailer's theological significance for

America and Americans. In the selections on *Reading Moby-Dick and Other Essays*, there is of course an extended treatment on reading *Moby-Dick* and a theological and post-theological reading of Melville's masterpiece. And, finally, in *A Quest for the Post-Historical Jesus*, Hamilton runs through portraits of Jesus from Tolstoy, Dostoyevsky, Emily Dickinson, and a host of good and bad novels and films, always seeking the way in which their portrayals of Jesus coincide or don't with the experience of the death of God.

This explicit treatment of the literary and creative expression of the experience of the death of God is complemented by Hamilton's own creative experimentation with theological forms. He uses, at different times, to generally very good effect an interview with himself (*On Taking God Out of the Dictionary*); "T.V. Plays" (*On Taking God Out of the Dictionary*) and dialogues (*Moby-Dick* and *Post-Historical Jesus*); and short stories (*On Taking God Out of the Dictionary*). He eschews systematic work in favor of the fragment, especially the literary fragment.

Hamilton's interview with himself in the opening pages of *On Taking God Out of the Dictionary* is a good case in point to illustrate his strength as a writer in a discipline that often makes do with clumsy translations from the German. He uses the form to address issues of the genesis of the death of God theology, the title of the work, the role of the media in creating and uncreating theological sensations, his fickle theological colleagues, the shifting emphasis of his work from "detective" to "killer" modes, and his own sense of historical irony about the place of radical theology—all without boring the reader. This in itself—to address issues of history, methodology, and social placement in an interesting fashion—gives the lie to all those boring first chapters of dissertations that all of us in the profession thought we had to write at one time or another.

He does not use his own considerable talents as a writer simply to contextualize his own work, however—he also works in that time-honored form, the dialogue, often in the form of film or television scripts to make larger theological points. He cleverly uses that old-fashioned preacher's trope, the walk along the beach with Jesus, at the end of *A Quest for the Post-Historical Jesus* to illustrate the tenuous nature of our knowledge about our mysterious Lord and how much projection is involved in our constructions of what we find important. Again, to be able to use the forms of the culture to illustrate the larger theological points is part and parcel of his own commitment to the arts and their creative work in theology.

This creative vision is there throughout the earlier phases of detective and killer as well, and a concern for (and, I believe, some suspicion of) the creative aspect permeates Hamilton's entire creative work. The strongest parts of his work are when he is restrained by a sober Jesus-centered ethical and moral vision, and the parts when he is not anchored by that vision read as the most self-indulgent and dated (the optimism of the Beatles as a theological inspiration). Some minor quibbles notwithstanding, however, Hamilton's work comes across as freshly and movingly as when it was first causing a sensation back in the 1960s and 1970s. It remains to be examined, then—why did we stop reading it?

Why Eclipsed?

The second focus of this essay, after a description of the main emphases of Hamilton's work, is to explore some reasons why few have taken his vision of the death of God as seriously as, say, some folks seem to have taken Altizer's view. There are many possible answers to this problem, some of them more likely than others. There is a serious question whether or not any sort of atheistic discourse has resonance in the greater American scene.[18] There is the question of the media backlash—how, insofar as *Time* magazine made and unmade other theological movements (e.g., Tillich or Niebuhr), they were not also responsible for Hamilton's eclipse. There is the question of the institutional commitments, which Hamilton himself cites, among those who might perhaps share his views but still needed a seminary job and therefore could not alienate their more conservative supporters. This last point can always be coupled with a critique of the personal and institutional cowardice of some who believe that we are living in the time of the death of God yet fail to proclaim that fact as the most important religious one of the last century. All of these are possible, and indeed, contributory elements in a total answer as to why Hamilton's views, so lucid and powerful, have been on the decline.

In addition to these practical answers, some theological ones must also be considered. This proclamation of the death of God, simply and clearly, is the narrow way. It is the harder path, and there are few that find it. The broad and easy way is to continue to use forms and language that are outmoded, simply because it is habit or because the community demands it (as an example, think of Jewish marriage rites that entail the purchase of a woman, like a field or an ox; or Christian ones that entail that a woman obey her husband). Related organically to this notion is also that fact that the death of God has not been for years, if it ever really was, a simply descriptive exercise. In this, perhaps, Hamilton's early views were naïve—there were and continue to be demonic forces that do not want their Gods to die. They want to keep the divine zombie corpse animate for their own evil purposes. The murdering, vicious tribal Gods of fundamentalism in particular have rushed in to fill the vacuum left by the death of the Christian God. As Hamilton warned, the demons have come in and made themselves at home.

The eclipse of Hamilton's vision of the death of God is thus theologically understood as the effect of sin, in a very classical sense. It is the sin of not doing the hard and necessary work. It is a sin of leaving things undone—in this case, not finishing God off for good.

Further Reflection

Having thus explored some of the reasons for the decline of Hamilton's notion of the death of God in theological discourse, popular and academic, the following questions remain: do any parts of it need to be jettisoned as we attempt to resurrect it? Are some parts of it too problematic to be helpful? What can be unflinchingly affirmed? There are several areas that are too problematic to be maintained, and several that will continue to bear fruit in the years to come. Some of the problematic areas include his treatment of various liberation movements and his early optimism with regard to human capabilities. What will remain helpful is a methodological emphasis on Jesus (which I think bears expanding to a variety of Christian theological enterprises) and the role that Jesus (and again, by extension, other theological enterprises) can play in the life of faith. With his reading of Bonhoeffer, the call here is to follow Jesus without God. His attempt to construct a fully Christian theological endeavor without God is what will continue to be his legacy.

Liberation Movements

In Hamilton's earlier-noted suspicions of feminist theology are the seeds of the largest disappointment of his ethical/prophetic moment—his treatment of Latin American liberation themes and thinkers. Certainly some of his critiques of Sobrino and Boff are appropriate—he calls into question their uncritical appropriation of the most anti-Semitic parts of the Gospels, for example. He almost certainly has liberation thinkers in mind when he notes that Christianity almost always, even when it says the right things about liberation and brotherhood and Karl Marx, has a hard time not giving the impression that it is a little richer and deeper than Jewish faith.[19]

Even this legitimate critique, however, has some disappointing elements. The first of these is a somewhat old-fashioned and at times unstated anti-Catholic bias. Here the worldly, well-educated Euro-American Protestant seminary professor criticizes the less-educated (although not in reality!) Latin American Catholic priest-activist-theologians for either not being as concerned with his issues (anti-Semitism) or for being not educated enough in the "information that matters" (the latest in Jesus scholarship).

One always hopes that such attitudes will disappear from academic theology, and yet they continue to resurface, always disappointing.

The second disappointing element is one that is almost universally shared by academic North American and European academic theology (up to the present day) as it addressed and addresses questions brought by third world theologians. It is the mistake of dealing with these theological movements as if they were the next trend in academic theology, unconnected from the liberation struggles and grinding poverty that is their social context. So, to say to the Boffs and Segundo that their Jesus isn't sufficiently critically analyzed misses the entire point of what they are trying to do.

Hamilton's larger critique of the liberation movements in general, however, is that they are not sufficiently radical in their orientation to God and Jesus and Christian faith. Calling liberation theology "so practically interesting, so disappointing as theology" he critiques Segundo for "finding the Jesus his community desires."[20] Why he does not relate this as a parallel to his own loyalty to Jesus in his American context is puzzling. It cannot be because he finds Segundo insufficiently critical. Hamilton himself notes that it is not what critical scholarship can discover about Jesus that is normative but the picture of the apocalyptic Christ and the demands it makes on one to stand with neighbor, enemy, unfortunate. How does Sobrino not stand in the same tradition? Sobrino is grasped by the "Man for Others" who will stand against the ecclesiastical and political authorities even unto death, on the side of the poor. Why this is different than Hamilton's view on Jesus is completely unclear. This is truly disappointing. It is not a lack of political sympathy—Hamilton was against Central American expansionism. It does seem to be a theological criticism, but it is hard to find a reason for it. Even if they *might* fail on the "intellectually possible" side of Hamilton's goal of "seeking to define the conditions under which Christianity might still be intellectually and morally possible,"[21] they have the morally possible side in spades.

What Abides: Jesus/Christ, Love, Action

His inability to appreciate liberation movements notwithstanding, Hamilton has several elements in his thought that are worth preserving for further theological reflection. The first of these is the way in which he can appropriate Jesus and Christ in a post-historical fashion, beyond and outside of critical debates about Jesus as such.

It is at this point that thinking of the "Post-Historical Jesus" can offer a clue for the direction of further theological reflection. Moving beyond the debate about the "historical Jesus" is essential. Following Hamilton, I am almost entirely uninterested in Jesus as he "was" or "might have been." How Jesus was does *not* help us. I am interested in Christian theology as it comes to identify God with love, with babies, with neighbors, with "the least of these," with enemies (!), with "two or three" gathered together, with feeding the hungry, clothing the naked, visiting the sick. The historical Jesus may or may not have said or held any or all of these views. It's hard to say.

It is here that Hamilton is helpful for us. His bookends for the cultural exploration of Jesus in *A Quest for the Post-Historical Jesus* are revelatory and prophetic. In the first section, his own discussion of Jesus, he points out that we have little or no access to the historical Jesus, and what we do have is problematic. Once we critique even these pictures from what Hamilton calls a "cultural" perspective—objecting to their anti-Semitism or sexism for example—we reject at that point the possibility of the historical-critical method to help us arrive at "norms of faith and practice." Mary Daly helps us here: "Jesus might have been a feminist. If he was, great. Even if he wasn't, I am." The question becomes irrelevant, and almost always an exercise in either eisegesis or navel-gazing. This is a classical instance of the *incurvatus in se*.

And the second bookend, the conclusion of the work, continuing Hamilton's penchant for dialogues, is a conversation with a sort of contemporary fictional Jesus. Hamilton confesses to Jesus, "I wanted you to be left-liberal"—and Jesus eludes even those points that continue to grasp Hamilton. "The least of these" still have a claim, because Hamilton owns that claim upon him. "Whatever validation [of his "experience" or reflection upon Jesus would occur] by what took place in my life and work in the months to come."[22] Not by correlation with the historical probability, or by demonstration. But simply by its being a claim that grasps us.

Finally, after showing us ways to reappropriate the post-historical Jesus, what Hamilton offers to us is a fully Christian theology that is at the same time developed without God. This is at once the stumbling block and the genius of his work. It is, as mentioned earlier, one of the reasons that his work, although unanswerably lucid, remains the narrow way of the radical theologians. Christians, and especially American Christians, like to think that God exists, cares about them, and will engage in commerce—hearts and minds in exchange for eternal life. To live a Christian life simply because something in the Christian story or its theological presentation grasps one, not because there is some reward at the end, is a hard truth to swallow. Nevertheless, it is one that is both, as Hamilton himself says, morally and intellectually possible. Live in love. Do the right thing. Tell the truth. Be Jesus to the neighbor, the least of these, the enemy. Do it all without the expectation or hope of reward, but simply because one cannot do other and still claim the title of Christian. On second thought, I may need to take back everything I said about this being the narrow way. It might be the only way that being Christian is still possible in the world.

Notes

1. See the recent volumes edited by Lissa McCullough, John Caputo, and Jeffrey Robbins.

2. The phrase is Richard Rorty's.

3. The detective and killer tropes are explicitly evoked by Lloyd Steffen in his excellent and sympathetic "The Dangerous God: A Profile of William Hamilton," *The Christian Century* (September 27, 1989): 844. The artist trope is from my own analysis.

4. See Rosemary Ruether's essay in this volume for an evaluation of Vahanian's contribution to discussion of the death of God in the 1960s.

5. William Hamilton, *Radical Theology and the Death of God* (New York: Bobbs-Merrill, 1966).

6. William Hamilton, "The Shape of a Radical Theology," *The Christian Century* (October 6, 1965).

7. This is a point that Cobb and other process theologians would not dispute. The redefinition of God and the end of the God of classical theism is very much their project as well. It is not for nothing that Altizer and Cobb edited volumes on the other's work and both sensed a deep kinship in their basic commitments.

8. William Hamilton, *On Taking God Out of the Dictionary* (New York: McGraw-Hill, 1974), 179.

9. Personal conversation, cited in Lloyd Steffen's "The Dangerous God."

10. William Hamilton, *Reading Moby-Dick and Other Essays* (New York: Peter Lang, 1989), 178.

11. Ibid., 179.

12. Ibid., 179.

13. All citations, Ibid., 179. Thus Hamilton anticipates Vattimo's "weak thought" by twenty years or so. See Gianni Vattimo and René Girard, *Christianity, Truth, and Weakening Faith: A Dialogue*, trans. William McCuaig (New York: Columbia University Press, 2010).

14. Hamilton, *Reading Moby-Dick and Other Essays*, 171.

15. Ibid., 174.

16. Ibid., 174.

17. Ibid., 175.

18. As Patricia Killen notes in her book *Religion and Public Life in the Pacific Northwest: The None Zone* (San Francisco: AltaMira, 2004), belief in God seems to be one of those "American" traits—however one wants to define God.

19. Hamilton, *Reading Moby-Dick and Other Essays*, 157.

20. William Hamilton, *A Quest for the Post-Historical Jesus* (New York: Continuum, 1994), 67.

21. Ibid., 12.

22. Ibid., 288.

5

Holocaust, Mysticism, and Liberation after the Death of God

The Significance of Dorothee Soelle

Sarah K. Pinnock

I was on sabbatical when I started writing this chapter, which meant that casual conversations about my work focused on research instead of teaching. Each time someone asked what was keeping me busy, I said that I was writing about the death of God. What resulted was a small informal survey of general opinion about God's death. To my surprise, I discovered that a common response was amusement. When did God die? According to whom? To most people it is obvious that there are countless believers in God, nations praying to God, and conflicts sanctioned by God. Feeling somewhat defensive, I would explain that my work studies the repercussions of the much-publicized death of God movement from the 1960s. But to show that the movement is still relevant, I would mention that the death of God has generated new understandings of God, rather than disbelief. That response led to raised eyebrows, as if the pronounced "death" was merely academic sleight of hand. After a few minutes, these friendly exchanges would drift to more interesting topics such as my new baby.

I must agree that the slogan "death of God" seems deceptive. The major figures associated with the movement, such as Thomas J. J. Altizer, William Hamilton, Gabriel Vahanian, Paul van Buren, and Richard Rubenstein, are not conventional atheists. Although they agree in rejecting God as a scientific explanation, controller of history, or authoritarian father, these authors explore what can fill the space left by the removal of God. While they make radical departures from institutional religion, they generally continue to affirm God's relevance. Lest the term "radical" suggest that they invent something brand new, it is instructive to note that they maintain connections to Scripture and theology. Following the pattern of

Protestant thought—and this holds true even for Rubenstein as a Jewish thinker—death of God theologians claim to discover new meanings and more authentic forms of faith in God. As such, it is clear the death of God is also a birth.

Looking back at the movement forty-five years later, it is the birthing that holds most promise for the present. While I admire the movement for its intellectual bravado and postmodern prescience, if these features are its sole source of value, then its interest is purely historical. In that case, the death of God may be debated indefinitely in rarefied academic circles and the ordinary person is justified in viewing it as outdated. However, I object to such dismissal and hold that God's death has deep ethical and social ramifications.

Back in the 1960s, the death of God caught public interest in the era of antiwar and civil rights protests by offering the exciting notion that God was changing drastically along with society. Around that time, black theology, feminist theology, and liberation theology emerged to address social injustices and Holocaust theology arose in response to the horrendous evils of genocide. Rubenstein's Holocaust response notwithstanding, the death of God movement in general seems remote from concerns about social and economic equality. Summing up his assessment from an African American perspective, Hubert Locke considers the death of God movement to be a privileged, white male enterprise that does not reflect the beliefs of civil rights activists or the need for social justice.[1] It is not true that death of God thinkers completely ignore developments in society, for they are motivated by the crisis of meaning in a secular age, although Locke is correct that they do not thematize social inequalities of class, gender, and race.[2]

I am convinced that the death of God movement is constructive intellectually and ethically. To investigate the enduring impact of the movement, I shall trace the repercussions of the death of God in my own thinking and in the writings of German Protestant theologian Dorothee Soelle (1928–2003). In so doing, significant connections emerge between the death of God movement, post-Holocaust reflection, political, feminist, and liberation theologies responding to suffering, oppression, and injustice.

Autobiographical Reflections

The death of God has been a preoccupation since my undergraduate days in the late 1980s. My first vivid memory concerns the religion major's seminar I took about methodology in the study of religion. My professor read aloud Friedrich Nietzsche's parable of the madman in the first class. I recall the excitement generated by this ominous prophecy from a century ago. Without hesitation, I was convinced of the sagacity of the madman and in the context of the seminar, I came to view the academic study of religion as a symptom of this crisis in history. I saw scholars of religion as erstwhile collaborators with the death of God in mounting arguments to discredit faith. Nietzsche's parable reflects attacks on God by his predecessors Feuerbach and Marx, and anticipates twentieth-century figures such as Durkheim, Freud, Camus, and others. But not all scholars of religion intend to disabuse believers. The terminology of approaches to religious studies distinguished between descriptive and reductive, and the death of God was a reductionist critique that dismissed the reality of the divine. Academic writers were evidently responsible for killing God—but not only them. Nietzsche's madman compares churches to sepulchers and blames the death of God on "all of us," which I took to mean not only modern skeptics but also everyday persons who neglect religious practice.[3] This accusation rang true to me growing up in southern Ontario. I had observed secularization among my peers. I also saw churches struggling to prove their relevance to youth in the face of declining membership and attempts at renewal in order to attract members with new forms of worship and ministry.

As a student actively involved in Christian groups, I was disturbed by the madman's prophecy. I grew up in an evangelical Baptist family, and my father, Clark H. Pinnock, was a well-known theology professor at McMaster Divinity College. Intending to blaze my own trail, I pursued a pre-med program for three years at the University of Toronto hoping to become a doctor and researcher in molecular biology and immunology. But this field was not what I expected. The rote memorization, repetitive lab work, bleak hospital environment, and materialistic competitiveness of my peers repulsed me. By my junior year, I concluded that medical science would not be a fulfilling career. After intensive self-examination, I decided to change universities and start a new major. My interests ranged from science to classics, religion, philosophy, anthropology, and psychology. I applied to study fine art. I knew that I wanted a large measure of independence and intellectual challenge in my profession. In the end, the deciding factor in choosing religious studies was its holistic breadth. I felt that it encompassed most of my main interests, even aspects of medicine and science. I liked the fact that religion was more holistic than philosophy or the social sciences and how it posed difficult questions about knowledge, morality, and life on earth. The chief problem with majoring in religion was that I seemed to be imitating my father. The other problem was the perennial question, always posed by my current students, about employability, which I solved by deciding at age twenty-one to become a professor.

I received a BA and an MA at McMaster University in the Religious Studies Department in the Faculty of Social Sciences, strictly separated from the Divinity College where my father taught systematic theology to students heading for careers in ministry. Of course, this separation was particularly sensitive for me. Religious studies as a department took pride in its neutral and secular viewpoint, where critical scientific methods hold sway and religious truth claims are bracketed and evaded. I absorbed this approach separating my studies and my evangelical Christian involvements. But despite this attempt to build a wall between academic and personal thinking, I noticed that fellow religion majors were often looking for appealing religious ideas and coming to terms with their backgrounds. Unavoidably, students' religious standpoints were relevant even when they were suppressed, not only in my case but also among friends enamored with Asian religions. As the religion majors' seminar in methodology pondered Nietzsche's death of God, many of us were facing a process of negation as we came to terms with childhood assumptions and influences.

In addition to Nietzsche, Dietrich Bonhoeffer influenced my thinking about God's dying. Reading Bonhoeffer's *Letters and Papers from Prison* in my final undergraduate year gave me an opportunity to consider challenges to notions of God's power. At that time, I was not aware of Bonhoeffer's influence on the 1960s death of God movement, but his radical notions about embracing secularization fascinated me. In enigmatic letter form, prior to his execution in a Nazi prison in April 1945 on suspicion of assisting a plot to assassinate Hitler, Bonhoeffer criticizes traditional theism and advocates God's vulnerability. Although he is a pastor, Bonhoeffer announces a shift to religionless Christianity. He praises questioning of God as a sign of freedom from dependence on God to fill the gaps left by science and reason. He opposes metaphysical supernaturalism. Christians should live "as if there was no God" without using God as a "working hypothesis" in science, politics, morals, or philosophy. On July 16, 1944, he writes: "The God who is with us is the God who forsakes us," "before God and with him we live without God," and "God allows himself to be edged out of the world and onto the cross."[4] Bonhoeffer makes paradoxical statements denying and affirming God, which are not worked out in his letters. I found Bonhoeffer's notion of religionless Christianity an admirably daring response to the Holocaust and modern science. For me as an undergraduate, this discovery opened up the possibility of radical theology.

At the same time that I was encountering the notion that God is dead in modernity, I was also becoming fascinated by what meaning certain divine attributes might continue to hold. Augustine's *Confessions* was the topic of my senior thesis, supervised by an early church historian. But after multiple readings, rather than choosing a historical topic, I became intrigued by the philosophical and aesthetic aspects of Augustine's Platonism, which he sought to reconcile with the Bible. Then I became fascinated by Plotinus's *Enneads* and the notions of perfect goodness and oneness. In the end, I wrote about the paradox of divine freedom and necessity in Augustine. Continuing to explore difficult points in theology, my master's thesis studied the concept of omnipotence in Thomas Aquinas and objections by process philosopher Charles Hartshorne, which led me deep into theodicy debates about divine goodness and power. Exploration of divine attributes gradually shifted to focus on the problem of evil.

In 1992, I entered the doctoral program in philosophy of religion at Yale University. As in my master's degree, I chose to explore the weaknesses of philosophical theism faced with the problem of evil, which drew me toward Christian and Jewish Holocaust theology. My concern began to shift from God's nature to human suffering, particularly social group suffering due to oppression, prejudice, or genocide. I reached the conclusion that in situations of severe suffering, the theodicy question "why God?" fails to be resolved. My reasons included the philosophical inadequacies of theodicy arguments, but also the autobiographical reflections of Holocaust survivors, and the contributions of black theology and liberation theology. The testimonies of people who suffer show how faith manifests hope despite evil and despite lack of satisfying theodicy answers. In my dissertation, *Beyond Theodicy*, I explored objections to theodicy and practical faith responses such as I-Thou relations, hope, resistance, and mystical faith.[5]

Still today I object to theodicy explanations about why God allows suffering for philosophical, theological, historical, ethical, spiritual, and pastoral reasons. Neither an omnipotent God nor a suffering God is adequate. Even if God orders history providentially, God's goodness is tarnished by suffering massively and unevenly distributed. If God relinquishes control to humans, God is a spectator to evil and creation is a tragic experiment where divine intervention is withheld. In my view, the failures of theodicy indicate the death of God of philosophical theism and orthodox Christianity. The best answer to this crisis is not a new concept of God but mystical faith and ethical awareness that redemption depends on human action. Mystical unknowing recognizes the gaps left by theodicy and the scandal of God and evil. To recommend mystical faith is not to endorse naïve embrace of contradictory beliefs or rote repetition of dogmas. Rather, with critical reflection on Scripture and tradition, a mystical response to evil realizes that openness to God is transformative even despite God's death or absence.

Mystical language offers a non-theodicy response to evil as well as an alternative to patriarchal theology. Many female religious thinkers have been drawn to mystical thinking as a way to overcome authoritarian images of God, respond to evil, and gain authority for women's voices in male-dominated discourses and institutions. One recent example that I admire is the feminist Holocaust theology of Jewish thinker Melissa Raphael. Raphael observes that the hiddenness of God, proclaimed by male Holocaust theologians, represents the absence of the God who rules over history. Likewise, disappointment with God after the Holocaust by death of God thinker Richard Rubenstein is rooted in patriarchal expectations of God's power. While rejecting an omnipotent God, Raphael proposes that women's Holocaust experiences reveal God's presence. God can be discovered in the concentration camps in relationships of care—washing, warming, feeding, dressing—among women. Even in suffering and squalor, acts of touch display the female face of God in loving attention and consolation.[6] Other feminist thinkers, Jewish and Christian, also develop approaches to God in nature and human relationships that are nonpatriarchal and post-theistic. Alongside the turn to a relational and vulnerable deity, mystical language is employed to explore God's intimacy and nearness. Rejecting theodicy as a counterpart to classical theism, many feminists eschew the justification of evil and develop responses to suffering that involve hope, resistance, and empowerment.[7] There are deep affinities between responses to the Holocaust, feminist critiques of theodicy, and various responses to suffering in black, womanist, Latin American, Latino/a, political, and liberation theology. Parallels involve attention to systematic suffering, ethical resistance, and mystical acceptance of reality.

Autobiographical musings are always partial. But my intellectual journey provides a recent case study about the impact of the death of God movement from the 1990s onward. To further reflection on the contemporary relevance of the movement, I turn to an established theological writer who brings the death of God to bear on Holocaust, feminist, and liberation theology.

The Impact of Dorothee Soelle

Soelle is a German post-Holocaust liberation theologian who had a formative influence on my thinking. I first encountered her book with the stark title *Suffering* as a graduate student conducting research on theodicy. I read more of her writings and become so impressed that I considered making her the subject of my dissertation, although I was not able to find supervision among Yale faculty to study her writing. Although I pursued other avenues, my interest was undiminished and in the last year of my doctoral studies, I received a German Academic Exchange (DAAD) one-year fellowship at the University of Hamburg, which enabled me to meet with Soelle in person from 1997–1998. I took her seminar on Theology and Literature, audited courses in theology, and conducted library research in Hamburg. With her husband Fulbert Steffensky, we shared suppers of whole-grain bread and cheese at her spacious home in a leafy suburb. Our conversations displayed her passion for myriad social issues such as fair trade, environmentalism, immigration, third world development, feminism, the peace movement, anti-Semitism, and ecumenical dialogue. I also saw her joy in being a grandmother and observed the aesthetic dimension of her faith reflected in her enthusiasm for singing Lutheran church music and quoting German poetry. At that time, her self-designated *magnum opus* on mysticism, *Mystik und Widerstand*, had just been published in German.[8] We remained in contact and a few years later, I decided to edit a book on her theology, gathering contributions from her contemporaries, colleagues, and students in North America. Unexpectedly, her funeral sermon became the preface for the book because she died suddenly from a heart attack on April 27, 2003.[9]

Soelle's prolific writing career made her the best-known female German theologian of the twentieth century. The conservative university establishment in Germany never granted her a professorship in a faculty of Protestant theology because of her outspoken critical views, her interdisciplinary approach to theology and literature, her desire to balance motherhood with academics, and her accessible writing style, which did not fit conventional definitions of *Wissenschaft* (scientific knowledge). She was a published poet, and she considered theology itself a form of poetic language. From 1975–1987, she served as a professor at Union Theological Seminary in New York where she became well known to an English-speaking readership, while returning for part of each year to Hamburg. One of Soelle's notable achievements was to bring theology into contemporary life, for ordinary readers as well as scholars. Through her social involvements, she contributed to multiple contextual theologies including political, liberation, feminist, post-colonial, and post-Holocaust.

In the following pages, I trace Soelle's theology as a trajectory of the death of God movement shaped by contemporary social issues and culminating in socially transformative mysticism. My starting point is her book-length response to the death of God, concurrent with the U.S. death of God movement. The next section studies her constructive "post-theistic" theology centering on God's incarnation in human life, particularly in suffering and resistance to oppression. To conclude, I reflect on mystical language as an effective response to the death of God, drawing on Soelle's longest and final book, *The Silent Cry: Mysticism and Resistance*.

Soelle's Theology after the Death of God

Soelle's first book is titled *Christ the Representative: An Essay in Theology after the 'Death of God,'* published in German in 1965 and translated into English in 1967.[10] Her prolific writing career made her famous among scholars and laypeople as the first feminist German theologian. Like other death of

God thinkers, her main interlocutors are modern European philosophers and theologians. She follows the genealogy of the death of God back to Hegel and Nietzsche in the nineteenth century. God's death is not primarily an intellectual stance, although first articulated by philosophers. As a sociological phenomenon, the death of God is an event that conditions Western history. According to Soelle, God's death matters because it affects persons concretely as bereavement. She diagnoses the experience of God's death as a painful condition of ongoing uncertainty that cannot be resolved by appeal to objective truth or a leap of faith. Secular scientific society is unable to fulfill the human longing for meaning and personal identity.[11] This traumatic experience of being insecure and alone in the world has spread along with secularization in the twentieth century.

In *Christ the Representative* Soelle takes a post-theistic position that is characteristic of her theology as a whole. She declares the bankruptcy of traditional theism with its mythological conceptions that fill the gaps left by scientific knowledge, a critique advanced by her theological forbearers Dietrich Bonhoeffer and Rudolf Bultmann. Since God is no longer needed as a working hypothesis in morality, politics, and science, religious certainty has become impossible. God is not experienced as present or alive, but secular society cannot fully replace God. It would seem that God is lost, but this is not so, for only now does "the truth that Christ represents the absent God first take on its full significance."[12]

Soelle searches for an understanding of Jesus the Messiah that corresponds to contemporary experiences of freedom and uncertainty in the era of the death of God. In some ways, she takes on the same challenge as Thomas Altizer for whom God's annihilation is required for divine incarnation in Christ. As the title of her book indicates, Soelle employs the notion of Christ as "representative" to explain how he mediates God. Soelle identifies the main problem in Western society after the death of God as the inability to find identity and meaning. She also concludes that traditional Christian doctrine is not suited to meet this need because it operates on assumptions of human heteronomy and passivity, rather than autonomy. She rejects the doctrines of substitution or sacrifice, where Christ replaces humanity before God. She shifts emphasis away from the mythical or archetypal act of Christ saving humanity from sin, which corresponds to a spiritual understanding of salvation disconnected from the realities of history. Representation does not lapse into dependence or immaturity but safeguards human uniqueness and irreplaceability.[13] Christ as representative expresses God's powerlessness in the world and dependence on humanity.

Not only does representation respond to the anomie of people who experience the death of God, but it also underlines the provisionality of Christ's role, which has ethical import. In the past, the doctrine that

Christ secures redemption and fulfills God's kingdom has justified exclusion, prejudice, and the demonization of non-Christians. Where the church feels the strongest politically and dogmatically, claims Soelle, it becomes a totalitarian institution perpetrating violence. At the height of Christendom, the inquisition, death sentences, and pogroms against Jews were driven by dogmatic theological certitude and the spiritualization of salvation. The Holocaust is the apogee of violence against Jews condoned by the churches. As a German who witnessed World War II and its aftermath—Soelle was sixteen when the war ended—acceptance of the death of God involves repudiation of triumphalist doctrines.

It is not the triumphant "final Christ" but the "provisional Christ" who operates in the era of the death of God. To realign Christian attitudes toward Jews after Auschwitz, Soelle declares the provisionality of Christ's act of salvation. She suggests that Christians adopt a more Jewish understanding of redemption in history where God's kingdom is expected on earth. Soelle makes the strong claim that "Christ enables non-Jews to become Jews; that is to say, he enables them to live in postponement."[14] This view is realistic about obstacles to realization of God's kingdom where peace, justice, and redemption are human responsibilities. Using doctrinal language, Christ represents persons before God, and reciprocally Christ represents God in the world. Both God and Christ depend on human beings to assent actively to representation.[15] Unlike Altizer, Soelle does not dissolve God into Christ, nor does she comprehend evil within the dialectic of God's revelation. Her prophetic orientation toward the Bible is shaped by dialogue with Jewish thought and the ethical imperative to resist evil.

There are significant points of contact between Soelle's death of God theology and the position of Richard Rubenstein. They both write theology after Auschwitz, and they agree that theology is an expression of a given society. In modernity, God is in doubt. Soelle would agree with Rubenstein's statement that we live "in the time of the death of God," while she would object to Altizer's hubris in proclaiming "God is dead" as a metaphysical reality. Rubenstein too holds that in the death of God era, speech that is creative and poetic is best for expressing the ambiguous status of God.[16] Likewise, Soelle considers literature and poetry the most effective expressions of theology in a secular era.[17] Theology is embedded in culture, and it requires creative language to express searching for God who always surpasses human comprehension.

In keeping with her turn to literature and narrative, Soelle focuses on the meaning of Jesus Christ in response to God's death. However, in diametrical opposition, Rubenstein argues that thinkers who replace God with the Messiah are actually shirking its radical implications. Attacking Thomas Altizer and William Hamilton specifically, these Christian authors

cannot confront the death of God because Jesus's death on the cross has
salvific value. Jews can deal more honestly with God's death because they
do not replace God with God incarnate in Christ. Rubenstein observes that
"God simply doesn't die in Judaism" according to the Torah and tradition.[18]
Therefore, for Jews, the death of God breaks with tradition whereas for
Christians the death of God evokes images of crucifixion and resurrection.
Rubenstein believes that the appropriate response to the death of God is
mourning in a world devoid of hope and illusion.[19] He finds truth and pathos
in Dostoyevsky's observation that if God is dead, everything is permissible,
including murder. For Rubenstein, soberly affirming God's death in Judaism,
the consequences are grim realism.

Soelle would agree with Rubenstein that Auschwitz displays the failure
of the world to become God's Kingdom and makes a mockery of confidence
in human freedom. She would also accept his criticism of Christological
understandings of God's death proposed by Altizer and Hamilton that
show optimism about the future. The Dionysian jubilation and apocalyptic
confidence where Altizer embraces radical human freedom are foreign to
Soelle, who treats the death of God as an inevitability of our historical
moment, a disorienting and traumatic event. Like Rubenstein, she finds the
issue of freedom less pressing than the problem of evil. For both of them,
the "theistic God" lacks credibility after Auschwitz.[20] Rubenstein generalizes
that the "difference between Christian and Jew" is that the gospel ends
in hope, whereas the Pharisees and rabbis evidence tragic acceptance of
the broken condition of humanity.[21] But I propose that the provisional
understanding of redemption, advanced by Soelle, can be framed as an
effective Christian response to Rubenstein's critique where Christ represents
hope that is provisional, postponed, and unfulfilled. The conclusion of *Christ
the Representative* displays the close connection between the Holocaust and
the death of God, where Soelle announces that God "has been, *and still
is,* mocked and tortured, burnt and gassed."[22] What is required after the
death of God is taking on responsibility to oppose evil and bring closer
approximations to justice. Rubenstein is right to criticize some Christian
thinkers for celebrating the death of God, but Soelle demonstrates a
Christian alternative centered on God's submergence in history rife with
suffering.

A final point of convergence between Rubenstein and Soelle lies
in their constructive visions. Both authors explore mystical language and
embrace religious pluralism. Rubenstein seeks God in nature, paganism,
the mystical traditions of Jewish Kabbalah, and Buddhist philosophy. He
explores a mystical-dialectical pantheism where destruction is inherent
in God who transcends the categories of good and evil. But at the same
time, he affirms the role of traditional Jewish ceremonies invoking God as

meaningful for communal identity.[23] As we shall see, mystical expression is important throughout Soelle's writings as a response to suffering and an articulation of hope. In her later work, her thinking becomes pluralistic as she draws from Hasidic, Buddhist, Hindu, Islamic, and Native American sources to explore religious experience in nature and community.

Post-Theism and Suffering in Holocaust and Liberation Theology

As her theology matures, Soelle moves away from systematic theology and Christology toward existential engagement, liberation praxis, and literature. In the era of the death of God, traditional theology must be surpassed. In *Thinking about God* (1990), Soelle fondly recalls a conversation with Martin Buber in Jerusalem where she told him that she was a teacher of theology. He paused before replying slowly: "Theology—how do you do that?"[24] Soelle was extremely impressed with this reply, emblematic of the pitfalls in God-language. This memorable reply underlines the inadequacy of academic theology that discusses God as an "It" in contrast with the living experiences of God found in the Bible. The Bible relays narratives of I-Thou relation, as Buber defines it, consisting of personal encounter, mutuality, and reciprocity. Even when God is experienced as dead or in eclipse, faith relation remains I-Thou with other persons and the absent God.[25]

In attempting to make theology relevant for contemporary times, Soelle advances the efficacy of literary theological language including prayer, poetry, myth, and narrative. These discourses maintain a relational character and overcome the abstract and arcane vocabulary of traditional theology. Literature can offer what Bonhoeffer calls a "non-religious" interpretation of Christian concepts.[26] Although both literature and theology point toward what ultimately concerns us and what extends beyond us, literature does a better job for ordinary people in communicating the relevance of faith's aspirations. The shift to literature, also found among U.S. death of God theologians, is a response to secular and scientific irrelevancy of God-language in modern culture.[27]

Soelle pursues the implications of the death of God in *Suffering*; however, she does not propose a theodicy that justifies God. Theodicy falls into the same errors as academic theology in objectifying faith experience and reifying God. Soelle uses an impressive array of nontheological references in her book *Suffering* including popular song lyrics, interviews with factory workers, letters from Latin America, Vietnamese antiwar poetry, and quotations from classics by Sophocles, Dostoyevsky, and Brecht. While she innovates in her theological method, she also proposes changes in content. In response to the Holocaust, she cannot accept an omnipotent God who is a spectator of mass suffering and atrocity. She cannot accept a

God of justice who permits massive injustice in order to allow the exercise of human freedom. This God of classical theism is a sadist. He must die. Soelle states that "in the face of suffering you are either with the victim or the executioner—there is no other option."[28] After Auschwitz, Soelle agrees with Rubenstein's conclusion that the God of the Bible who is the providential ruler of history and protector of the people of Israel is unavoidably the author of the Holocaust.[29] She also shares the radical impulses of Hamilton, van Buren, and Altizer toward a secularized Christianity. In addition, she rejects the omnipotent author of evil on feminist grounds as a patriarchal despot, one antithetical to liberation ethics.

In *Suffering*, Soelle rejects explanations for why God permits suffering and focuses on how to make suffering meaningful, which involves mystical relation with God. The theodicy question "why God?" is replaced by the question "whom does suffering serve?"[30] Most suffering is meaningless, but Soelle does find room for accepting suffering "for God's sake." This affirmation is not the same as masochistic acceptance of pain as God's will. Instead, the purpose of accepting suffering is to help others, expose injustice, or show solidarity with an oppressed group. To make suffering meaningful does not depend on theodicy, or explaining God's plan, but on a person's reaction and creative engagement. Suffering, mysticism, and social transformation are closely related. Only in a mystical capacity, exemplified by Jesus, does suffering become dedicated to God's service.[31]

Attention to victims of suffering is central to both Holocaust theology and liberation theology. Latin American writers explore the economic causes of suffering, poverty, and resistance. Feminist thinkers add another dimension to liberation theology by exposing suffering particular to women based on insights about patriarchy in society, the Bible, and the church. For Soelle, attention to suffering includes not only victims of genocide but the poor, women, minorities, and the persecuted.[32] In *Christ the Representative*, Jesus is the representative of the absent God deferred to the eschatological future, and in her later work, the focus shifts to Jesus as a model for humanistic ethics spurred on by hope in God's kingdom. Rather than claim that Jesus's suffering was unique, Soelle views his experience as repeatable. Jesus died on the cross because he remained dedicated to nonviolent resistance against corrupt political powers. In *Suffering*, she juxtaposes reflection on Jesus's prayers and loneliness in the garden of Gethsemane with two other narratives—an autobiographical letter by a member of the Danish resistance who was shot to death by the Gestapo in 1945 and a diary entry written by Italian writer Cesare Pavese in 1940 a few years before he committed suicide. Jesus was not heroic but powerless, yet his commitment to love was stronger than death. He exemplifies the mystical affirmation of suffering, freely accepted for the sake of solidarity with others who suffer. To say yes to suffering is "to see life as a whole as meaningful and to shape it as happiness."[33] For Christians, taking up your cross means standing with the victims. Jesus models voluntary solidarity with the poor and oppressed, participation in suffering, and hope for those who struggle against violence.

Soelle enlarges on the implications of the death of God pursued in *Christ the Representative*. In *Thinking about God*, she summarizes reasons for her post-theism. Traditional theism rests on Aristotelian metaphysics where God is located at the apex of the order of being, self-sufficient and invulnerable. The theistic concept of divine omnipotence is a misguided attempt to apply perfection to God's power.[34] Soelle locates God in the world, as do U.S. death of God thinkers. She also demythologizes theological language to expose the existential search for meaning that motivates faith.[35]

Her understanding of Jesus Christ found in the world corroborates the end of theism. There is a certain resemblance here to Altizer's kenotic Christology where God becomes incarnate in the world. Both authors hold that God is immanent in the world, inseparable from human history. Also like Altizer, she continues to speak of God and employ theological or mythological language drawn from Christian doctrine and given new meanings. Nevertheless, Soelle makes no use of Hegelian dialectic, nor does she move in an apocalyptic direction. She would reject Altizer's coincidence of opposites joining the sacred and profane as a failure to repudiate and resist evil in the world.[36] Altizer's assertion that God totally empties himself into flesh is one more attempt to fit God into a philosophical system, and not only does it repeat the reification of theism, but it also has shocking implications in response to the Holocaust. For Altizer, as for Hegel, all of history including massive suffering is justified within the divine dialectical movement, thus, the Nazis like Pharaoh were God's chosen instrument.[37] Despite his radicality, Altizer's justification of history is no more an adequate theodicy than the divine providence of classical theism. Soelle would undoubtedly side with Rubenstein, who finds Altizer's theology offensive in subsuming the Holocaust in the dialectic of history and redemption.[38]

To explore the implications of her post-theism, and her reinterpretation of theological tropes, it is instructive to reflect on her understanding of divine suffering. In *Theology for Skeptics*, Soelle titles one chapter "God's Pain and Ours," where her intention is to "snatch God out of patriarchy's clinch and overcome the theodicy question as a false question."[39] Beginning with reflection on literature, Soelle frames her objections to theism using *The Trial of God* by Elie Wiesel. Set in Russia in the seventeenth century, Jewish villagers conduct a trial accusing God of cruelty toward those who love him in the context of brutal pogroms. No one in the village is willing to defend God at the trial until at night a stranger arrives. The stranger praises God's omnipotence and Jewish fidelity, and he commands the villagers to

glorify and worship God. After the trial ends, when everyone puts on their
Purim masks, the stranger dons a devil's mask and ushers in a marauding
gang to commit yet another pogrom. Wiesel's *The Trial of God* is about how
accusation may be a gesture of love for God.[40] Soelle approves of protest
to and rejection of an omnipotent God who condones suffering and death.
But the death of this God is followed by mystical seeking of divine presence
hidden in human experience and suffering itself.

Challenges to theism generated by the Holocaust are also voiced by
liberation theologians who protest the plight of the poor in Latin America.
Since the 1970s, Soelle has advocated a "first world" liberation theology
in solidarity with developing countries globally. In "God's Pain and Ours,"
she moves from Wiesel's *Trial of God* to consideration of Archbishop Oscar
Romero in El Salvador. She considers his assassination in 1980 because of
his advocacy on behalf of landless farmers against a military regime. She
ponders why the theodicy question concerning why God allows suffering
is not central for Romero, for whom Christ is an example of resistance to
oppression on behalf of the poor. God is on the side of those who suffer,
God is involved in liberation, and God depends on humans. For her as a
German, it is the comfortable detachment of a bourgeois or "first world"
purview that explains preoccupation with asking why. For someone involved
in political resistance, Soelle concludes that the most important question
should be: "How do our pains become God's pain, and how does God's pain
appear in our pains?"[41] What matters is mystical identification with God
that sustains hope and solidarity. Her post-theism differs from traditional
Christology in dealing only with God as found in this life and this world.
God's pain is defined in human terms as sorrow over the barbarity and
injustice of the world. God's pain represents collective compassion for those
who die suffering and a collective commitment to alleviating suffering.
There is no ontological or metaphysical theism and no God of the gaps to
explain events. To experience pain as God's pain requires participation in
the process of liberation. It includes involuntary suffering from poverty or
illness exacerbated by lack of medical care and voluntary suffering accepted
in solidarity with those who suffer. Suffering gains meaning directed toward
hope for God's Kingdom, or to use non-mythological language, utopian hope
for a world where no one is oppressed or hungry and sharing and relation
occur in a global community of peace.

Soelle is adamantly against the view that Holocaust suffering is
redemptive as a whole. Suffering may be redemptive only by choice, and
many victims of trauma are too broken by pain to make this choice. Yet
rare though it may be, voluntarily accepted suffering embodies "God's pain."
Soelle affirms human agency to transform the potential destructiveness of
suffering into something hopeful.[42] God's pain is human pain characterized

by acceptance, love, hope, and solidarity with all those who engage in the struggle for liberation, living and dead. God has no other hands than ours and God needs us. The post-theistic God is radically embodied and dependent.

Soelle uses mythological language for its symbolic vividness and existential expression. But is God real? In one telling passage, she considers how she would respond to someone who has absolutely no use for the concept of God but who agrees with her about accepting suffering as necessary for solidarity and activism for social justice. Her reply is experiential. What it means to embrace "God's pain" is to be borne up by hope and joy and convinced that resistance to suffering is not in vain. This positive valorization of struggle is a mystical experience and part of the mystery of life.[43] Feeling unity with others and believing in a cause are mystical experiences because they connect a person with something larger, something that transcends individuality and the present. Is the resurrection real? It is not bodily resuscitation, according to Soelle. Rather, the resurrection expresses the conviction that resisting political oppression is meaningful and enduring and a powerful message of justice and oneness in love understood politically. Jesus is not dead because he is remembered. Is incarnation exclusive to Jesus? No, for divine incarnation in the world is continual and involves solidarity with and among those who suffer. She remarks that "even today, the powerful do not succeed in extinguishing this love of justice."[44] Faith involves living in hope and resisting oppression.

For Soelle, the death of God is required by the Holocaust, feminism, and liberation. It is the death of the authoritarian God of patriarchy and colonialism, the providential God incompatible with scientific explanation and the omnipotent God who usurps human freedom. The content of God-language is humanistic, while the experience of searching for something beyond one's individual self is mystical.

Conclusion: Mysticism after the Death of God

Soelle begins her career with the death of God and ends with mysticism, but these two strands are interwoven throughout her writings. Not coincidentally, the affinity between mysticism and the death of God is also displayed in the North American death of God movement. Both Altizer and Rubenstein employ mystical approaches to give birth to God. They use dialectic, paradox, and negation to formulate an esoteric theology of unity between God and the world. But unlike these authors, her mysticism is not metaphysical but practical and activist in orientation. Soelle's thought provides an occasion for exploring the convergence of mysticism and death of God theology with contemporary challenges of oppression and economic inequality. Her theology continually returns to the question: what difference does faith make to how I live? Mysticism directs attention toward ethical concerns and the death of God transfers responsibility to human beings.

Soelle's thought provides an occasion for exploring the convergence of mysticism and death of God theology with liberation ethics. In *The Silent Cry: Mysticism and Resistance*, she investigates five places of mystical experience thematically—nature, eroticism, suffering, community, and joy—illustrated by Christian mystics, alongside Jewish, Buddhist, Sufi, and Native American examples. Mystics are not only saints, gurus, or famous figures. The capacity for mysticism is democratic and pluralistic, theistic and non-theistic. Mystics may feel intense oneness, ecstasy, longing, or even abandonment. Although mystical responses to suffering are prominent in Soelle's work, mysticism is not concerned only with travails. Mystics may feel intense happiness and a powerful connection to all of nature and humanity. This optimistic perspective is expressed in Soelle's last writing project on the mysticism of death. Published posthumously, this manuscript focuses on the importance of love and hope rather than loss. From a mystical perspective, death is a place of encounter with God.[45] Experientially, mysticism admirably expresses the contemporary epistemic crisis generated by the death of God. For instance, the *via negativa* expounded by fifth-century mystic Pseudo-Dionysus posits that God cannot be known or described because human conceptions are inadequate. The medieval English text *The Cloud of Unknowing* develops techniques of prayer to seek God in hiddenness, darkness, and forgetting. In the tradition of negative theology, German mystic Angelus Silesius conceives of God as pure nothingness, and Soelle praises Meister Eckhart who is famous for his apparently atheistic prayer: "And so I ask God to rid me of God." From this point of view, not only must God die but also the ego that claims to know God.[46] Mystics face a crisis of knowledge and security and thus anticipate secular challenges to faith.

Mystical expression is uniquely equipped to negotiate ambivalence toward God and even rejection of God. In contemporary times, science rejects God's causal relationship with the world, feminism objects to authoritarian ideals of divine power, the Holocaust discredits God's goodness, and Marxism accuses religion of perpetuating oppression. For Soelle, all of these critiques have validity and challenge traditional attributes of God. However, the appropriate response is a mystical approach to God and not a new concept of God. Poetry and literature offer narrative languages that speak to the existential concerns of faith and preserve connections with tradition. Her thinking provides evidence for my contention that mysticism can express the radical claims generated by the death of God.

Ethically, mysticism is valuable because it gives broader meaning to human life, beyond the individual to other people and the planet, and generates resistance to social injustices. In *The Silent Cry*, Soelle admiringly cites Levinas's statement that "Ethics is not the corollary of the vision of God, it is that very vision," which she paraphrases as the conviction that "resistance is not the outcome of mysticism, resistance is mysticism itself."[47] Her post-theism accentuates human responsibility for resisting social oppression while stressing that mystical attitudes sustain activism.

Soelle's social and political humanism may seem like a radical departure from the Christian tradition. But biographically, Soelle identified as a Christian and actively participated in the German Lutheran Church. She found inspiration in choral singing, led retreats for laypeople, and attended national denominational gatherings. Frequently, she cooperated with Roman Catholic activists protesting war, oppression, poverty, and injustice, and she took an ecumenical attitude toward other religions as well as other churches. She engaged in Jewish-Christian dialogue, which she considered imperative after the Holocaust. Her faith in God was not doctrinaire but based on admiration for the prophetic and mystical inspiration of the biblical tradition as well as religious classics of hymnody, poetry, and literature.

Soelle expresses her insights about God simultaneously in religious and secular terms. Characteristic of her unflinching honesty in the face of harsh realities, she devoted the last years of her life to reflecting on the mysticism of death before her sudden fatal heart attack in 2003. She advises fellow Christians to discard "faith-crutches" such as belief in an individual existence after death or in a God of good fortune who rewards his followers. Like a secular person, she takes a naturalistic position on the end of life and rejects belief in an afterlife. However, her mystical interpretation of death infuses human impermanence with hope. In the last pages of her book, she poses the question: "Is everything over when I die?" Her candid response is poignant:

> No, everything is not over. Everything continues. Everything I lived for, everything I tried to do with other people, everything I started and everything I failed at—it all goes on. I won't be eating anymore, but bread will be baked and eaten. I won't be drinking anymore, but the wine of brotherly and sisterly love will continue to be shared. I will no longer breathe as this individual, this woman of the twentieth century, but the air I breathed will be there, for everyone.[48]

This statement expresses her Christian conviction that nothing can separate us from the love of God, which in humanistic terms means that nothing can separate us from the continuation of life, love, and hope. According to Soelle, the core of mysticism is discovery of meaning and value that extends to other people and the planet. Such mysticism is inherently ethical and eminently appropriate after the death of God.

Notes

1. Hubert G. Locke, "The Death of God: An African-American Perspective," in *The Death of God Movement and the Holocaust*, ed. Stephen R. Haynes and John K. Roth (Westport, CT: Greenwood Press, 1999), 91–97.

2. Although social inequalities are not explicit material for reflection, death of God authors may recognize them as important on a personal level. For example, William Hamilton's support for Christian activism is displayed in his remark that "the theological work that is to be truly helpful . . . is more likely to come from wordly contexts than ecclesiastical ones, more likely to come from participation in the Negro revolution than from the work of faith and order." William Hamilton, "The Death of God Theologies Today," in *Radical Theology and the Death of God*, ed. Thomas J. J. Altizer and William Hamilton (New York: Bobbs-Merrill, 1966), 48.

3. Friedrich Nietzsche, "The Gay Science," in *The Portable Nietzsche*, ed. and trans. Walter Kaufmann (New York: Penguin, 1966), 95.

4. Dietrich Bonhoeffer, *Letters and Papers from Prison*, ed. Eberhard Bethge (New York: Collier Books, 1972), 360.

5. Sarah K. Pinnock, *Beyond Theodicy: Jewish and Christian Continental Thinkers Respond to the Holocaust* (Albany: State University of New York Press, 2002). As alternatives to theodicy, I consider two types of practical responses to suffering: Gabriel Marcel and Martin Buber, who offer interpersonal "existentialist" individual-ethical responses, and Ernst Bloch and Johann Baptist Metz, who give Marxist-influenced "political" social-ethical responses.

6. Melissa Raphael, *The Female Face of God in Auschwitz: A Jewish Feminist Theology of the Holocaust* (New York: Routledge, 2003).

7. Dorothee Soelle, *Suffering*, trans. Everett R. Kalin (Minneapolis: Fortress, 1975); I. Carter Heyward, *The Redemption of God: A Theology of Mutual Relation* (New York: University Press of America, 1982); Grace Jantzen, *Power, Gender, and Christian Mysticism* (Cambridge: Cambridge University Press, 1995); Wendy Farley, *Tragic Vision and Divine Compassion: A Contemporary Theodicy* (Louisville: Westminster/John Knox, 1990); Sharon Welch, *A Feminist Ethic of Risk* (Minneapolis: Fortress, 1990); Kathleen M. Sands, *Escape from Paradise: Evil and Tragedy in Feminist Theology* (Minneapolis: Fortress, 1994).

8. Dorothee Soelle, *The Silent Cry: Mysticism and Resistance* (Minneapolis: Fortress Press, 2001), trans. of *Mystik und Widerstand: 'Du stilles Geschrei'* (Hamburg: Hoffmann und Campe, 1997).

9. See Baerbel von Wartenberg-Potter, "Funeral Sermon," in Sarah K. Pinnock, ed., *The Theology of Dorothee Soelle* (New York: Bloomsbury T&T Clark, 2003).

10. Dorothee Soelle, *Christ the Representative: An Essay in Theology after the 'Death of God,'* trans. David Lewis (Philadelphia: Fortress, 1967), trans. of *Stellvertretung: Ein Kapitel Theologie nach dem 'Tode Gottes'* (Stuttgart: Kreuz Verlag, 1965).

11. Ibid., 10–12.

12. Ibid., 131. Her understanding of God's weakness and suffering is an elaboration on Bonhoeffer's statement in a letter on July 16, 1944, that "only a suffering God can help." *Letters and Paper from Prison*, 361.

13. Ibid., 132.

14. Ibid., 111.

15. Ibid., 123. Dianne Oliver explores the chronological development of Soelle's Christology in "Christ in the World," in *The Theology of Dorothee Soelle*, 119–127.

16. Richard Rubenstein, *After Auschwitz: History, Theology, and Contemporary Judaism*, second ed. (Baltimore: Johns Hopkins University Press, 1992), 250.

17. The poetic nature of Soelle's theological language is explored in Andrea Bieler, "A Calling in a Higher Sense," in *The Theology of Dorothee Soelle*, 71–89.

18. Rubenstein, *After Auschwitz*, 249.

19. Ibid., 259.

20. Ibid., 248.

21. Ibid., 265.

22. Soelle, *Christ the Representative*, 151; emphasis added.

23. Rubenstein, *After Auschwitz*, 174.

24. Soelle, *Thinking about God*, 2.

25. Martin Buber, *I and Thou*, trans. Walter Kaufmann (New York: Touchstone, 1970).

26. Martin Rumscheidt, "A Calling in a Higher Sense: The Poetics of Dorothee Soelle" in *The Theology of Dorothee Soelle*, 77. Bonhoeffer, *Letters and Papers from Prison*, 344, July 8, 1944.

27. William Hamilton is similar to Soelle in turning to literature for theological expression, waiting for new words to address God, emphasizing practical responsibility, and living ethically in the world. One primary influence on both Hamilton and Soelle is Bonhoeffer. William Hamilton, "The Death of God Theology," *The Christian Scholar* 48, 1 (Spring 1965) reprinted in William Robert Miller, *The New Christianity* (New York: Dell, 1967), 336.

28. Soelle, *Suffering*, 32.

29. Rubenstein, *After Auschwitz*, 157.

30. Soelle, *Suffering*, 135.

31. Ibid., 145.

32. Soelle, *Thinking about God*, 72.

33. Soelle, *Suffering*, 108.

34. Soelle, *Thinking about God*, 173.

35. Soelle responds appreciatively to the existentialist interpretation of the Bible developed by Rudolph Bultmann in *Political Theology* (Philadelphia: Fortress Press, 1974), trans. of *Politische Theologie: Auseinandersetzen mit Rudolph Bultmann* (1971). Paul van Buren also engages in a demythologizing project; however, he uses experiential and ethical categories and distances himself from doctrinal and church language that Soelle continues to use. Paul van Buren, *The Secular Meaning of the Gospel* (New York: Macmillan, 1963).

36. Thomas J. J. Altizer, *The Gospel of Christian Atheism* (Philadelphia: Westminster Press, 1966), 96.

37. Thomas J. J. Altizer, "God as Holy Nothingness," in *What Kind of God? Essays in Honor of Richard L. Rubenstein*, ed. Betty Rogers Rubenstein and Michael Berenbaum (Lanham, MD: University Press of America, 1995), 352.

38. Richard L. Rubenstein, "Radical Theology and the Holocaust," in *The Death of God Movement and the Holocaust*, 45–48.

39. Soelle, *Theology for Skeptics*, 66.

40. Ibid., 62.

41. Ibid., 71.

42. Soelle's notion of voluntary redemptive suffering implies a high level of agency that cannot apply to victims of trauma, including many Holocaust victims. For such victims, protest or silence is more appropriate than insistence that God shares the pain. Flora A. Keshgegian, "Witnessing Trauma," in *The Theology of Dorothee Soelle*, 93–108.

43. Soelle, *Theology for Skeptics*, 79.

44. Ibid., 107. Soelle's humanistic interpretation of Jesus Christ focusing on ethics links her with death of God movement founders William Hamilton and Paul van Buren, although she is more concerned with preserving connections with the church and traditional theological vocabulary.

45. Dorothee Soelle, *The Mystery of Death*, trans. Nancy Lukens-Rumscheidt and Martin Lukens-Rumscheidt (Minneapolis: Fortress, 2007), trans. of *Mystik des Todes: Ein Fragment* (Stuttgart: Kreuz, 2003), 117.

46. Soelle, *The Silent Cry*, 68.

47. Ibid., 199.

48. Soelle, *The Mystery of Death*, 130.

II

The Second Coming of Radical Theology

6

The Death of God and the Politics of Democracy

·•·———·•·

Jeffrey W. Robbins

In an observation often repeated with its political implications developed but its theological implications left only implied, Alexis de Tocqueville famously wrote, "The people reign over the American political world like God over the universe. It is the cause and aim of all things, everything comes from them and everything is absorbed in them."[1] By this, and almost a half-century before Nietzsche, Tocqueville acknowledged democracy as the political instantiation of the death of God. By the people's assumption to rule, the role once consigned to God—or at least to God's assigned representative in the person of the monarch—was now usurped. Democracy thus spells not only the end of the divine right of kings but also the death of God understood as a transcendent authority lording over, or dictating, earthly human affairs. To the extent that we live in a democratic age, to the extent that we allow democratic governance to settle our differences and determine our collective fate, there can be no God to save us. We are our own lords and masters. Or at least, such is democracy's political aspiration and presumption.

However, while Tocqueville was prescient in his observations and analysis of American religious and political culture, this notion of democracy as the political instantiation of the death of God was not a theo-political fate he was prepared to accept. On the contrary, in the introduction to *Democracy in America*, he went so far as to describe his realization of democracy's "irresistible revolution" as a "kind of religious terror" impressed upon his soul.[2] In this way, Tocqueville was a reluctant modernist who sought to domesticate the unsettling impact of democracy. And, as this chapter shows, he saw civil religion as the primary tool for this project of domestication. So, as I argue here, just as democracy is rightly seen by Tocqueville as a political and cultural revolution that marks the twilight of the ancient regime and the dawn of a revolutionary new world, so too must its radical religious and theological implications be understood. And further, whereas Tocqueville recoiled as a result of his self-described religious terror, this chapter will pursue the full democratic potential latent to a religion untethered from state control and unleashed by the transformations wrought by the changed conception of divine power once the sovereignty previously held in reserve by God alone has been seized by the people's own prerogative to rule.

Finally, by way of introduction, the contemporary political and cultural theorist Jacques Rancière has written of the "hatred of democracy" that runs throughout the history of Western political thought and practice. This logic of hatred presents democracy as the ruin to legitimate political order. Rancière defines democracy neither as a form of government ruled by popular sovereignty nor as a form of society determined by the power of commodities but instead as "the action that constantly wrests the monopoly of public life from oligarchic governments, and the omnipotence over lives from the power of wealth."[3] By defining democracy as action, Rancière provides not only a timely intervention against the misuse of democracy's language of freedom to justify military aggression and the abuse of law but also an original theory of democracy that belongs together with Aristotle's first analysis of democracy as a state-form and Tocqueville's first analysis of democracy as a social force. But what is most significant about Rancière's unveiling of this logic of hatred is how it helps us better to detect and understand the reactionary political theology employed to stem the tide of democracy's revolutionary social torment. In other words, Tocqueville's religious terror is symptomatic of a much broader trend that prevails throughout the history of Western political discourse. And thus, though he is rightly credited as the first great modern theorist of democracy, he nevertheless fits within that ancient and enduring pedigree exposed by Rancière.

Let me offer the following, therefore, as the theme and thesis to the proceeding analysis: With Tocqueville as our case in point, we might say that to understand and embrace more fully and truthfully the politics of democracy, we must first be prepared to profess the theology of the death of God. Anything less belongs to the logic of the hatred of democracy as exposed by Rancière.

Tocqueville's *Democracy in America*

Soon after Tocqueville's *Democracy in America* was published, John Stuart Mill touted it as "the first philosophical book ever written on Democracy, as it manifests itself in modern society."[4] In his authoritative study of Tocqueville, Sheldon Wolin develops Mill's observation further: "Tocqueville was the first political theorist to treat democracy as a theoretical subject in its own right and the first to contend that democracy was capable of achieving a genuine, if modest, political life-form."[5] By this development of the first comprehensive theory of democracy, Tocqueville also gave birth to a new genre of political theory, one that concentrated on political culture and thus freed democratic theory from the framework of constitutionalism bequeathed by modern liberal political philosophy. Instead of democracy being defined in terms of electoral politics and a representative system of government, Tocqueville pictures it, in the words of Wolin, "not only as a form of government but as a massive social pressure resulting from the actions of countless free individuals." "Democracy represents," Wolin continues, "the weight of diffused power."[6]

Power diffused—and consequently, defused—to Tocqueville's mind, this is both democracy's blessing and curse. It is a blessing because, as Tocqueville observed throughout his travels in America, a participatory democracy provided its own political education. If the modern age in contrast to the ancient regime was characterized by its egalitarian culture whereby the democratic revolution was made irresistible, then it was precisely this political education that was required to make the members of society into true citizens. As Tocqueville explained in his chapter on "self-interest rightly understood," for democracy to work, it did not and does not require altruism from its citizens, only a certain level of engagement, a politics of self-interest that eventually develops into the recognition of long-term common interests. This is why he counsels the use of democracy to moderate democracy, because in so doing that which is traditionally conceived as democracy's great vice—namely, majority rule—can become its virtue. In other words, the remedy to democratic excess comes not by way of some external, nondemocratic means but within the political culture of democracy itself. As Wolin argues, "Democracy did not require an elite to instruct it in the ways of its own politics. Tocqueville went even further and broke with the long-standing tradition in political thinking that saw no remedies to democracy's ills except from some wise and disinterested 'outside' agent who could somehow dilute a democracy system with a 'mixture' of non- or antidemocratic principles."[7]

Democracy does not require its power to be diluted because it always already is a mixture of competing interests and wills. To repeat, democracy represents the weight of diffused power, a power that even resists power's natural inclination at consolidation. It is in this sense that democracy is correctly understood as a power game, or more precisely, a power play by those long kept outside the proper political domain. If the end result of democracy is a political education that makes members of society into actual citizens, it must not be forgotten that, at least by Tocqueville's reckoning, it begins in common grievances. Reminiscent to what the radical democratic theorist Jacques Rancière argues in *The Hatred of Democracy*, democratic politics must be seen for what it is, that is, as a takeover from those who are "naturally" in power, a great social upheaval and overturning from which there was no turning back.[8]

For Tocqueville, then, democracy is a modest revolution, an eminently practical form of politics arising out of the historical necessity of a radical cultural transformation. "The democracy represented by Tocqueville," Wolin writes, "was the best that modernity might realistically hope for":

> Although Tocqueville did not identify democracy with the most exalted political life, a life of disinterested service to the common good and the striving for a politics of *grandeur*, he found in it a plenitude of civic vitality, an intensity of involvement in common concerns by large numbers of citizens, and a lack of bitterness among social groups that was unmatched. . . . Among their citizens he recognized a new political animal, not the rustic, virtue-loving member of Rousseau's community of the general will, but an ordinary being who learns to acquire a political identity, first and foremost, out of physical necessity and self-interest, but then, as civic concerns gradually become an integral part of his life, to find that he cannot do without them.[9]

Not only was this modest positive appraisal of democracy part of Tocqueville's general theory, but it was also in part his own political strategy. While his observations were based on his travels in America, his audience was post-revolutionary France whose political climate was even more skittish with regard to democracy's revolutionary fervor than most. By his argument that democracy can be used to moderate the effects of democratization, therefore, Tocqueville was using America as an illustration. While America was uniquely gifted in achieving its democratic revolution without the need for a revolution in society, it also stood the permanent risk of losing its own gains in the forging of a political citizenry. Tocqueville viewed such a risk as intrinsic to, if not the fatal flaw of, democracy. If democracy's blessing is the high level of civic participation that is essential to the moderating effects of its political culture, then without this civic and political engagement democracy can easily devolve into a tyranny of the majority whereby public opinion stifles dissent and the egalitarianism that is democracy's hallmark becomes indistinguishable from uniformity. It is in this way that democracy is a curse, because ironically by the diffusion of power, the individual loses his or her individuality. Put otherwise, in an irony noted by Tocqueville, democracy actually leads to *less* freedom of thought. In a democratic culture wherein equality is the greatest virtue, the risk is everything becomes the same.

Indeed, this cultural uniformity, which Tocqueville saw as part and parcel of democracy's tendency toward political neutralization, was the very problem that Wolin argues was "the abiding concern of Tocqueville's thinking, the referent point by which he tried to define his life as well as the task before his generation"[10]—namely, when political life is driven by the apolitical forces of culture and the economy, then how can the political be revived? Put otherwise, is a democratic politics a self-contradiction? After all, as we learn from Tocqueville, when democracy is constituted by a diffused power, it is "less consciously shaped by an active demos than by its interaction with the new forms of power represented by public administration and private industry."[11] This was the great paradox of democracy that Tocqueville observed: It begins with the taking of power by individuals and groups refusing their subservient status but leads to a generalized sense of powerlessness. As Tocqueville put it, "The most striking characteristic of the times is the powerlessness of both men and governments to direct the course of political and social changes."[12]

There was no question that there was a radical, even revolutionary, change at hand. With the dawning of the modern world and the democratic revolution it wrought, the social order was upturned, the ancient regime passing away. And with it, the old constellations of power were losing their hold. The paradox is that this was clearly the doings of humankind but had the force of a historical and cultural necessity without a directing will—"an irresistible revolution." "By the nineteenth century," Wolin writes:

> theorists were confronting a world of diverse powers and dominations, which humankind had brought into existence but no one had legislated. There were concentrated powers, like those of emergent industrial capitalism and the centralizing nation-state; diffused powers, such as those represented by small entrepreneurs, local notables and an unorganized citizenry; and mysterious powers, which came into existence when large masses of people were aroused by appeals to liberty, patriotism, and nationalism.[13]

As the first comprehensive theorist of democracy Tocqueville singles out the central paradox of democracy that goes to the heart of how modern power is constituted. The transfer of power from God to the people is not a simple or one-way transaction such that the original notion of political sovereignty is kept intact. On the contrary, the divine sovereign will that was single and undivided has now become diffused and no less mysterious:

Politics was relocated from an absolute center and diffused throughout society. Even power's forms changed in ways that would have astonished ancient or mediaeval thinkers, accustomed as they were to locating power in some person or class. Authority in the modern world is no longer personified in a king or a great family. It is anonymous, as diffused as politics itself, yet nonetheless powerful. Its form is cultural, its agent the unconscious majority, its expressions intangible rather than material, its power more the conditioning resulting from simultaneity of belief rather than from self-conscious concerted action.[14]

While constitutional measures provide for some semblance of power sharing, by attending to the domain of political culture one can see how social forces exert an almost irresistible, though anonymous, will. Borrowing the arresting image from Marx and Engels in *The Manifesto of the Communist Party*, "Modern bourgeois society . . . is like the sorcerer who is unable to control the powers of the nether world he has called up by his spells."[15] It is on this point that Tocqueville and Marx were in complete agreement. By the constitution (or diffusion) of modern power, political life is subsumed by economic and cultural forces.

In the face of this felt sense of powerlessness, one could just as readily give oneself over to despair as join together in the revolutionary temper of the times. How to counter this sense of powerlessness is where Tocqueville and Marx part company. While Marx embraces the revolutionary nature of modern power that gave the moral justification to the proletariat's struggle against capitalist rule, Tocqueville was the reluctant modernist who eventually conceived democracy in terms of a "postrevolutionary culture that would be antirevolutionary."[16] With Marx, as Wolin observes, "revolution is pitted against revolution, a titanic struggle between two world-changing, world-destroying powers." Whereas for Tocqueville, "The very point of [his] conception of a culture whose purpose was to make democracy safe for the world was not to prepare democratic man for political action but to neutralize him."[17]

As Wolin sees it, this essential conservatism on Tocqueville's part, which becomes more pronounced between the first and second volumes of *Democracy in America*, reflects his aristocratic ambivalence in welcoming the onset of modernity. No one to Wolin's mind saw the democratic implications of modern life more clearly than Tocqueville, and indeed, he might have been "the last influential theorist who can be said to have truly cared about political life,"[18] but in the end his political strategy at making democracy palpable led to a shift in his own emphasis from democracy as a participatory practice toward a mere means of self-expression and personal satisfaction. As Wolin laments, Tocqueville not only saw but hastened "a redirection of the demos, away from politics toward personal satisfactions." This shift was as imperceptible to most as it was surprising in its ease and efficiency: "All that is needed to produce a politically neutralized demos is a combination of structured work haunted (but not demoralized) by unemployment; public education that provides the utensils to consume popular culture; and representative government that regulates mass politics according to a timetable of periodic elections leaving the rest to commentary by the clerks."[19]

Democracy and the Death of God

Nowhere is the ambivalence on the part of Tocqueville more apparent than when it comes to his treatment of religion. Tocqueville's views on religion in America are well known. He is the first to set out the irony of religion in America whereby the disestablishment of religion is key to the religious vitality within society. By untethering religion from state support and sanction, religious life in America apparently becomes more responsive to modern culture. Its adaptive nature ensures its relevance as religious leaders and groups are forced to compete in an open marketplace of ideas. At the same time, while religious belief and identification remain high, their impact might very well be negligible: by religion's responsiveness, which is essential to its continued vitality, religion in America is more a reflection than a directing force of social and cultural powers. In this way, just as democracy almost precludes the possibility of the political statesman, it is also a breeding ground for religious charlatans.[20] This is not so much a critique by Tocqueville as it is a demonstration of the moderating effects of democratization and thus further proof of democracy's palpability for a post-revolutionary world. By allowing it free rein, democracy makes use of religion as a method of social control, as it was the one societal force that exhibited the soft power to cool the revolutionary ardor of equality. As Wolin explains:

> The democratic passions of the Many would have to be toned down, even repressed, and discouraged from direct expression without, however, differentiating them. This had to occur within society rather than through political processes. The obvious means was religion—or at least it seemed to Tocqueville the obvious remedy, given the deep impression left on him by the wholly salutary role of religion in the United States.[21]

Yet beyond or beneath this well-known domesticated vision of civil religion in America lies a much darker image from which Tocqueville recoils. In the introduction to *Democracy in America*, he tells the reader that "the whole of the book in front of the reader has been written under the pressure of a kind of religious terror exercised upon the soul of the author."[22] His immersion in American culture, which he describes as seeming to have the necessity of "the habit of changing place, of turning things upside down, or destroying,"[23] engenders within him a crisis of faith. As Wolin describes it:

> Tocqueville was not a practicing believer in the institutional sense but he was far from being a resolute atheist or agnostic or skeptic. He might be called an uncertain theist who was assailed by religious anxieties arising from a nagging worry that the universe was being governed either by a dying deity, a god who, like the absolute monarchs, had lost his potency, or by a god who had changed his mind, and transferred his favor from aristocracy to the multitude. His deepest fear was the deity might be neither and that men were condemned to live in an abandoned world, a chance arrangement devoid of any immanent meanings.[24]

Tocqueville's anxiety over "a god . . . who had lost his potency" finds expression in a well-known correspondence from 1835. "After all," he observed, "it may be God's will to spread a moderate amount of happiness over all men instead of heaping a large sum upon a few by allowing only a small minority to approach perfection."[25] While some have interpreted this as an argument from Tocqueville that the modern spread of democracy was providential, Wolin instead points out the hesitancy in Tocqueville's voice. By writing that it "may be God's will," it is clear that at least in Tocqueville's mind, it may *not* be God's will just as well: when it comes to the revolutionary changes wrought by democracy in the modern world, who could know the mind of God, and who could tell whether God's will was even determinative for life in this world or not? All that could be said with assurance was that, in the words of Wolin, there was a "fundamental shift in the order of divine dispensation," a fact of modern life that Tocqueville meets with great apprehensiveness and leads to what he himself describes as his "struggle against God." The modern democratic age staked its preference on the happiness of the many over that of the few. But with this regime of equality that Tocqueville fears produces a culture of uniformity, where does God stand? Where do God's political preferences lie? To this question Tocqueville was destined to remain forever uncertain. The most he could do was admit his quarrel with God: "What seems to me decadence is thus in His eyes an advance; what wounds me is agreeable to Him."[26]

Such is the nature of Tocqueville's religious torment as he reluctantly comes to terms with an advancing democratic culture in which his presumed natural privileges as an aristocrat are slowly but ineluctably being stripped away. But what is most significant for our purposes in this story is its ramifications for political theology. We have already seen how with the constitution of modern democracy and its nature of diffused power we are left with a politics not only where sovereignty has been transferred from God to humanity in a one-way transaction; rather, the nature of political sovereignty itself has been transformed, suggesting the terrifying prospect for Tocqueville at least of a politics without sovereignty, a society bereft of any conscious directing will and thus entirely whim to the irresistible social and cultural forces at play. Modern democracy, in other words, represents a diffused, unlocatable, and anonymous form of power. Tocqueville's quarrel with God over democracy, therefore, can be seen as Tocqueville's efforts not simply to salvage his own privileged station but actually to save God himself from his own apparently willed annihilation and to do so by staving off the cultural revolution that was democracy's irresistible force. Tocqueville is angry with God for not having the sense to foresee what Tocqueville himself saw looming on the horizon in which the people's presumption to power alters the very nature of power itself all the way from the ground up, from the innocent actions of the individual civic activist championing his or her rights to the conception of divine sovereign power, now tragically hidden and removed from the affairs of humankind.

Not only is Tocqueville angry with God, caught as he is in a kind of "religious terror" wherein his quarrel with God is played out before the public, but again, much like Marx, he also adopts the posture of the religious prophet making pronouncements as if he knows the future. Democracy is that irresistible revolution, which Tocqueville tells us, "has progressed over so many centuries, surmounting all obstacles, and which is still advancing today amid the ruins it has caused."[27] Not only do his observations and predictions make the case for a kind of historical determinism at work in culture, but also, as Wolin demonstrates, the tone throughout *Democracy in America* is one of apprehensiveness and foreboding. It is a strange and tragic fate, on the one hand, to be plagued by religious anxieties, fearing one's world has been abandoned by God or that God has rendered himself utterly anonymous by the weight of democracy's social force and, on the other, to posture oneself as the voice of God, as the lone seer of what the future foretells, all the while not even sure that God cares, let alone that there is a God who still has power to act.

To be clear, from a theo-political perspective, with democracy it is God's power that is at stake. If the democratic nature of diffused power leaves politics without sovereignty, then what does it make of God? As Wolin asks,

"What kind of god is suited to a democratic age?" And the related question, "What was the cosmology projected by democracy?"[28] Concerning the latter, Wolin again gives us the key:

> Assuredly [the cosmology of democracy is] not the riotous atheism of nonbelievers, a free-for-all of anarchic forces. Tocqueville would claim that democracy's "principal effect on philosophy" was to promote "pantheism." . . . Possibly he may have been thinking of Spinoza's conception of a total system in which every being is [the] reflection of an order that derives from one substance, God. Tocqueville's pantheism was closer to an ideology, a projection of a mass belief-system.[29]

Here we can see Tocqueville's religious terror at work with the notion of the individual's experience of massiveness, of being lost and swallowed up in the indiscriminate, the realization that the most powerful forces at work in society are unlocatable, untraceable, anonymous.

In short, once Tocqueville became aware of the latent political theology of democracy, he recoiled from what he saw. When met face to face with the theo-political implications of the democratic revolution, Tocqueville's conditional embrace turned to outright hesitation. Democracy comes to be seen as "a desire to dissolve all differences," even "the primary division of things" between "creation and creator."[30] Because this so obviously smacked of idolatry, because its presumption was too much to bear, and because it precluded all prospects of the individual rising above the undifferentiated mass, it was here that Tocqueville issued his clarion call: "Within the different systems which help philosophy in its attempt to explain the universe, pantheism seems to me one of the most likely to entice the human mind in democratic ages. All those who are smitten with the nobility of man must join forces and fight against this idea."[31] Believers of the world, unite!

While democracy may well be an irresistible revolution, in the end for Tocqueville a line must be drawn. If God does not have the will or power to act, or the sense even to know when enough is enough, then the task falls to humanity. By salvaging the prospect of the individual from the undifferentiated mass, Tocqueville also stumbles upon political theology and the effort at saving God from God's own annihilation. Democracy, he says, goes too far by conjuring up a world of which it knows nothing—a world ultimately devoid of God. While the civil religion in America is commendable both as a training ground for political citizens and as a tool of moderation, if not social control, it is *the latent death-of-God theology* that goes hand in hand with the democratic revolution that Tocqueville resists. In short, it is the theology of democracy that makes the politics of democracy ultimately untenable.

Of course, even by this very strategic distinction on Tocqueville's part between the civil religion and theo-politics of democracy, Tocqueville shows himself to be a man of the modern world. By doing the work that in his mind should belong to God, Tocqueville puts himself in the place of God. Democracy's massive social pressure and the weight of diffused power prove themselves yet again as the sovereignty that was once the exclusive domain of divine power, a power that now passes itself on to humankind and, in the process, renders itself anonymous as well as irresistible. Once the people reign over the political world "like God over the universe," that power cannot be easily or readily returned to its source. The God of sovereign power is dead, and democracy is its political instantiation.

Rethinking Religion

Tocqueville was right to recognize the radical potential of the altered political theology ushered in by the modern democratic age. Where he failed is in not trusting his own original salient reading of how the nature of democracy's diffused power works. The benefit of democracy is the recognition that the world is left to be what we make of it. It is this truth that has both inspired people to act and prompted dread. With the cultural revolution wrought by the social force of democracy, it is easily shown how religion is likewise left to be what we make of it. Just as assuredly as democracy is the political instantiation of the death of God, with this fundamental shift in the order of divine dispensation, religion is reborn, given a new lease on life as it claims for itself a central role in the transformation of the social and political order. After all, it should come as no surprise that the two volumes of Tocqueville's *Democracy in America* are published around the same time as Ludwig Feuerbach's *Essence of Christianity*, for in each we have a theorist coming to terms with what has by then become obvious within society and culture—namely, religion is of humankind's making, even as it simultaneously remakes humankind in its image.

While the insight that religion is of humanity's making fundamentally alters the religious terrain, it need not be seen as an attack on orthodoxy or as an extension of the Enlightenment suspicion of religion as dogma and superstition. More than anything else, what it means is a transposition of religious authority from the established centers of learning and power to that of ordinary people. Religious belief, therefore, remained strong. But it is the ability to define that belief, and even more, to channel its energy and enthusiasm, that is altered. It is a question of toward what ends religious passions serve—is it a method of social control for a world weary with revolution or fuel in the fire continuing the work the democratic revolution left undone? These are the questions pursued by the historians Gary Nash and Nathan Hatch in their masterful studies of early America.

Nash's book, *The Unknown American Revolution*, is an attempt at writing a democratic history of the American Revolution, a history which would "expand our conception of revolutionary American society and to [help us] consider the multiple agendas . . . that sprang from its highly diverse and fragmented character."[32] In this book he demonstrates the integral role played by religion in the radical revolution to reinvent American society. As Nash argues, "The American Revolution was not only a war of independence but a many-sided struggle to reinvent America. It was a civil war at home as well as a military struggle for national liberation."[33] By chronicling this "revolution within the revolution," or the struggle for democracy that coincided with or even laid the groundwork for the fight for independence, Nash reminds us how during the early days of the American republic, just as now, there was a battle between those who placed a premium on freedom, security, and order verses those driven by concerns for equality and equity. Further, just as independence does not necessarily constitute democracy, democratic action does not necessarily require independence as its prerequisite. Therefore, though the war for independence was eventually won, the democratic revolution for a free, just, and equal society is never complete. In Nash's words:

> To think of the American Revolution as incomplete is very different from arguing that it was a failure, even for those with the most expansive ideas about a truly free, just, and equal society. Revolutions are always incomplete. Almost every social and political convulsion that has gone beyond first disruptions of the *ancien régime* depended on mass involvement; and that in itself, in every recorded case of revolutionary insurgency, raised expectations that could not be completely satisfied. In this sense, there has never been such a thing as a completed revolution.[34]

As for the mass involvement and the raising of expectations that Nash has in mind, integral to this story is the role played by the radical religious visionaries, itinerant preachers, and newly emboldened communities astir with the religious passion that came with the belief that they were direct agents of God. The religious effect on the emerging American democracy can first be seen in what is commonly referred to as the First Great Awakening, which was a series of religious revivals that swept through the colonies during the middle of the eighteenth century at least a full generation before the actual war for independence was fought. The main catalyst was the

English Calvinist George Whitefield, who toured the American colonies
as a traveling evangelist. Whitefield was nicknamed "the Grand Itinerant,"
indicating that though he was ordained as a priest by the Church of England,
though he had a formal theological training within the Calvinist tradition
and was a friend and contemporary of John Wesley (the founder of the
Methodists) during his studies at Oxford, his primary identity and influence
was as "a preacher who is not confined to one particular church and pulpit
but who proclaims the Word wherever he can find listeners."[35] With the great
success of the emotionally stirring sermons by Whitefield, the colonies had
perhaps their first united and unifying cultural experience. It was as though
everyone had either heard Whitefield for themselves or knew of someone
who had. In this way, the first Great Awakening proved instrumental in the
birth of a national consciousness and the making of a political federation. In
this way, an examination of the politics of religion during this period shows
how *the cultural led the political* as this shared religious experience helped to
form a collective identity.

More native to our present concerns, while historians perceive the
Great Awakening as one of the first common and unifying experiences
within the American colonies, equally important was its message of social
leveling, which was seen by many contemporaries as especially incendiary.
As Nash writes, "Whitefield challenged traditional sources of authority,
called upon people to become instruments of their own salvation, and
implicitly attacked the prevailing upper-class notion that the uneducated
masses had no minds of their own."[36] The effect of this message, again in
the words of Nash, was the "[relocation of] authority collectively in the
mass of common people."[37] Needless to say, one would imagine that there
would be many established interests that resented, feared, and resisted this
movement. One contemporary, for instance, accused the traveling itinerants
such as Whitefield of being "a set of incendiaries, enemies not only of the
Established Church, but also common disturbers of the peace."[38] Worried
Anglican clergymen in Virginia were able to convince the governor "to
restrain 'strolling preachers' who conjured up a world without properly
constituted authority."[39]

While in hindsight this widespread and emotionally potent series
of religious revivals might have proven enormously effective in creating a
common culture and forging the beginnings of a national identity, during its
time its leaders were seen by many as irresponsible and unrefined agitators.
The notion that they were conjuring up worlds without the legitimate
authority to do so leaves the impression that they worked more as sorcerers
and magicians than as authentic preachers of the gospel. They offered an
unapologetically radical egalitarian interpretation of the gospel. In so doing,
they upset the established social order and planted the seeds of democracy

within the emerging culture of the American colonies. Nash spells out the radical democratic implications of this movement well:

> The Great Awakening provided a "radical model" for revolutionary activists. . . . The Awakeners created a mass movement; they challenged upper-class assumptions about social order and the deference due to established figures; they seceded from churches they regarded as corrupt and built new, regenerated ones in their place, even without license; they forced religious toleration on those arrayed against it and broke apart attempted unions of church and state; they fractured established churches such as those in Virginia and thereby threatened the existing social order.[40]

In short, neither the revivalist preachers nor the converts they attracted knew their place or observed the proper decorum. The First Great Awakening can and should be seen as a democratic movement not only because it endowed individuals with the gumption if not the right to question authority, but also because it left individuals organized and mobilized as collective congregations in its wake. It is not that the emphasis on personal conversion merely undermined the authority of established churches and the existing social order, but rather that a new locus of authority was established—an authority whose legitimacy lay squarely with the people acting as agents of God.

Likewise, Nathan Hatch's *The Democratization of American Christianity* shows how religion played a democratic, even revolutionary, role in early American history. Specifically, Hatch examines the period in U.S. history between 1780 and 1830, a transitional period that he argues transformed not only the structure of American Christianity but also American political life. What we see abounding in this period are "mass movements that were deeply religious and genuinely democratic at the same time."[41] And by these "deep and powerful undercurrents of democratic Christianity" the United States was distinguished from the rest of the modern industrial world.[42] With this unique history and culture, observers and scholars have long been at odds at explaining exactly the role religion plays in American society. Once considering its theo-political implications, is it as devastating and world-altering as Tocqueville suggests? Or, on the contrary, is the continued prevalence of religious belief and activity in the United States a sign of a retrograde culture, one which operates by the very dynamics of social conformity laid out by Tocqueville making belief in God the absolute social norm?

Hatch acknowledges this confusion and debate, making it central to the argument he proposes about how the shakeup in the locus of religious authority not only reflects but hastens the radical cultural and political transformation American society was undergoing at this time. "As common people became significant actors on the religious scene," he writes, "there was increasing confusion and angry debate over the purpose and function of the church. A style of religious leadership that the public deemed 'untutored' and 'irregular' as late as the First Great Awakening became overwhelmingly successful, even normative, in the first decades of the republic."[43] This new style of religious leadership was reflective of the new class of individuals invested with the authority to speak, preach, and lead, a transfer of power that was of course not granted without a fight. Hatch labels this phenomenon "religious populism," which is defined according to the "passions of ordinary people" and which has the "charisma of a democratic movement." As by now we should come to expect, as a democratic movement, it was met with resistance, the suspicion being that it was an uncivil, anarchic force in society, made up of "common folk not respecting their betters, organized factions speaking and writing against civil authority." And to be sure, as Hatch makes clear, this conflict was "not merely a clash of intellectual and theological differences but also a passionate social struggle with power and authority. Deep-seated class antagonism separated clergy from clergy." On the one side were "those who defended clerical authority as a right of a gentry minority." On the other were "rough-hewn leaders who denied the right of any one class of people to speak for another."[44]

According to Rancière's analysis, this class antagonism, cloaked in the guise of respect and civil authority, is not coincidental but part of the structural opposition to democracy revealed from the ancient times to the present. But with Hatch, his emphasis is not on the resistance to religious democratization but the constructive work done by various religious populist movements led by, and in response to, common people. As Hatch writes, "Christianity was effectively reshaped by common people who molded it in their image and who threw themselves into expanding its influence." And further, "The rise of evangelical Christianity in the early republic is, in some measure, a story of the success of common people in shaping the culture after their own priorities rather than the priorities outlined by gentlemen such as the framers of the Constitution."[45] In the words of Alexander Campbell, the founder of the Disciples of Christ who set out to restore the primitive form of Christianity unencumbered by creeds or denominations, this story of success amounted to "a declaration of independence of the Kingdom of Jesus."[46] As he described it, this was an independence hard earned, for it required nothing less than renunciation of the traditions and errors from one's theological education and religious heritage: "My mind was, for a time, set loose from all its former moorings," Campbell explains. "It was not a simple change: but a new commencement . . . the whole landscape of Christianity presented itself to my mind in a new attitude and position."[47]

Likewise, the Methodist evangelist Charles Finney likened this religious transformation to a Copernican revolution whereby religious life was adapted to "the language of common life."[48] This is why, when it comes to Hatch's own assessment, he writes that "this vast transformation, this shift away from the Enlightenment and classical republicanism toward vulgar democracy and materialistic individualism in a matter of decades, was the real American Revolution."[49]

Once recognizing ordinary people's ability and willingness to shape religion to their own needs—whether defined spirituality or politically in terms of social transformation—Hatch identifies three ways that these popular religious movements "articulated a profoundly democratic spirit." First, they extended the Protestant Reformation conviction of the priesthood of all believers by denying the distinction that set the clergy apart from ordinary people and refusing the deference owed to learned theologians and traditional orthodoxies: "All were democratic or populist in the way they associated virtue with ordinary people rather than with elites, exalted the vernacular in word and song as the hallowed channel for communicating with and about God, and freely turned over the [reins] of power."[50] Second, by taking ordinary people's spiritual needs and impulses "at face value rather than subjecting them to the scrutiny of orthodox doctrine and the frowns of respectable clergymen," the people were effectively enfranchised and empowered. Third, not only were ordinary people empowered, but also one-time outsiders and fringe leaders now were now more fully incorporated into the religious and social landscape. These religious outsiders, "flushed with confidence about their prospects" and with "little sense of their own limitations," now "dreamed that a new age of religious and social harmony would naturally spring up out of their efforts to overthrow coercive and authoritarian structures. This upsurge of democratic hope, this passion for equality, led to a welter of diverse and competing forms, many of them structured in highly undemocratic ways."[51]

With that last statement making conditional Hatch's otherwise positive appraisal of this religious and social transformation, he leaves the reader to ponder the still paradoxical role religion plays in American society and, by extension, the theo-political paradox of democracy itself. As Hatch writes in his conclusion:

> Forms of popular religion characteristic of [the early American] cultural system bound paradoxical extremes together: a reassertion of the reality of the supernatural in everyday life linked to the quintessentially modern values of autonomy and popular sovereignty. . . . By raising the standard "no creed but the Bible,"

Christians in America were the foremost proponents of individualism even as they expected the open Bible to replace an age of sectarian rivalry with one of primitive harmony. Like the egalitarian credo of the early republic, this vision has taken a powerful hold on the American imagination despite the disparity between the quest for unity and actual religious fragmentation and authoritarianism.[52]

The Dialectic between Religion and Democracy

Contrasting Nash and Hatch with Tocqueville, we can say that their concern is not so much with religion's moderating effects on democracy as much as it is the dialectical relationship they see between religion and democracy: religion is democratized as it simultaneously becomes a force for democracy continuing where the democratic cultural revolution leaves off by empowering ordinary people to craft a world of their own making. Tocqueville recognized the unsettling theo-political implications of this democratic revolution as divine sovereign power is now transferred—and thus, dispersed and diffused—to the people. Nash and Hatch extend this analysis to the social and political impact of democratized religion. In a democratic age, religion cannot and could not remain a means of social control to moderate the effects of democracy's otherwise irresistible social revolution. Instead, it too is subject to that revolution and from the very start is drafted into its efforts at social and political transformation if only because its open access provides an ever-present ladder of opportunity for ordinary people to have their voices heard.

In short, while Tocqueville's analysis implied a distinction between the civil religion and theo-politics of democracy, commending the one and recoiling from the other, Nash and Hatch make clear that no such distinction is possible. Religion in America was not and is not merely the moderating influence Tocqueville portrayed. On the contrary, just as the latent political theology led Tocqueville to a state of religious terror as it revealed an anonymous God now whim to the weight of democratic social forces, so too was the religious life in the early republic radically destabilized, even as it proved to be a constantly destabilizing, world-transforming force, if only because it was the primary means by which common people were politically empowered. Put otherwise, we might say while it was on the theo-political terrain that the terrifying change democracy represented was revealed to the likes of Tocqueville, the religious terrain made manifest the ongoing struggle to complete the work left undone by the democratic revolution still underway within American society. In this way, the religion and political theology of democracy were one and the same: both testified to the tumult that was democracy's coming of age in the form of the people's coming to power.

To conclude, while Tocqueville is rightly credited as developing the first comprehensive theory of democracy, his theory ultimately falls short by its failure to follow through on its own theo-political implications. His observations and analysis tacitly acknowledged democracy as the political instantiation of the death of God. Nevertheless, his strategic efforts at demonstrating democracy's palpability for a post-revolutionary world rested on his argument that religion essentially served as a moderating force. As Wolin shows, this led Tocqueville disingenuously to make the New England town meetings, where the legacy of a high-brow form of Calvinism was still decisive, the norm in his treatment of religion in America, while the tradition of radical democracy was excised from his published writings. The former, which practiced a domesticated form of civil religion, was seen as a laboratory for political citizenship; the latter, which Tocqueville described as "the experiment of a democracy without limits," was seen as wildly uncivil and uncontained.[53]

Recalling Rancière's unveiling of the logic of the hatred of democracy, we can see how Tocqueville fits within that ancient and enduring pedigree, caught as he is in that classic double bind: on the one hand, recognizing democracy as an irresistible revolution by the force of its massive social pressure and, on the other, seeking above all else to demonstrate democracy's palpability by showing the means by which its irresistible force might be nevertheless contained and its politics more effectively managed. As Rancière might put it, by his emphasis on the moderating impact of civil religion to those who like him might otherwise be deeply troubled by the theological implications of democracy, Tocqueville effectively inserts a "dead-man-god" to comfort modern humanity in its "great distress as orphans condemned to wander in the empire of the void."[54] This image of a "dead-man-god" is crafted in terms of modern liberal philosophy as a concession to the revolutionary torment wrought by democracy. But as a God conceived to fill the void left vacant by the death of God, it is at best only a stopgap measure and thus utterly impotent to counter or redirect the revolutionary social forces it is meant to tame.

Notes

1. Alexis de Tocqueville, *Democracy in America*, trans. by Gerald E. Bevan (New York: Penguin Books, 2003), 71.

2. Ibid., 15.

3. Jacques Rancière, *The Hatred of Democracy*, trans. by Steve Corcoran (New York: Verso, 2006), 96.

4. As quoted in Sheldon S. Wolin, *Tocqueville between Two Worlds: The Making of a Political and Theoretical Life* (Princeton: Princeton University Press, 2001), 8.

5. Ibid., 59.

6. Ibid., 99.

7. Ibid., 194–195.

8. Rancière, *The Hatred of Democracy*, 96.

9. Wolin, *Tocqueville between Two Worlds*, 166.

10. Quoted in ibid., 5.

11. Ibid., 308.

12. Quoted in ibid., 13.

13. Ibid., 14.

14. Ibid., 199.

15. Karl Marx and Frederick Engels, *The Manifesto of the Communist Party* (Chicago: Charles H. Kerr, 1906), 21.

16. Wolin, *Tocqueville between Two Worlds*, 336.

17. Ibid., 17, 336.

18. Ibid., 5.

19. Ibid., 378.

20. As the sociologist of religion Steve Bruce observes in his brief on Tocqueville's observations of the nature of religion in U.S. society, "[Whereas] the state church system found in much of Europe contained little incentive for the clergy to recruit a congregation . . . , the clergy of the American churches only ate if they recruited members who were willing to feed them. The key to prosperity was not sucking up to the elites but appealing to the people. In a voluntary system there is a very strong incentive for preachers to build churches, to make their message popular, and to work hard to build a following." In Bruce, *Religion in the Modern World: From Cathedrals to Cults* (Oxford: Oxford University Press, 1996), 132.

21. Wolin, *Tocqueville between Two Worlds*, 323.

22. Tocqueville, *Democracy in America*, 15.

23. Quoted in Wolin, *Tocqueville between Two Worlds*, 109.

24. Ibid., 108.

25. Alexis de Tocqueville, *Memoir, Letters and Remains of Alexis de Tocqueville*, vol. 1 (Boston: Ticknor and Fields, 1862), 377.

26. Quoted in Wolin, *Tocqueville between Two Worlds*, 186.

27. Tocqueville, *Democracy in America*, 15.

28. Wolin, *Tocqueville between Two Worlds*, 327, 314.

29. Ibid., 314.

30. Ibid., 315.

31. Tocqueville, *Democracy in America*, 521.

32. Gary Nash, *The Unknown American Revolution: The Unruly Birth of Democracy and the Struggle to Create America* (New York: Penguin Books, 2005), xiv.

33. Ibid., 1.

34. Ibid., 453–454; emphasis in original.

35. Ibid., 142.

36. Nash, *The Unknown American Revolution*, 9.

37. Ibid., 10.

38. Quoted in Henry Mayer, *A Son of Thunder: Patrick Henry and the American Revolution* (New York: Franklin Watts, 1986), 34.

39. Nash, *The Unknown American Revolution*, 10.

40. Ibid., 11.

41. Nathan O. Hatch, *The Democratization of American Christianity* (New Haven: Yale University Press, 1989), 58.

42. Ibid., 5.

43. Ibid.

44. Ibid., 5–9.

45. Ibid., 9.

46. Quoted in ibid., 186.

47. Quoted in ibid., 71.

48. Quoted in ibid., 197.

49. Ibid., 23.

50. Ibid., 10.

51. Ibid., 10–11.

52. Ibid., 213.

53. See Wolin, *Tocqueville between Two Worlds*, 136–137.

54. Rancière, *The Hatred of Democracy*, 31.

7

Extraordinary Ecclesiology

.•·———·•·

Radical Theology in Practice

CHRISTOPHER DEMUTH RODKEY

> The church is several things. She is a treasure chest which is often closed, which we must open again and again.
>
> —Paul Tillich, *The Irrelevance and Relevance of the Christian Message*, second edition

A common criticism of radical Christian theology in the United States is one of *praxis*: what kind of church would remain if a religious community accepted it? Recognizing that radical "death of God" theologies are at the very least *post-ecclesial*, if not *anti-ecclesial*, the question of *praxis* is legitimate; any theology that remains "Christian" must wrestle with the question of communal life and the corporate expression of faith. Radical theology was probably not meant by radical theologian Thomas Altizer at first to be an *extra-ecclesial* phenomenon; Altizer was forbidden from entering the Episcopal ministry on the basis of psychological fitness, even while he himself served as a lay minister to an interracial mission on Chicago's South Side.[1] Few modern theologies have the distinction of being strictly forbidden by certain denominations—one should recall that the Southeastern College of Methodist Bishops in 1968 issued a reductionist statement declaring the death of God theology to be entirely incompatible with the denomination's teachings. Altizer did not pick a fight with the Methodists; the Methodists picked a fight with Altizer.[2] The Thomas Altizer papers at Syracuse University are a testament to this fact: this archive contains boxes and boxes of letters from Methodist pastors and women's societies, resolutions passed by

Methodist church boards and various Methodist student movement organiza-
tions, and letters from children's Sunday School classes.

Although radical theology demands from its thinker and practitioner
solitude, radical theology is not *necessarily* a lonely or solipsistic calling. To
be sure, being clearly anathematized by orthodox Christianity, and having
the Christian media intentionally ignore a small movement of reformers,
forces a small group of radical thinkers to go underground and into hid-
ing.[3] Radical theologians pride themselves on their iconoclastic intellectual
positions: Mary Daly[4] cried at the opening of her futurist manifesto *Quintessence*, "Even if I were the only one, I would still be a Radical Feminist!"[5]
A brief study of 1960s death of God theologies demonstrates that even
those within this small movement were going in different directions on
their own and that there are significant theological and political differences
between Altizer, for example, and Gabriel Vahanian. Clearly, though, any
Christian theology must acknowledge that while one's own individual theological voyage may be in complete solitude, the communal voyage promises
better living and better futures.[6] As a Christian reform movement, radical
theology demands the existence of a community; as a subversive missionary
movement, few adherents may be expected with the confidence that radicalism in Christianity always initiates a far-reaching influence, as in the case
of the Radical Reformation.

The Radical Reversal

There are a few characteristics of radical theology that might loosely tie
this small group together; one I wish to focus upon that is relevant to pastoral practice is the "radical reversal" present in Altizer's radical theology.
Within the context of his theological method of *coincidentia oppositorum*,
the apocalypse of history is a sacred diachrony: Godhead moving *forward*
and *downward* through history into the incarnation of Christ. In the present age this *forward* and *downward* motion continues in the "eternal death
of Jesus," provoking and invoking a piercing interruption of the Nothing
as *Geist* seeping through the vacuum and noise[7] of the gravediggers of God
surrounding us.

The most stunning of the radical reversals implicit throughout Altizer's
thinking is borrowed primarily from William Blake, who embodies this reversal in his "Everlasting Gospel":

> The vision of Christ that thou dost see
> Is my Visions [sic] Greatest Enemy
> . . . .
> Thy Heaven Doors are my Hell Gates
> . . . .

Both read the Bible day & night
But thou readst black where I read white.[8]

Elsewhere, Blake explicitly reveals the traditionally understood Christian God to be none other than the Satan himself, admitting to having "worshipd [sic] the Devil" and not the "God of worldly things."[9] Following Blake, Altizer's theology is a *contrarian* theology—one that Walter Bruegemann calls a "pervasive and perverted understanding of the prophets"—in its reversal of Christ and Satan and its own prophetic self-understanding that, in spirit, prophetic theology radically reverses prophetic theologies.[10]

To be sure, for Altizer the embodiment of a radical reversal in radical theology is consistent with the metaphysics of reversal, the *coincidentia oppositorum*, in its loyalty to the diachronic, apocalyptic[11] *logos* of history that is disclosed in the Scriptures. In other words, a radical Christianity must be a contrarian Christianity that seeks faithfully to reverse the stagnant heteronomy of the more common, *unreversed* orthodox Christianity. Recalling that for Blake "[t]he voice of honest indignation is the voice of God," such a radical theology is one whose *pervasive* and *perverted* heresy could only originate in response to a perverted Christianity as *honest indignation*, one which seeks to unravel Christianity to reveal the *Gospel* of the divinely enfleshed heretic, Jesus.

Examining Altizer's interpretation and use of Blake in his method will prove helpful in understanding the theological implications of the radical reversal. Throughout much of Blake's writings there is a clear presentation that authentic Christianity is quite the opposite of any Christianity remotely practiced. Blake writes in "The Everlasting Gospel" within the context of a world becoming more secular, "The Moral Christian is the Cause/ Of the Unbeliever & his Laws," and later, "That they may call a [*crime*] shame & Sin/ [*The*] Loves [*sic?*] temple [*where*] that God dwelleth in/ And hide in secret Hidden Shrine/ The Naked Human form divine," adding, "Blaspheming Love" is "blaspheming thee."[12] As a reversal of traditional, *ecclesial* Christianity's compulsion against the diachronic movement of Godhead, radical Christianity affirms the Godhead of history moving into an "eternal death" rather than an "eternal life."[13] This eternal death of Jesus is the perpetuation of the crucifixion and dismemberment of the death of God. As "[t]he forward-moving occurrence of advent and perishing," Lissa McCullough explains, an ongoing apocalypse of Godhead is known "theologically as the passion of God, even as the passion of God enacts itself through this history of advent and perishing."[14] This perishing is both *in* and *through* our human flesh, the residual temples of the sacred.

The radical reversal gives way for a theology of the Kingdom of God. In the present, then, transcendence is itself (*kenotically*) emptied out, dismembered, and enfleshed; in the vacuousness of the present, Godhead is

made actual through actualization.[15] *As enfleshment, we actualize Godhead.*
"The very everydayness of true parabolic language," that is, the apocalyptic
language of Jesus, Altizer writes, "bespeaks an immediate presence in a world
of voice. Parabolic enactment occurs on earth and not in heaven, in 'flesh'
as opposed to 'spirit.'" *Now* is the kingdom of God; "[n]ow is the time of
decision, and this nowness reverses every trace of a beyond which is only a
beyond . . . likewise, there occurs here a reversal of a world which is merely
and only world." This world "now stands forth in its immediacy, and that
immediacy is itself the time of decision." The voice of Godhead transfigured
through our flesh is "itself . . . praxis, the praxis of a world come of age."[16]

Speaking and actualizing Godhead out of enfleshment "stills the sound
of speech by breaking up and dismembering a vertical immediacy into a hori-
zontal presence," that is to say, "vertical presence recedes behind and before
the impacting center of voice and in that expanding horizon an immediate
identity passes into simile and metaphor" on the edge of language. It is to
dismember and *reverse* vertical *presence* into an *actual* immanence. Altizer
writes accordingly in *The Self-Embodiment of God*:

> The pure and emptying of voice is the pure transcendent of voice, a
> transcendence which is self-transcendence, for it is the self-enactment
> of the self-embodiment of voice. When the voice of "I AM" real-
> izes itself as pure transcendence, it fully empties itself of its original
> voice and identity. That emptying is the self-embodiment of the
> voice of "I AM," a self-embodiment which is a self-transcendence
> of the original identity of "I AM." Now the voice of "I AM" is a
> wholly self-actualized immediacy, and an immediacy wherein voice
> is totally present in hearing. But this presence, this self-actualizing
> presence, is a self-negating presence. Only the self-negation of the
> original presence is the immediate actuality of hearing. Pure hearing
> is the total embodiment of voice, an embodiment wherein voice
> is the otherness of itself. That otherness is the pure otherness of
> the original presence of "I AM." Therefore, in that otherness, the
> original identity of "I AM" realizes itself as "I AM NOT."[17]

Altizer concludes, "'I AM NOT' can be the fully embodied voice of 'I
AM.'"[18] McCullough observes that for Altizer, "[i]f the death of God inaugurates the 'triumph' of the kingdom of God, that 'triumph' nonetheless feels
like death, a totally consuming darkness, *faith is a kingdom in which the Godhead is broken up.*"[19] Self-negation, *kenosis*, incarnation, self-transcendence:
for Altizer, in each moment we step into a new world, and this new world
is a New Creation where we self-actualize the self-emptying Godhead. The
final and total transfiguration of flesh into an immanence within a *coinciden-*

tia oppositorum with Spirit is "only . . . resolved in our deepest theological vision" and is made actual through apocalyptic thinking.[20] Radical Christian *praxis*, then, must be at once incarnational and apocalyptic, embodying and reversing, enfleshing and spiraling *forward* and *downward*: self-subverting, self-dismembering, acting silently or loudly interrupting the banality of Nothingness in the present.[21]

Pastoral Practice

For Altizer's death of God theology, any conception of the Kingdom of God that refuses to accept its diachronic, kenotic metaphysics misapprehends any authentic portrayal of biblical Christianity. In other words, for the death of God theologian to say that the orthodox Christian's God is "dead" is to say, in addition to other implications of irrelevance, that the totalitarian, absolutist conception of God that is popularly worshiped in churches today is a reversal itself of an actual Godhead of history. This God *did once exist* as a primordial Godhead but has since self-annihilated and self-dismembered itself into history, beginning with the beginning: the act of creation. To go a step further, the orthodox Christian conception of God refuses to acknowledge any conception of an Absolute Hymen (the rupture of primordial, alien transcendence at the act of creation), let alone its breaking; the tearing of the Absolute Hymen of Creation, the initiation of *kenosis* and subjectivity in Godhead speaking Godself into existence, is *the* actualization in history that begins the Christian story that disseminates into your and my human flesh.[22] It follows, therefore, that a Christianity that worships a God long dead will not only worship death but *lust* for it—*necrophilia*—and perpetuate this lust through its ritual and liturgy.

Although radical Christian theology reverses orthodox Christianity, it is important to distinguish that orthodoxy is not the *only* poison in the world. As Mary Daly so powerfully argues throughout her writings, traditional Christianity is one face of the polycephalous "sado-religion" that she names, similarly to Altizer, as the "nothing."[23] Within the patriarchal sado-religion, the normative sado-state is "deadtime," where we are dismembered and "severed" from our own Words, from our powers of "spiration/creation." In Daly's earlier thought, the divine is Be-ing, or the "Verb of Verbs": nothingness commits *verbicide*, not only killing the Verb but stripping individuals of the Power of Naming, rendering language flat and enacting "babble-spheres" or "*verbigeration*," that is, "a continuous repetition of stereotyped phrases." In the nothing, the creative sources within become "amnesic" and "apraxic," preventing an individual from "being Really Present" in the present.[24] The nothing is the "double edge" that is the "presence of absence" and the "absence of Presence"; a "decentralized mass without organic purpose;

it expands like a tumor of the soul. . . . Phallic *absence of Presence* is lack of content and purpose," that is, "negation of meaning in a conversation, lack of affection or of intelligence in a face, nonresponse to a question, to an act of love," concluding, "[i]t is absence of soul."[25]

In the nothingness of sado-religion, reversals occur away from the *pure lust* or "biophilia" of the Verb, Be-ing; the lust for death, *necrophilia*, is a radical reversal of life-itself. To love life is radically to reverse the greatest reversal, even through small and seemingly insignificant steps. According to Daly, the necrophilial reversal has actual consequences through history and theologically explains the tragic history of women in what she calls the "sado-ritual Syndrome."[26] A radical Christianity names orthodox Christianity as part of this "sado-religion" and seeks radically to reverse this reversal, to negate the negation, of Christianity itself.

Radical Christian practice recalls that for Mircea Eliade, the *coincidentia oppositorum* "is one of the most primitive ways of expressing the paradox of divine reality."[27] It is the method through which the individual religiously *processes* reality, a reality that culminates toward an ultimate *conjectio oppositorum*—a *conjunction* of opposites—through the relationality and movement of the *coincidence* of opposites. The self-dismemberment of Absolute Hymen disclosed as the initiation of incarnation may then be understood to be a primary act for liturgical expression (as opposed to the Sabbath worship celebrating the apprehension of Absolute Hymen). If public worship is an act of colliding the sacred *with* or *in* the profane by corporately provoking Spirit through communal self-embodiment and self-embodying, an incarnational community understands and liturgically operates within a theological framework of *apophasis* or "camouflage." The communal eschatological hope is not only in the present but also in the hope for a perpetuating glimpse of Second Coming, or "supreme theophany."[28]

Coincidentia oppositorum in practice—the radical reversal—is a process by which the hiddenness of enfleshed Godhead *mystagogically* occurs in small radical communities. Today many "emergent" Christian communities use the term "incarnational community" fairly often, yet their doctrine remains loyal to a fixed, immutable Godhead who might be historically spoken of as a "Creator" but is not creating, moving, or self-giving in any ultimate sense.[29] This is to say that such thinking is not incarnational at all by virtue of the dead God that neatly fits into a metaphysical puzzle at the very top of the picture the puzzle nominally discloses. By reclaiming the dismemberment of Absolute Hymen—and thereby a diachronic metaphysics of Godhead— *coincidentia oppositorum* becomes a theological concept of the first order, connecting the interrelated theological concepts of creation, incarnation, Word, kenosis, Christ, passion, crucifixion, burial, descent, resurrection, enfleshment, atonement, divine perishing, transfiguration, life itself, and death.[30] Consequently, the cycle of the liturgical calendar embodies and commemorates these concepts and their progressions within divine history; and furthermore, *coincidentia oppositorum* connects these ideas to their negation, as in the case of I AM and I AM NOT. As such, these traditional theological ideas are to be understood as not only progressing from or out of each other, but they are *coincidental* reversals of each other, taking on new meaning at each turn of history as they are reenacted and restored.

Radical Christian practice, then, is not simply a blaspheming of orthodox Christianity, and not simply a radical attempt to reverse the sick, necrophilial Christianity that is popularly worshiped on Sunday mornings around the world. Radical Christianity *may* be these, but it is not *necessarily* or simply a reversal or negation of orthodoxy. Instead, radical Christianity blasphemes Christianity in its own reversal of biblical Christianity. Traditional orthodoxy scandalizes itself in its claim to be "biblical," as it is biblical primarily in the sense that the practice of proof-texting for doctrinal purposes has replaced any conception of incarnation. The error of orthodoxy may have begun with Paul, as Nietzsche proposed in his *Anti-Christ*,[31] but orthodoxy perpetuates the erasure of an actualized theology of creation in contemporary faith; in fact, an actualized creation is reversed by orthodoxy into so-called political Creationism.[32]

To this end, to go beyond blaspheming, radical Christian practice *reclaims* the radical reversal that occurs in Scripture. Too often Protestant liberalism has downplayed or apologized for the Scriptures in exchange for social justice or has proof-texted the Scriptures out of a social agenda, following the example of orthodoxy. The theological error is not necessarily an affinity for Scripture but begins with the erasure of Absolute Hymen and the worship of a dead God whose primordial transcendence is not understood as having been itself apocalyptically manifested in Scripture. Radical Christianity understands that social justice, if it is to be actualized, cannot truly be removed from an apocalyptic reading of the whole of Scripture, not just parts, and must be scripturally embodied in the public.[33] It follows for Altizer that orthodoxy has been blinded to understanding the ultimate reversal embodied and actualized in Christ, that "the whole body of Christian theology is grounded in the presumption that no new prophet arose in Jesus, and thus no truly new enactment or proclamation here which is not a repetition of an earlier revelation, and above all no truly new realization of God" that is "dissolved in the Christian Church, and is already forgotten by the second century, a negation which is the dissolution of the original Jesus."[34]

Radical Christian communities seek to establish the Kingdom of God in the present, not simply or necessarily through social holiness but by radically reversing Godhead as Holy Spirit. A radicalized understanding of the

Holy Spirit is a negation of nondiachronal Godhead as represented by the tearing open of sky at certain points of the Jesus narrative, culminating in the Day of Pentecost that follows the ascension. The reality of the Holy Spirit in the present then demands Pentecost to be the beginning of a new epoch in which the church perpetuates its Pentecosting. "Not only does an absolutely 'new' dawn ever more fully, but an absolutely 'old' is equally called forth," Altizer writes, "an 'old' which apocalyptically can be named as the old aeon or even Satan, but an actualization of Satan and the old aeon or the old creation only possible as the consequence of an absolutely forward movement." He explains the kenosis of Spirit further:

> Just as it was the prophetic revolution which first enacted the abso-
> lutely new, this is a revolution fulfilled in Jesus, and in that Jesus
> who enacted the final dawning of the Kingdom of God, a kingdom
> that is not primordial or ancient or eternal kingdom, but a kingdom
> that is and only is an apocalyptic kingdom, or that kingdom which
> *is* the absolutely new.[35]

New Kingdom-language invoked by radical Christians indicates a new understanding of Godhead is emerging that is necessitated and perpetuated by the newness of each moment of time moving forward. A *new* morphology of the sacred, the Holy Spirit emerges upon the horizon of the infinite of the Eternal Now.

Radical preaching reclaims the language of the Bible that is *both* (though not necessarily the same at once as a *coincidentia oppositorum*) a reversal of a former epoch *and* a reversal of the former now—the orthodoxies of the nothingness of the present and the orthodoxies of unreversed historical Christianity. Radical education reverses the heteronomy of the Sunday School—as Tillich himself blasphemed in his *Irrelevance and Relevance of the Christian Message*[36]—and enacts a life-span *mystagogy* where initiation into the faith in baptism is an invitation not only into eternal life but the sacred history of reversals: Godhead dismembering the face of the deep, the destruction of the great flood, the rainbow-promise made through droplets of water, the crossing of the Red Sea and the Jordan, etc. This invitation into eternal life through baptism is an invitation into the eternal death of God, not only by the initiate becoming a bearer of sacred history but *through* divine enfleshment. The Psalmist's cry to pass the mighty acts of the Lord onto the next generation can no longer be understood as an appeal to the past (through *pedagogy*, reclaiming our past childhoods) but as making the past relevant by its faithful reversal (*mystagogy*). Social justice is understood as—to employ by reversal a controversial phrase within my own denominational tradition—*biblical witness* rather than a biblical restoration or apprehension. Sacramental acts, most prominently the Eucharist, are interruptions of the nothingness of the world that, while moving forward, wishes to move backward.[37] To enact the Eucharist, for example, is to reclaim the canni-balistic parody of the rite as given in Scripture, connecting the ritual to the dismemberment of John the Baptist. The Eucharist is, in essence, more than Zwinglian memorial but an act of *re-membrance*, of reassembling the disassembled and dismembered body of Christ, ritually restoring the believ-ing community to abide within the death of God and for the death of God physically to graft into their individual flesh through consumption.

I am not advocating that radical Christianity *must* appear as these examples or suggestions from my own theology of pastoral practice. In fact, in various contexts and in the future, new reversals are needed that will dis-close the reversals implicit in the Scriptures. The actualization of an advent of the Kingdom of God requires continual and perpetual reversal; as such, the *coincidentia oppositorum* becomes a first-order category for pastoral theol-ogy as it is the foundational theological method within Altizer's thought.

Radical Ecclesiology

I have demonstrated that radical theology and pastoral practice may inter-sect within a context of a radical Christian community. To be sure, more examples and practical demonstrations need to be explored. The question of a radical ecclesiology, however, is different than *praxis* or polity. Yet the theological and attitudinal theological shift implied in the described pasto-ral practice suggests an ecclesiology that follows the method of *coincidentia oppositorum* as first-order theology.

First, radical Christianity is at the very least *post-ecclesial*, if not *anti-ecclesial*. In a 1990 essay aptly titled "Is the Negation of Christianity the Way to Its Renewal?" Altizer claimed that Christianity requires a "historically evolving faith and praxis,"[38] which recalls for this reader Friedrich Schlei-ermacher's "Fifth Speech" to his "cultured despisers," where Schleiermacher claims that "[t]he living spirit" of Christianity "slumbers oft and long." For Schleiermacher, Christianity may withdraw "itself into a torpid state, into the dead shell of the letter, but it ever wakes again as soon as the season in the spiritual world is favorable for its revival and sets its sap in motion," adding that "[t]hus in oft repeated cycle it renews itself in various ways."[39] Schleiermacher does not here refer to revivalism in the American preaching tradition but rather *negation* and *actual* liberation from the heteronomy of orthodox Christianity itself.

Gabriel Vahanian, in *Anonymous God*, equates the church as hav-ing left all semblance of connection with the earth. He writes, "[l]argely anticipating the image of the earth as a space ship, the classic image of the church has been that of a ship, all hands on board and each to a station, a station to each."[40] Recalling the ship-language of John Eck's debates with Martin Luther and the *anathematic* language of the Council of Trent (not to mention the Methodist bishops' polemic on radicalism), clearly, it seems, the radical theologian might have trouble finding a job on deck—in fact, she might find herself walking the plank! Vahanian's language recalls also the end of Walter M. Miller's classic science fiction novel, *A Canticle for Leibowitz*, where the Catholic Church sends herself into outer space as a passive means of human survival in the face of a coming nuclear holocaust. Miller probably meant this image to signify that the Church is the only hope for the world for human survival, but Miller's spaceship image is indicative of a vision of an *ecclesia* that passively stands along the sidelines of history, perhaps preserving ancient knowledge from a foregone era, yet unable to transform and transfigure the ultimate death of spiritual necrophilia.[41] Orthodoxy's apprehension of an actualized apocalyptic theology directly results in the human tragedy of nuclear apocalypse; the Church's only option is to escape the world it long ago forsook for a prioritized life after death. At the end of *A Canticle for Leibowitz*, the escape into outer space only continues the necrophilic sado-religion into zero gravity—a monk utters while boarding the spaceship, "*Sic transit mundus*," thus passes the world.[42] Vahanian writes that "if a world is to be raised from the church . . . in view of the kingdom of God, she must also commit herself to the enactment of social justice."[43] This enactment prioritizes *this* world where God is enfleshed over a removed plane of existence with pearly gates and mansions; rather, to blaspheme further, the kingdom of God is *at hand*, *near*, and *is in you*.

Second, a *post-ecclesial* and *anti-ecclesial* ecclesiology is a radical ecclesiology. A self-negating and self-subverting ecclesiology would be implicit for a radical ecclesiology; it is in fact the radical understanding of the present that is self-negating itself in the eternal crucifixion of Jesus as enfleshed in every human hand and face—the force of flesh pulling the Now *backward* and *upward* into the sado-nothingness while the enfleshed *theosis* challenges us *forward* and *downward* in history, in Hell. Radical ecclesiology is a "radical negation" of the church as we know it, though it is not an *exitus* or exodus.[44] Radical ecclesiology is not, as Charles Winquist observed, "a Sunday School theology," as "[i]t inhabits spaces in the weave of everyday discourses and insinuates formulations of extremity into the fissures of ordinary discourse, thereby generating *extraordinary* discourse."[45] In other words, a radical ecclesiology equips individuals to teach individuals how to engage and change the world in an *extraordinarily* Christlike manner rather than passively interpret the world for signs of its own destruction—a destruction with culpability resting in Christian passivity.

Tillich predicted that orthodoxy's apprehension of an *extraordinary* ecclesiology would have significant negative consequences for both church and society, "condemned to slow decay."[46] A radical, extraordinary ecclesiology blasphemes religion for the sake of religion, self-dismembers, self-subverts, and exorcises its own demons from within itself. As a self-critical extraordinary ecclesiology, the religious community is characterized by its own recognition of "demonization" of an "absolutization of the finite" within its own and others' walls, and never claims to have "The Answer" that cannot be epistemologically known.[47] As an actualized Pentecost creation, an extraordinary ecclesiology recognizes that, as with the Pentecost of history, Vahanian writes, "[o]ther tongues than one's own are being spoken."[48] Communal radical Christianity is extraordinary discourse, where one's solipsistic journey is voiced, shared, compared, diverged, and biblically grafted with the help of others—a lived and living faith, a *chosen* faith, weakened and humbled by its own dynamism. "The relevance of Christianity," Tillich wrote, "is asserted by its self-negation," and "[w]ithout this self-negation, Christianity is not true Christianity and is not relevant."[49] A radical ecclesiology opens communal space for this self-negation to be actualized through acts of community, justice, education, and liturgy.

For radicals the current state of the church need not be a cause for *exitus* but rather recognized as an *eucatastrophe*.[50] The *Gospel* of radical Christianity is that everything, including the church, requires a radical reversal, though the church is a large institution to budge. Yet there is hope for something extraordinary. If radical Christianity is a biblical faith, it is a *missionary* faith in a secularized and secularizing world that has recognized the orthodox *ecclesia* as an element of the nothing that pervades our present moment. The mission field is the present world that the church has neglected, dismissed, defrocked, and anathematized. As an "expatriate" theology, the Gospel mandate is now to *return to that which is alienated*, even if that return is by a different path (1 Kings 13: 8–10, Matt. 2: 12).[51] To return is to *reverse* the existing *ecclesia*, working *in spite of the Church* rather than *for the Church*, working "*in spite of God*" rather than "*for the sake of God*," while at once yearning and obsessing over the reality of enfleshed Godhead.[52] To rethink church, to have extraordinary discourse, requires a radical rethinking of Godhead, which implicitly requires a radically new ecclesiology that includes the human flesh and thinking itself as the bearers of the Holy, rendering *extraordinary* the banality of *ordinariness*. This new thinking now occurring requires both an *exitus* and a *return*, an extraordinary discourse continuing the *coincidentia oppositorum* of community and solitude, exit and return, belief and atheism. It must be a thinking that we *behold as making all things new* (Rev. 21: 5).

Notes

1. Mark C. Taylor offers some details of this in his foreword to Thomas Altizer's *Living the Death of God* (Albany: State University of New York Press, 2007), xii–xiii.

2. The Methodist's official declaration against Altizer is published as "Statement of the College of Bishops, Southeastern Jurisdiction," *The Mississippi Methodist Advocate* ns 19, 17 (February 2,1966): 6.

3. Mike Grimshaw, "Did God Die in *The Christian Century?*" *Journal of Cultural and Religious Theory* 6, 3 (2005): 7–23.

4. My inclusion of Mary Daly into the canon of radical death of God theologians may be unique or perhaps a novelty among other radical theologians. However, a careful and historically progressive reading of Daly, particularly her journal articles between *The Church and the Second Sex* (Harper Colophon ed., New York: Harper, 1975) and *Beyond God the Father* (Boston: Beacon, 1973), will demonstrate a Catholic writer engaged with Protestant death of God theology through a radical reading of Tillich. As such, these articles lead directly into the first chapter of *Beyond God the Father*, titled "After the Death of God the Father," which is arguably Daly's most read and most significant popular contribution to American theology. These articles include Mary Daly, "Dispensing with Trivia," *Commonweal* 88 (1968): 322–325; "The Return of the Protestant Principle," *Commonweal* 90 (1969): 314–317; "Mary Daly on the Church," *Commonweal* 91 (1969): 215; "The Problem of Hope," *Commonweal* 92 (1970): 314–317; "The Courage to See," *The Christian Century* 83 (1971): 1108–1111; "Abortion and Sexual Caste," *Commonweal* 95 (1972): 415–419; "A Call for the Castration of Sexist Religion," *Unitarian Universalist Christian* 27 (1972): 23–27; "The Spiritual Revolution," *Andover Newton Quarterly* 12, 4 (1974): 163–176; "The Women's Movement," *Religious Education* 67 (1972): 327–335; and Daly with Aquinas Ferrara, "Underground Theology," *Commonweal* 88 (1969): 531–534. All of these are discussed in Christopher Rodkey, "In the Horizon of the Infinite" (PhD diss., Drew University, 2008), 200–235.

5. Mary Daly, *Quintessence* (Boston: Beacon, 1998), xi.

6. Cf. Daly, "Abortion and Sexual Caste," 417; Mary Daly, "The Courage to Leave," *John Cobb's Theology in Process*, ed. David Griffin and Thomas Altizer (Philadelphia: Westminster, 1977), 85.

7. Cf. Christopher Rodkey, "Reconsidering Noise in Theology and in Praxis," *Doxology: A Journal of Worship* (2004): 72–91.

8. William Blake, "The Everlasting Gospel," *The Complete Poems*, ed. Alicia Ostriker (London: Penguin, 1977), ll. 1–2, 8, 13–14 (p. 851).

9. Blake, "Notebook in Epigrams and Satanic Verses," "To God," 629.

10. Walter Bruegemann, "The Triumphalist Tendency of Exegetical History," *Journal of the American Academy of Religion* 38, 4 (1970): 369–370 n. 10.

11. By "apocalyptic" I am employing Altizer's use of the term throughout this essay. "Apocalyptic" is the absolute newness of every moment of the eternal Now, enacted through the dialectic of history moving forward and downward.

12. Blake, "The Everlasting Gospel," 3, ll. 7–8; 5, ll. 63–68, 72.

13. Thomas J. J. Altizer, *Living the Death of God*, 68.

14. Lissa McCullough, "Theology as the Thinking of Passion Itself," *Thinking through the Death of God*, ed. Lissa McCullough and Brian Schroeder (Albany: State University of New York Press, 2004), 38.

15. Actualization here refers, in the process sense, to an actual event or actual occasion.

16. Thomas J. J. Altizer, *Total Presence* (New York: Seabury, 1980), 7. Cf. 2 Cor. 10: 3–5.

17. Thomas J. J. Altizer, *The Self-Embodiment of God* (New York: Harper, 1977), 70–71.

18. Ibid., 71.

19. McCullough, "Theology as the Thinking of Passion Itself," 44–45; emphasis added.

20. Altizer, "A Response," in *Thinking through the Death of God*, 223.

21. It is likely true that an obvious feminist concern might be raised here regarding the divine imposing child abuse upon its own constituency. I am not sure I can offer a genuine or sufficient response to this concern except that the abusing Godhead is one who abuses to maintain power, dispenses grace as a means of coercion, in nondiachronal models of the divine. In the radical conception, Godhead not only sympathizes with its children but empathizes with the abused and is in fact enfleshed with the abused.

22. D. G. Leahy, *Foundation* (Albany: State University of New York Press, 1996), 392ff.; Jacques Derrida, *Dissemination*, trans. B. Johnson (Chicago: University of Chicago Press, 1981), 261ff., 340ff.

23. For example, see Daly, *Quintessence*, 91. It is important to note that while my own conception of radical theology is informed by Altizer and Daly, along with others, Altizer and Daly are very different thinkers with contradictory ideas and terminologies. One explicit and striking similarity, however, is their use of the word "nothing."

24. Mary Daly, *Pure Lust* (New York: Harper San Francisco, 1984), 94, 147; *Quintessence*, 119–121.

25. Daly, *Pure Lust*, 147.

26. Mary Daly, *Gyn/Ecology* (Alyesbury, England: Women's, 1991), 133ff.

27. Mircea Eliade, *Patterns in Comparative Religion*, trans. Rosemary Sheed (London, NE: University of Nebraska Press, 1996), §159 (p. 419).

28. Thomas J. J. Altizer, "Mircea Eliade and the Death of God," *Commonweal* 29 (1979): 257.

29. See, for example, Brian McLaren, *A Generous Orthodoxy* (El Cajon, CA: Youth Specialties, 2004), 245ff.

30. Brian Schroeder, "Absolute Atonement," *Thinking through the Death of God*, 65. Schroeder here is referencing Thomas J. J. Altizer, *The New Gospel of Christian Atheism* (Aurora, CO: Davies, 2002), 104–105; *Genesis and Apocalypse* (Louisville, KY: Westminster, 1990), 158; and *The Contemporary Jesus* (Albany: State University of New York Press, 1997), xxi.

31. See, for example, my argument in Christopher Rodkey, "Nietzschean Christology," *The Fractal Self*, ed. Douglas Shrader (New York: Oneonta Philosophical Studies, 2000), 155–174.

32. Further examples of orthodox apprehension of the sacred include the movement to publicly display the Decalogue (or even public-square nativities), which embodies a reversal of any actual immediacy of the radical reversal implicit in understanding Zion (or Bethlehem) as an instance of the sacred descending forward and downward in history.

33. This is why, for example, during the 2008 American presidential election cycle, John Hagee defended Jeremiah Wright's use of the schema in his infamous "God Damn America" sermon at Trinity United Church of Christ in 2001; very different radicalisms recognize each other.

34. Thomas J. J. Altizer, *The Genesis of God* (Louisville, KY: Westminster, 1993), 170–171.

35. Thomas J. J. Altizer, *Godhead and the Nothing* (Albany: State University of New York Press, 2003), 148.

36. Paul Tillich, *The Irrelevance and Relevance of the Christian Message*, second ed., ed. A. Durwood Foster (Cleveland: Pilgrim, 1996), 18.

37. I devote more on the Eucharist as "drinking the nothing itself" and "black mass" in my dissertation, "In the Horizon of the Infinite," unpublished manuscript, 329–336.

38. Thomas J. J. Altizer, "Is the Negation of Christianity the Way to Its Renewal?" *Religious Humanism* 24, 1 (1990): 10.

39. Friedrich Schleiermacher, *On Religion*, trans. J. Oman (Louisville, KY: Westminster, 1994), 250.

40. Gabriel Vahanian, *Anonymous God*, trans. Noëlle Vahanian (Aurora, CO: Davies, 2002), 127.

41. Walter M. Miller Jr., *A Canticle for Leibowitz* (New York: Bantam, 1976 [1959]), 312–313.

42. Ibid., 312. It is worth mentioning that the aphoristic tenor of the very end of Miller's novel is worth noting—almost echoing the cadences of Walter Kaufmann's translation of aphorisms 123 and 124 of Nietzsche's *Gay Science* (trans. W. Kaufmann [New York: Vintage, 1967]).

43. Vahanian, *Anonymous God*, 128.

44. Thomas J. J. Altizer, "Response," *The Theology of Altizer*, ed. John Cobb (Philadelphia: Westminster, 1970), 76.

45. Charles Winquist, *Desiring Theology* (Chicago: University of Chicago Press, 1995), 135; emphasis added.

46. Tillich, *Irrelevance and Relevance of the Christian Message*, 19.

47. Ibid., 51–52; Mary Ann Stenger, "Troeltsch and Tillich," *North American Paul Tillich Society Newsletter* 29, 3 (2003): 12.

48. Vahanian, *Anonymous God*, 128.

49. Tillich, *Irrelevance and Relevance of the Christian Message*, 52. This kind of kenotic community may have legitimate feminist concerns, particularly in the anti body language at work in my theology. Clearly, I am using this language metaphorically, and I believe that this language is not necessary for truly radical Christian communities. I intend my theological language, however, to be drawn from Altizer's, which comes from a distinctly systematic, Anglican context.

50. I borrow this term from Tolkien to indicate a good catastrophe, as opposed to a dyscatastrophe (J. R. R. Tolkien, "On Fairy-Stories," *Essays Presented to Charles Williams*, ed. C. S. Lewis [Grand Rapids, MI: Eerdmans, 1968], 81). I connect this concept to the tension between *missa jubilaea* and *missa solemnis* in Altizer (see Thomas J. J. Altizer, "Response to David Jasper," *Contributions in Religion and Theology* 5, 2 [2007]: 172).

51. William Hamilton, *On Taking God Out of the Dictionary* (New York: McGraw-Hill, 1974), 44.

52. Vahanian, quoting Dietrich Bonhoeffer, in Gabriel Vahanian, "Theology at the End of the Age of Religion," *Concilium* 6, 2 (1966): 55.

8

The Death of God, Death, and Resurrection

Clayton Crockett

In truth, in very truth I tell you, a grain of wheat remains a solitary grain unless it falls into the ground and dies; but if it dies, it bears a rich harvest.

—John 12: 24

The death of God is the essential precondition for any serious theological thinking, and any theology that forecloses the death of God renders itself irrelevant to human thought and action or ultimately human life. In this chapter, I consider the more well-known dialectical understanding of the death of God, from Luther and Hegel to Altizer and Žižek. Here the death of God is the negation that leads to a negation of negation, a reversal that is a resurrection of God in some form, however specifically understood. Then I contrast this dialectical reading with a more nondialectical reading of the death of God, which I take from Deleuze's *Difference and Repetition*. Here the death of God is the pure and empty form of time, which is the transition to the third synthesis of time, that of the future. Life is impossible without death as its precondition. Resurrection is accordingly the flip side of the death of God, not understood as the mere resuscitation of a corpse but a coming-to-life that is the emergence of novelty, which is the result of a process of repetition of difference.

Nietzsche proclaims the death of God in his philosophy, which reverberates throughout twentieth-century thought. Although Nietzsche was an atheist, his understanding of the death of God primarily means the devaluation of the highest values, the idea that values like truth, reason, and morality ultimately break down into their opposite under the pressure of the values they instantiate. In our uncompromising search for truth, we are forced to admit that truth is a lie, because the ideal of truth distorts reality in its dynamic becoming, forcing it to fit into the categories of our knowing and understanding.

For many theologians, Nietzsche's philosophy represents an attack, undermining any possibility for authentic belief in God, although the most creative Protestant theologians of the twentieth century, Karl Barth and Paul Tillich, were strongly influenced by Nietzsche's thought. However, in the 1960s, when the death of God theology emerged, it appeared radical and strange because it affirmed that the proclamation of the death of God was the most authentic Christian belief. Initially, the diagnosis of the death of God was an indictment of contemporary culture, the determination that for postwar America God ceased to have any force or meaning. According to Gabriel Vahanian in his book *The Death of God*, "This age is post-Christian not only theologically but also culturally."[1] It is no longer possible for a human being authentically to become Christian. In its first manifestation, some death of God theology applied Nietzschean criteria to contemporary culture and determined that this culture was no longer Christian in an important way. For Vahanian, the understanding of the death of God was a profound critique and rejection of contemporary culture in the name of an evacuated Christianity. Vahanian later viewed the death of God more positively, as he developed a constructive theology of the secular.[2]

From the beginning of the death of God theology movement, Thomas J. J. Altizer has been its most famous and most influential representative. For Altizer, the death of God is not a negative but a positive phenomenon, and it is not a new event but the essence of Christianity itself. Altizer says that "only the Christian can truly speak the death of God, because the Christian alone knows the God who negates himself in his own revelatory and redemptive acts."[3] For his understanding of the death of God as the core of Christian faith, Altizer appeals to William Blake, Hegel, and Nietzsche. Here the incarnation and crucifixion of Christ as God accomplishes the complete and total death of God. The resurrection of Jesus is not a restoration of a transcendent God but the dialectical and historical progression of spirit as it sublates the difference between divinity and humanity. According to Altizer, "the death of God does not propel man into an empty darkness, it liberates him from every alien and opposing other, and makes possible his transition into what Blake hailed as 'The Great Humanity Divine,' or the final coming together of God and man."[4] Resurrection is not a restoration of divine transcendence but an irreversible process of divine self-annihilation.

This divine self-annihilation, however, it is good news, because it involves the liberation of humanity from its servitude to a transcendent deity.

For Altizer, Hegel is the central philosopher of the death of God, because Hegel's dialectic provides a logic to explain how God or Spirit alienates itself as spirit into nature and then reconstitutes itself on a higher level by transcending and sublating nature. The world is alienated from divinity, but then God incarnates Godself as human and dies. What dies on the cross is not simply the human being, Jesus, but God the Father as a transcendent agent. God really dies on the cross, and this is the good news of Christianity. Christianity understands the progression of history as the dialectical progression of absolute spirit, whereby the Holy Spirit sublates both the transcendent God and immanent humanity in a higher, more evolved form. The implications of this death of God are worked out in time as history, albeit from a Eurocentric and Christocentric viewpoint.

Hegel's idea of the dialectic proceeds by means of negation, where the split between God and nature or humanity constitutes a negation that is then negated in a negation of the negation, which is a positive, affirmative movement. The death of God is the reconciliation of spirit and matter, humanity and divinity, in a process that continues to work itself out both metaphysically and historically. Hegel draws the logic of his dialectical reading of Christianity from Martin Luther's understanding of the relationship between grace and law, worked out in Paul's letters. In his *Commentary on Galatians*, Luther explains that the law constitutes a form of death, or sin, that judges and condemns life itself. The law functions as a negation, but grace is the death of the law, or the death of death, which is a negation of the original negation: "The law of Moses accuseth and condemneth me; but against that accusing and condemning law, I have another law, which is grace and liberty. This law accuseth the accusing law, and condemneth the condemning law. So death killeth death: but this killing death is life itself."[5] The death of God becomes the name for this death of law that occurs by way of grace. Jesus's death crucifies and kills death itself insofar as it accomplishes the end of the law and the release from sin.[6] Paul's dialectic of grace and law as elaborated by Luther takes a metaphysical and progressive form in Hegel and Altizer, where it is not simply Jesus's sacrifice as the death of the law that occurs but the actual and entire death of a transcendent and external God.

Slavoj Žižek follows the basic thrust of this Hegelian and Altizerian reading of the death of God, except that he counters the stereotypical reading of sublation as the total overcoming of negativity. In fact, for Žižek the *Aufhebung* (sublation) of Hegel is not a higher and more complete synthesis but opens up and exposes the abyss at the heart of the dialectic. That is,

Žižek compresses the dialectic and shows how it tears itself up, revealing the death of God as God's death and emptiness. What Jesus represents is the actual incarnation and death of God, because God is like us, not in the sense of elevating humanity up to the level of divinity, but God is not one with Godself. In *The Puppet and the Dwarf*, Žižek claims that "[w]e are one with God only when God is no longer one with Himself, but abandons Himself, 'internalizes' the radical distance which separates us from Him. Our radical experience of separation from God is the very feature which unites us with Him" in a paradoxical way.[7] In his theology, Altizer elaborates an apocalyptic negativity, mainly as the precondition for a reversal, a total and absolute positivity because the darkest abyss conceals the most radical new beginning. Here Altizer is strongly influenced by the notion of, and often uses the phrase, *coincidentia oppositorum*, the coincidence of opposites, which means that the most extraordinary negativity obscures and goes hand in hand with the most incredible affirmation. On the other hand, Žižek, while he emphasizes the negativity of human being and thought by way of Hegel and Lacan, does not simply offer a means of overcoming it but rather an acceptance of the irreducibility of this negativity, and this is the true meaning of Christianity as well as the reason why Žižek calls himself a Christian atheist. According to Žižek:

> "man is man" indicates the noncoincidence of man with man, the properly inhuman excess which disturbs its self-identity—and what, ultimately, is Christ but the name of this excess inherent in man, man's ex-timate kernel, the monstrous surplus which, following the unfortunate Pontius Pilate, one of the few ethical heroes of the Bible (the other being Judas, of course), can be designated only as "Ecce homo"?[8]

From Hegel to Altizer to Žižek, the death of God becomes more internalized into Christianity and theological thinking, as well as the being of human being in philosophical terms.

The death of God can be understood in distinct ways, however, and we should be careful not to appropriate the death of God as a way to consolidate traditional forms of religion after a divergence that appears to be an opening or a negation, but then this negation or opening is itself negated by means of a vulgar Hegelianism. Here the death of God would not be not serious but would operate as a ruse or a power play.[9] If this is the case, then the death of God is only apparent, it is quickly converted to life, to the resurrection of the divinity and sovereignty of the same God with even more awesome power and might. And Christianity is still the privileged means of access to this God who is unscathed even by death.

In its Hegelian or crude, quasi-Hegelian version, resurrection is a progressive advance beyond the death of God. You must have at least two stages: 1) death and 2) resurrection (although for Žižek, resurrection is a transformed awareness upon further reflection of this death, so the second stage occurs only in thought). In contrast to this predominant, dialectical understanding of the death of God, I want to offer a more Deleuzean understanding of what the death of God means. This alternative reading is intended not simply to oppose the Hegelian and Christian death of God but to open up another space for theorizing what the death of God means and entails that is not necessarily tied to Hegelian dialectics or Christian apologetics. In this version, as I explain later, resurrection is not separated from death, but death properly understood *is* resurrection, and resurrection is life—not simply the magical resuscitation of a corpse but the passage or cut that allows for creative transformation and renewal.

In order to consider a more Deleuzean image of the death of God, it is also necessary to transform our understanding of theology. Both Altizer and Žižek radicalize theological thinking and show how it is vitally tied up with philosophical thought, but they do not completely transform it. Deleuze does not develop a new understanding of theology, but he offers hints in that direction, most famously and explicitly in a quotation from the appendix to *The Logic of Sense*. In a discussion of Pierre Klossowski and modern literature, Deleuze writes:

> In another respect, it is our epoch which has discovered theology. One no longer needs to believe in God. We seek rather the "structure," that is, the form which may be filled with beliefs, but the structure has no need to be filled in order to called "theological." Theology is now the science of nonexisting entities, the manner in which these entities—divine or anti-divine, Christ or Antichrist—animate language and make for it this glorious body which is divided into disjunctions.[10]

Here theology does not presuppose the commitment to specific (Christian) beliefs but attends to the structure or form of any beliefs whatever. Following Deleuze, the postmodern theologian Charles Winquist envisions theology in a postmodern, secular context as a kind of exigency that remains after the death of God, where "what is lost with the death of God is a fixed meaning of presence that grounds identity in difference."[11] Winquist characterizes theology as "a minor literature within a dominant discourse and vehicular language" that is nontheological in any explicit way.[12]

Deleuze's notion of the death of God is less explicitly Christocentric than Altizer's and Žižek's, and in *Difference and Repetition* he explains it in reference to time. In chapter 2, "Repetition for Itself," Deleuze elaborates three syntheses of time, which roughly correspond to present (habit), past (memory), and future (eternal return). The transition from the second to the third synthesis occurs along a break that is opened up by Kantian transcendental philosophy. According to Deleuze, "If the greatest initiative of transcendental philosophy was to introduce the form of time into thought as such, then this pure and empty form in turn signifies indissolubly the death of God, the fractured I and the passive self."[13] Instead of setting the self in time in an ontological sense, Kant places time within the self, and this division between the active (apperceptive) and passive self (the self that is the object of human representation) splits the self in two.

Why would the splitting of the self lead to the death of God? Because Descartes founds the modern idea of God upon the self as the *Cogito*. "God survives as long as the I enjoys a subsistence, a simplicity and an identity which expresses the entirety of its resemblance to the divine."[14] Deleuze claims that the pure and empty form of time that Kant isolates at the heart of the self also accomplishes the death of God. This is a nondialectical, non-Hegelian version of the death of God.[15] The pure and empty form of time constitutes the third and final synthesis of time for Deleuze, and it is the break or caesura of this form of time that opens onto a future. The past, the present, and the future are all distinct forms of repetition, and it is the third form of time that concerns the eternal return, and Deleuze's appropriation of Nietzsche.

The "repetition of the future as eternal return" is a kind of repetition that "affects only the new, what is produced under the conditions of default and by the intermediary of metamorphosis."[16] The conventional reading of Nietzsche's idea of the eternal return is the return of the same, the idea that everything returns exactly and identically. Deleuze claims that this is a misunderstanding of the eternal return: only what becomes returns or what becomes differently. The eternal return is repetition by excess, and it excludes all identity, including "my own identity, the identity of the self, the world, and God."[17] If Deleuze is right, and only that which is different returns, then there is no self-identity that can be substantialized or eternalized, including that of God.

To think the death of God is to think the death of the self and the impossibility of human and divine identity. This death, however, is an opening, a passage not to some higher form of identity but to a future that is different because it returns, or repeats. Only what is different returns, so becoming is repetition, but the content of repetition is always a distinct reiteration rather than the repetition of the same identity. This death does not lead to a future resurrection, but in fact it is directly resurrection. Resurrection properly understood is the new, the different that emerges out of the process of repetition or iteration that becomes the future. We can attempt to cling to our identity, but it is a false identity and a more reactionary kind of death, death as claustrophobic suffocation.

Although (pace Altizer) Deleuze's notion of the death of God is not technically Christocentric, it is relevant to Christianity and the resurrection of Jesus. In his *Systematic Theology*, the Protestant theologian Paul Tillich claims that Christ is the name for the New Being. According to Tillich, "New Being is essential being under the conditions of existence, conquering the gap between essence and existence."[18] Despite Tillich's ontological language that suggests a transcendence of essence and existence in a higher identity, I read Tillich in light of Deleuze. From a more Deleuzean viewpoint, we can see the New Being as the sign of repetition-as-difference, which is not any kind of static or identical being at all but rather names the process of eternal return. What Jesus signifies here is essentially futural, a calling into existence of the new. This way of understanding the resurrection, which I delineate later, spans from Tillich through Deleuze to Alain Badiou, John Spong, and John D. Caputo.

In contemporary historical and philosophical-theological thinking, a transition occurs during the late twentieth century from Jesus to Paul. After several waves of historical Jesus research, beginning in the nineteenth century and extending through the seminal work of Albert Schweitzer in *The Quest for the Historical Jesus* and culminating in the work of the Jesus Seminar and John Dominic Crossan, we can see a shift in emphasis toward a more significant engagement with Paul.[19] In terms of Continental philosophy, the atheist French philosopher Alain Badiou set off an important theoretical debate with his book *Saint Paul: The Foundation of Universalism*, published in French in 1997 and translated into English in 2003.

Badiou does not believe in the literal resurrection of Christ, as he assumes Paul does. But Badiou claims that Paul's thought represents the construction of a new, universal form of subjectivity. In a provocative reading of Romans 7, Badiou says that "all of Paul's thinking here points toward a theory of the subjective unconscious, structured through the opposition life/death."[20] The law, as Paul understands it, instantiates death in the subject, because it cuts off the subject from his or her object of desire. Law takes the form of a prohibition, where the person may not have access to the object of her desire. Life is posited on the side of the object, as what is desired, whereas the subject is in a mode of death, because she exists in a state of separation from life. Sin is the automation of desire as revealed and proscribed by the law. Sin is the name given to this way of being in a state of death, because life is on the side of the "involuntary automation of living desire," whereas the self is rendered impotent and powerless.[21]

According to Badiou, faith is a kind of subjectivation, a dynamic way of bridging the gap between subject and life. The object is not attained but is associated with death, so that the law and the object are on the side of death, whereas grace and faith bring the subject to life. This mode of subjectivation structures "the subject of a universal truth," beyond any particular ethnic, cultural, or national identity.[22] This universalism is a kind of resurrection, because it associates the subject with life rather than death: "Resurrection summons the subject to identify himself as such according to the name of faith (*pistis*)."[23] Resurrection is a kind of subjectivation; it closes the gap opened up by the law that prohibits the subject from possessing its object of desire.

Badiou says that for Paul, there is no gap between subject and subjectivation, and this mode of existence is faith, which is also a state of grace and love beyond the deadly clutches of the law. Resurrection is an event that brings the subject (back) to life. Paul is not a moralist, advocating this or that set of conventions; he is deeply concerned with psycho-theological problems of law and death. Christ is not resurrected in the sense of the reanimation of a dead body, but the gospel of Christ is the good news of how Christ's overcoming of death "saves" us. Salvation is not the *letter* of resuscitation of a corpse but the *spirit* of "a lawless eruption, unchaining the point of powerlessness from automatism."[24] Badiou defines salvation as the claim "that thought can be unseparated from doing and power."[25] Salvation is a kind of liberation of thought and a universalization of subjectivation that occurs only in and then through the law. Salvation is accomplished by the event, an unforeseen occurrence that structures the subject as a subject out of fidelity to it. The law is death, but at the same time faith is the recognition of grace of an event of subjectivation as the death of death, the overcoming of the law and restoration of the subject to life. The question is whether this process should be understood dialectically and temporally: first the law and then the event of grace; first death, then resurrection and restoration to life. I am arguing here that it is one and the same process, two sides of the same coin. The realization of death in and as separation from the object of desire, when fully realized, is the subjectivation of the subject beyond this law and thus a kind of resurrection.

Badiou preserves the form of Christian truth and subjectivity, even though he empties it of content. I think that Badiou can be read more dialectically, along the lines of Hegel, Altizer, and Žižek, or more nondialectically, as closer to Deleuze. In the latter case, the event constitutes a break or a cut that opens onto a future, and resurrection is the flip side of the death of both the subject and of God. In his major philosophical works *Being and Event* and *Logics of Worlds*, Badiou develops a mathematical ontology of multiplicity, where an event subtracts from this ontological multiplicity and instantiates a world that can be formalized according to distinct logics. Badiou critiques Deleuze for being too enthralled by the categories of the One and of Life, but his notion of resurrection can be viewed as deploying a certain logic of life, even if Badiou wants to avoid any pathos or romanticism surrounding the term.[26] In *Logics of Worlds*, Badiou defines resurrection as a "destination, which reactivates a subject in another logic of its appearing-in-truth."[27] This reactivation of the subject is not simply a repetition of identity, but can be seen as a repetition of difference in Deleuzean terms. Badiou affirms that "a resurrection presupposes a new world, which generates the context for a new event, a new trace, a new body."[28] Since resurrection creates a new world and a new subject, it is a radical repetition or reiteration. In fact, the death of a world requires the death of any God or overarching transcendent power sustaining it, even though Badiou provides rules or logics for the transcendental operations of appearing in worlds.

I am suggesting that resurrection in Badiou, which is developed in terms of a radical reading of Paul, has affinities with repetition in Deleuze, despite the divergence of their ontologies. In a more biblical and existential way, we can examine the evidence surrounding the claims for the resurrection of Jesus, even though this evidence and these claims are highly controversial. Here we shift from Paul—who was unconcerned with the historical, personal existence of Jesus and the particulars of his resurrection—to Peter.

According to Spong, the key to understanding the gospels as narratives about Jesus is to realize that the majority of the gospel stories are post-crucifixion and post-resurrection narratives. In his book *Resurrection: Myth or Reality?*, Spong argues that "a literal view of the resurrection narratives of the New Testament is not sustainable."[29] Most of the Synoptic Gospels center on Peter and evince a Galilean rather than a Jerusalem context. Spong claims that Peter and the other disciples fled when Jesus was arrested and did not witness the crucifixion. It was only months later that Peter had a transformative experience of Jesus as risen, and an understanding of his death as an intentional sacrifice.

It was in the midst of his intense grief that Peter had this experience that became known as the resurrection, and it occurred back in Galilee rather than in Jerusalem. Spong argues that most of the stories about the pre-resurrected Jesus are actually *post*-resurrection narratives, interpreted through the frame of Peter and his friends' experiences and understanding. The stories of walking on the water, rebuking Peter and the other disciples for unbelief, miracles, and even the last supper can be seen as post-hoc accounts within the context of a community coming to terms with Jesus's death and finding a way to make sense of it. Peter and his friends shared communal meals of fish and bread and exchanged memories of Jesus, and "somehow, seeing the risen Christ was associated with sharing the common meal, with participating in the meaning of the broken bread."[30]

This experience was not the literal seeing of a reanimated corpse but a transfigurative vision borne of intense grief and feelings of guilt and betrayal, combined with a deeper reflection about what Jesus's teachings meant in light of his violent death. Eventually, Peter and the other disciples returned to Jerusalem to proclaim the resurrection of Jesus, but this was associated not with Passover but with the Jewish festival of Tabernacles. According to Spong, "It was the symbols of Tabernacles that came to be thought of as the symbols of the Jerusalem resurrection—a Palm Sunday procession, the cleansing of the temple, the empty booth, the sweet-smelling spices, the ceremonial meal, and the angelic messenger who announced the resurrection."[31] Spong makes a persuasive case that Peter originates the claim that Jesus was resurrected in a Galilean context and that this tradition precedes both the stories of the empty tomb and the descriptions of Jesus's resurrected physical body. Ultimately, Spong believes that Peter's vision of Jesus as revealing and embodying the living God is credible, and he says a prayerful "[y]es to life after death—because one who has entered a relationship with God has entered the timelessness of God."[32] Although I sympathize with his belief, I do not exactly share his formulation of it, insofar as the resurrection of Jesus means individual human life after and beyond death in identitarian terms.

A more Hegelian/Altizerian/Žižekian interpretation, however, would see the death of Jesus as resurrected entirely into the life of the community of believers, as the Holy Spirit, without remainder.[33] Here life appears as progressive in a historical sense rather than literally transcendent. With Deleuze, though, we can think about the death of Jesus as the death of God, *as the death of identity that opens onto a future*, a repetition of difference beyond identity. In terms of the *Logic of Sense*, Jesus provides a body that suffers passion and death, which is the reality of his crucifixion, whereas his resurrection refers to the *sense* of this death, which appears nonsensical in conventional terms. For Deleuze, there are two series: a series of signs and a series of bodies, and the series of signs express what the series of bodies endure.[34] An event is the sense that the series of signs express, but the impetus for an event is embedded in (a) body and occurs as a wound. Events are actualized in sense as the expression of a trauma, a cut, or a wound, which is why "every event is a kind of plague, war, wound or death."[35]

Christ is the sign of a death/body that is proclaimed by Peter and Paul as life, an event that has revolutionary sense. The cut of the crucifixion is the intensity that drives the repetition that constitutes Christianity, and this process is singular to Christianity but not exclusive to it. We could also think about cosmic Buddha-bodies, ethical Jewish bodies, whirling Sufi bodies, and subtle Hindu bodies, among others, that constitute different dispersals and distinct relations between body and to sense.

It is not that Jesus dies, and then he is resurrected, and that event holds the promise for our own resurrection after death so long as we believe in it. It is not that Jesus dies, and he is then resurrected in us, the community of believers in Christ. It is that the message of Jesus's death is the resurrection, purely and simply. Christ dies, and this is precisely good news. Everyone dies. In his book *The Weakness of God*, John D. Caputo provides a thinking of resurrection that has affinities with Badiou/Paul and Spong/ Peter, but is distinct from both, and I want to try to tease out this difference.

In his reading of the Lazarus story in chapter 11 of *The Weakness of God*, Caputo claims that "rebirth and resurrection—that is what the kingdom is all about."[36] The resurrection that Jesus performs in the case of Lazarus is the "singular transformation from death to life," but it is a not a magical transformation that reverses the decomposition of a rotting body.[37] Caputo discusses the time of the world in terms of ruined time, which is evil. Not that worldly temporality is evil, but the crushing of possibilities is evil, the destructive power of pain and death. In contrast to ruined time, Caputo brings in what Levinas calls "the time of salvation," which pertains to the event. Salvation means "being saved from ruined time for a new time."[38] Caputo uses Levinas here, but we could also think of Badiou and Deleuze.

On the one hand, the redemption of a person, like Lazarus, seems to mean either the resuscitation of his body or the elevation of his soul to a state of eternal life, but I do not think that Caputo's view of time is either reversible or dialectic/dualistic. Salvation is a miracle of new life, but it is wholly situated "not in a heavenly pleasure but in the pain of the present."[39] We can only be saved by the other, by the appearance of a new birth, a child as the miracle of a new beginning, beyond death but not outside of death. According to Caputo, "Neither time nor salvation, neither rebirth nor resurrection, is possible in the solitary ego."[40] Reading Caputo in the context of Badiou and Deleuze, resurrection can be understood not as the self-transcendence of the ego into another, higher (soul) form of ego. Rather, life is a resurrection or rebirth, because it is predicated upon and condi- tioned by death, even as death is only possible for what lives. Lazarus is not a person who was dead and then was physiologically restored to life by some magic spell cast by Jesus, and Jesus is not another (very special, even super-human) person who was physiologically restored to life magically by a transcendent divine being. Instead, Jesus allows his mourners to transvalue Lazarus's life, to see it as truly alive with possibility and to let it spark life and transformation in the lives of his family and friends, and Jesus's life and death can inspire us to life as well.

As I read Caputo, Spong, Badiou, and Deleuze, the message of Jesus is that death is resurrection and rebirth, and that the only kind of death that does not constitute resurrection is the suffocation death of an enclosed or imprisoned ego. So long as we try to preserve and maintain our ego, our persistent identity, we can only die. But only insofar as we release our identity and recognize that we are not, the death of the self is the resurrec- tion because it is the gate by way of becoming anew. Becoming is becoming

differently, becoming in and as difference, and the death of God and self
are the only possibilities for resurrection, because that death is resurrection
itself, which is immediately divine. We can either reactively cling to life,
which delivers it over to death, and then our death seals this death-in-life,
cutting it off in an impossible manner; or we can embrace and accept death
as the opening up and out of ourselves as we recur differently and eternally
but not as us.

The death of God is not simple atheism but a radical atheism that
converges with radical faith. Conventional understandings of atheism are
not radical enough. Either religion is seen as a cultural sublimation (and/or
illusion) to counter the natural fear of death, or atheism is seen as producing a simple subtraction of God from the world, leaving a hole from which
meaning bleeds out. According to Ernst Becker in his influential work *The
Denial of Death*, the awareness of death creates unbearable anxiety that
is then sublimated into cultural formations. But recent sociological work
on human practices of death show that this anxiety over death is itself a
cultural formation rather than a natural instinct. Culture appears first, as a
result tool-making and using technology, domestication of fire and cooking
of food, and language.[41] It is only much later, as Allan Kellehear explains,
with the advent of agriculture, that pastoral death becomes a challenge to
be accomplished well and finally in the modern industrial age a problem to
be managed in various ways.[42]

Some religious critics of atheism complain that it leaves a God-shaped
hole that must be filled with other meanings, unless God can be properly
restored. On the other hand, as Peter Rollins points out, "The God-shaped
hole can be understood precisely as that which is left in the aftermath of
God," which means that the radical lack or death of God is a kind of pupil
or black hole that constitutes a singularity that produces effects on space,
time, and existence. Instead of covering over this hole with a superficial
theism or humanism, we should view this hole as "a wound that heals."[43]
Every event is a wound, according to Deleuze, because it affects bodies. But
it also heals because it transmutes body into sense.

> It is at this mobile and precise point, where all events gather together
> in one that transmutation happens: this is the point at which death
> turns against death; where dying is the negation of death, and the
> impersonality of dying no longer indicates only the moment when
> I disappear outside of myself, but rather the moment when death
> loses itself in itself, and also the figure which the most singular life
> takes on in order to substitute itself for me.[44]

The death of God is resurrection; it is the time of salvation because it opens
up on the future to the repetition of difference that is life.

Notes

1. Gabriel Vahanian, *The Death of God: The Culture of Our Post-Christian Era* (New York: George Braziller, 1966), 139.

2. See, among other works, Gabriel Vahanian, *Anonymous God* (Aurora, AO: The Davies Group, 20030.

3. Thomas J. J. Altizer, *The Gospel of Christian Atheism* (Philadelphia: Westminster Press, 1966), 102.

4. Ibid., 107.

5. Martin Luther, "A Commentary on St. Paul's Epistle to the Galatians," in *Martin Luther: Selections from His Writings*, ed. John Dillenberger (New York: Doubleday, 1962), 117.

6. See ibid., 121: "So my sin that it should not accuse and condemn me, is condemned by sin, that is, by Christ crucified."

7. Slavoj Žižek, *The Puppet and the Dwarf: The Perverse Core of Christianity* (Cambridge, MA: MIT Press, 2003), 91.

8. Ibid., 143.

9. For a critique of this strategy, see John D. Caputo, *The Weakness of God: A Theology of the Event* (Bloomington: Indiana University Press, 2006), 84. Caputo distances himself from the death of God, particularly its Hegelian supercessionary manifestations, but he also affirms a kind of death of God in the sense that we can no longer believe in "the God of metaphysics, and, in particular, the God of sovereignty and power and omnipotence," in John D. Caputo and Gianni Vattimo, *After the Death of God*, ed. Jeffrey W. Robbins (New York: Columbia University Press, 2007), 147.

10. Gilles Deleuze, *The Logic of Sense*, trans. Mark Lester with Charles Stivale (New York: Columbia University Press, 1990), 281.

11. Charles E. Winquist, *Desiring Theology* (Chicago: University of Chicago Press, 1995), 114.

12. Ibid., 127.

13. Gilles Deleuze, *Difference and Repetition*, trans. Paul Patton (New York: Columbia University Press, 1994), 87.

14. Ibid., 86.

15. We could say that Deleuze is right ontologically, that there is no separation between death and resurrection, but Žižek's interpretation of Hegel is right epistemologically or in terms of conscious recognition: there is always a delay between the recognition of death as death and the realization of death as resurrection. So thinking and understanding operate dialectically, but the truth or reality of the matter is that resurrection as repetition of difference is a nondialectical process.

16. Ibid., 90.

17. Ibid., 91.

18. Paul Tillich, *Systematic Theology*, vol. 2 (Chicago: University of Chicago Press, 1957), 118–119.

19. See, for example, John Dominic Crossan and Jonathan L. Reed, *In Search of Paul: How Jesus's Apostle Opposed Rome's Empire and God's Kingdom* (New York: HarperCollins, 2004).

20. Alain Badiou, *Saint Paul: The Foundation of Universalism*, trans. Ray Brassier (Stanford: Stanford University Press, 2003), 80.

21. Ibid., 83.

22. Ibid., 81.

23. Ibid.

24. Ibid., 84.

25. Ibid.

26. For his critique of Deleuze, see Alain Badiou, *Deleuze: The Clamor of Being*, trans. Louise Burchill (Minneapolis: University of Minnesota Press, 2000).

27. Alain Badiou, *Logics of Worlds*, trans. Alberto Toscano (London: Continuum, 2009), 65.

28. Ibid., 65.

29. John Shelby Spong, *Resurrection: Myth or Reality? A Bishop's Search for the Origins of Christianity* (New York: HarperCollins, 1994), 105.

30. Ibid., 202.

31. Ibid., 279.

32. Ibid., 292.

33. This formulation sounds very much like Rudolf Bultmann's understanding of the resurrection, which is influential upon Altizer, but Altizer also understands the resurrection in more explicitly metaphysical, dialectical, and Hegelian terms. Žižek has recently been talking about the resurrection in ways that are more similar to Bultmann—for example, at the session with Altizer on "Whither the Death of God: A New Currency" at the 2009 American Academy of Religion Annual Meeting in Montreal, although Žižek does not cite Bultmann specifically so far as I know. See Rudolf Bultmann, *The New Testament and Mythology and Other Basic Writings*, trans. Schubert Ogden (Minneapolis: Fortress Press, 1989), 1–43.

34. Ibid., 23.

35. Ibid., 151.

36. Caputo, *The Weakness of God*, 237.

37. Ibid., 238.

38. Ibid., 241.

39. Ibid., 252.

40. Ibid.

41. See Richard Wrangham, *Catching Fire: How Cooking Made Us Human* (New York: Basic Books, 2009).

42. Allan Kellehear, *A Social History of Dying* (Cambridge: Cambridge University Press, 2007). For a critique of Becker, see 56–58.

43. Peter Rollins, *How (Not) to Speak of God* (Brewster, MA: Paraclete Press, 2006), 55.

44. Deleuze, *The Logic of Sense*, 153.

9

Becoming

. ◆ ——— ◆ .

Andrew W. Hass

In all the modern Western variations of the "death of God," from Hegel, Feuerbach, Marx, Nietzsche, and Freud, to early avant-garde artists (Duch-amp et al.), to the Frankfurt School and post-Holocaust thinkers (Adorno, Celan, et al.), to the American "death of God" theologians (Altizer et al.), to contemporary philosophers (Badiou et al.), to present-day material atheists (Dawkins et al.), there remains one consistency: the insistence on a radical and absolute immanence. Whatever we may talk about as God's "death," it invariably assumes the eradication of any transcendent realm not simply from our experience but, more to the point (and beyond Kant), from all possibility. The death of God means, unequivocally, the death of the transcendent and the comprehensive, consummate sovereignty of the immanent. Nothing can come from the outside any longer; all reality, all substantiation of reality, indeed, all possibility of reality, must come from within, from amid the confines of what we call the human, or the natural, or the material plane of existence. *This* world, *post Dei*, is now *all* we have.

The following will question whether this must necessarily be the case, whether the very idea of "death of God" is beholden to what is one of the most tenaciously lasting binaries in our history of Western intellec-tual conceptions and consciousness, the transcendent-immanent polarity, or whether in fact it can, as part of its future trajectory, operate and go "beyond" that polarity, without in some way reverting to it. Can the death of God become something other than a species of immanentism, or than the very genus itself?

When we think of immanence, we generally assume, tacitly or not, an immanence within some sphere that stands over against some other sphere outside of it. Or as Deleuze and Guattari state it, immanence has been most often interpreted as immanent *to* something else, or in a dative relation to a Something that is inevitably not within that immanence. So the moment we introduce this "to," we "can be sure that this Something reintroduces the transcendent."[1] Thus we inculcate a dualism that is a polarity: one property or condition must always be understood in its alignment, or better, contra-alignment, with the other. But, as Deleuze and Guattari argue, there is an immanence, and a decisively modern immanence, that is immanent only to itself—a "plane of immanence" that does not yield to any outside.[2] This is the condition of immanence that follows upon the death of God. It is no longer the case of an Outside of our experience but only a within, a wholly self-sealed within. Nothing can penetrate this within, nothing external can break in, not because it has become so hard-shelled it is resistant to any alien intrusion—a kind of Kantian limit of phenomena to noumena—nor because the Outside has wholly secluded itself outside, a kind of apophaticism or a neo-orthodox withdrawal of the divine. It is because there no longer *is* an Outside, a transcendent beyond, a revelatory possibility. In Adorno's words, there is "no other possibility than an extreme ascesis toward any type of revealed faith."[3] *This* is all that is available to our reckoning and belief—where "this" becomes a meta-haecceity, the thisness of the "this" that consumes all immanental thinking, the here and now that consigns us to live absolutely within our own means, foreclosed to transcendental concepts or names. "God is unnameable, today, in that his name, or his names, are lacking," writes Jean-Luc Nancy.[4] We are left to names of our own devising. "Within our own means" would be the arch phrase inscribed over the entrance to this thoroughly (post[post])modern temple.

There has been much attempt recently to rescue transcendence from the ubiquity of this way of thinking.[5] Many have tried to show that transcendence is always lurking either in immanental thought or in the "this" of our world experience. And many sites or exposures have been put forward for this "new" transcendence: freedom, desire, ethics, image/representation, literature, the sublime, the Real, the nothing (as silence, void, abyss, nihilism), the other/Other, transnationality, network culture, humanitarianism, and on it goes. What is remarkable in all these attempts is that so many result in conflating the one into the other, so that we speak now of a "transcendent immanence" or an "immanent transcendence." What is supposedly outside our experience becomes located within that experience and so another feature of that experience; or what is supposedly within our experience becomes located outside that experience and so really not of that experience at all. The old poles keep resurfacing and, if now mutually informing, the dualism remains intact. Mark C. Taylor describes it this way: "The history of modern theology and religion grows out of the repeated 'alternation' between the monism of immanence and the dualism of transcendence," where the monism gives way to dualism (liberalism to neo-orthodoxy, say) or the dualism gives way to monism (neo-orthodoxy to death of God, say). Taylor's account, or his neologism, is still at work, we could claim, though now more subtlety disguised in a merging of the two terms. For Taylor, the "question that remains at the end of modernity is whether this altarnation figures an immanent transcendence that subverts the nihilism of both belief and unbelief."[6] But even Taylor's "immanent transcendence" will privilege the former term, and we wonder whether "transcendence" here—and in all such cases—is not simply another way of saying "inscrutable experience," while "immanence" in "transcendent immanence" is not simply another way of saying "scrutable metaphysics." The temptation to question such moves here is great, but then, that temptation has fueled so much of the academic critical analysis concerning the leaving behind of metaphysics, going back to Husserl and Heidegger (and earlier). As Heidegger launched his own existential project by breaking with Husserl on the grounds that his mentor and his phenomenology did not truly overcome the subject/object problem of modern Western philosophy ("transcendental subjectivity" as a kind of metaphysics needed for scientific reflection), so others have since made much academic capital in showing that Heidegger did not truly overcome Western metaphysics, or then later, that Derrida did not truly vanquish metaphysics, or that even the death of God movement does not truly avoid metaphysics.[7] However profitable, separating out the two terms of transcendence and immanence has always proven a complicated business, just as now conflating them proves to be uncertain, and the many admirable attempts made recently might suggest that, if nothing else, the conceptual dualism in this polarity is one that may never be overcome with any degree of finality.

But what if we were to hazard a way to put to the side this dualism, even if just for the moment, by suggesting there may be a way beyond the immanentism that engulfs the death of God that does not revert to a transcendence, however disguised? Of course we must be very careful with this term "beyond," as Caputo and company have already shown us in their volume *Transcendence and Beyond*. But what if we were to risk the claim to go beyond the binary of immanence and transcendence by invoking a third term that sits either between or before or outside the binary—*becoming*? This would hardly be a new move. The invocation of a "third term" of course recalls Hegel, and we know that the idea of becoming well precedes Hegel in the tradition of religion and philosophy, going back, in the West, as far as Heraclitus. But what if, to use Žižek's phrase, the "condition of impossibility is the condition of possibility,"[8] that what seems impossible to overcome as a binary is precisely the condition that might, in becoming, allow us to overcome it? Indeed Žižek, a Hegelian, has already been prompting us in this direction:

> In a properly Hegelian way, our painful progress of knowledge, our confusions, our search for solutions—that is to say: precisely that which seems to *separate* us from the way reality really is out there—is already the innermost constituent of reality itself. . . . Our process of approaching constituted objective reality repeats the virtual process of Becoming of this reality itself. The fact that we cannot ever "fully know" reality is thus not a sign of the limitation of our knowledge, but the sign that reality itself is "incomplete," open, an actualization of the underlying virtual process of Becoming.[9]

In order to hazard this possibility, it would do us well first to mark out, albeit briefly, the principle nodes of the modern conceptions of becoming. These can be generalized as three: 1) Hegel, 2) Nietzsche/Heidegger, and 3) Whitehead.[10]

If the dialectical thinking of Hegel was put forward to overcome the principle dualisms of his modern predecessors—subjectivity and objectivity, essence and appearance, freedom and necessity, faith and knowledge—acting over all of these might be that of transcendence and immanence. We are familiar enough with how Hegel's absolute idealism has since been construed in terms of a radical immanence. Spirit externalizes or phenomenalizes itself as the whole of immanent reality, and both the so-called Left-Hegelians and Right-Hegelians saw this being worked out in the very social conditions of our living, in what Habermas has described as a "partisanship of philosophy's becoming practical."[11] But too little attention has been given to the nature of becoming in this dialectic, even though it features in the very heart of the dialectical operation of reflection.

The first major expression of this becoming appears in the *Phenomenology of Spirit*, a title that already signals the immanence of the transcendent (at least in the conventional senses of these terms, which of course Hegel will go on to adjust). There, the becoming conscious of the Spirit, through self-reflection, drives the entire philosophical narrative, as a kind of grand *Bildungsroman*. The narrative movement, as the unfolding or maturation of Spirit's self-consciousness, ends in Absolute Knowing, but this knowing is of a Spirit that knows itself as sacrificed to its other, that is, as emptied out both into the externalization of Nature, "its living immediate Becoming," and into the temporality of History, "the other side of its Becoming."[12] We could go further and say this Becoming is the very enactment of the text itself—the text's self-becoming, Spirit made phenomenal in the narrative presenting itself *qua* narrative. But in whatever form, Nature, History, or

Narrative, the Spirit *becomes*, both itself and not itself, and in this becoming the necessary internal operation of Reality itself is thus constituted.

The necessity of becoming, in dialectical emergence, is more rigorously worked out in the later *Science of Logic* of 1812. This text begins with the dualism of Being and Non-Being (or Nothing), to which reconciliation must somehow accrue. That accrual, as dialectic, comes by means of becoming, the third term, which now introduces the concept of movement into what before had only been states. Becoming is not simply the unity of being and nothing, but their *unifying*, so that the two move from being states to being "distinct moments."[13] These moments are constantly passing over into each other—"the hour of their birth is the hour of their death"[14]—and they remain "distinct" or they subsist, Hegel says, only through becoming (and thus they are not self-subsistent[15]). This is the truth of their existence or nonexistence: they are forever coming-to-be and ceasing-to-be, simultaneously, at all times in their movement, so that just when the one disappears, the other appears, and the other becomes the one, while the one becomes the other. In Hegel's words: "becoming is the vanishing of being in nothing and of nothing in being and the vanishing of being and nothing generally; but at the same time it rests on the distinction between them."[16]

Here in Hegel is the beginning of conceptualizing becoming as the very foundation of reality and truth. The essence of Being is its very not-Being but only in a becoming that unifies these essential "moments" in a movement (here too through a reconciliation of time and space, as much as of existence and essence), which, as in the *Phenomenology*, allows them to appear in the very stuff, or immanence, of our world. But in order for this appearance to take place, Hegel could not remain at pure becoming. For how, in the continual movement of becoming, could being, of anything, ever become determinate? How could becoming appear to us unless it became something other than a mediating term, something determinate in and of itself? The dialectical process therefore necessitates—and there is always necessity in Hegel's dialectics—that becoming too be overcome or sublated. Becoming "stabilizes" only by sublating itself through the unifying process whereby Being and Non-Being, now together as a singularity, can be determined in its wholeness. And this whole operates, as it always does in Hegel, on a different level than the individual parts. The whole of becoming is the self-sublation that allows us to "see" becoming as something other than an abstraction, just as in the *Phenomenology* the whole of the Absolute is made manifest in the world as Nature and History (or Narrative). From distinction (Being and Non-Being) comes a unifying (becoming), which itself becomes distinct, having "settled into a stable oneness." This oneness is becoming itself: "It is the dialectical immanent nature of being and nothing themselves to manifest their unity, that is, becoming, as their truth."[17] Later in the *Logic*, Hegel will describe this sublation in negative terms, as the negation of negation: "becoming is essence, its reflective movement, is *movement of nothing to nothing, and so back to itself*. The transition, or becoming, sublates itself in its passage; the *other* that in this transition comes to be, is not the non-being of a being, but the nothingness of a nothing, and this, to be the negation of nothing, constitutes being."[18] But whether seen as the wholeness of unity or the negation of nothing, becoming, beyond the purity of its mediating role, comes into its own as something self-subsisting.[19] In trying to elaborate this self-subsistence, Hegel attempts here to institute becoming as something constitutional in the very makeup of Reality as it appears to us. For Reality *only appears to us* by nature of this becoming, even if in that becoming becoming too is sublated.

Nietzsche will try to un-sublate becoming, as much as he tries to un-sublate the very notion of Hegelian self-reflection and dialectical movement. What Nietzsche reacts against is any concept of a "stable oneness." By turning becoming into a distinct and stabilized unity, becoming for Nietzsche loses its power as *movement*. "Inertia needs unity," he asserts in a later fragment, whereas "plurality of interpretations is a sign of strength."[20] So Nietzsche wants becoming to remain in plurality, never in sublated wholeness. There are two ways he attempts to do this: one is by the notion of eternal return, the other by a generative understanding of nihilism within the will to power. And the two are interlinked.

In eternal return of the same, Nietzsche tries to distance himself fully from Hegel by undercutting any notion of development to or within movement. Unlike dialectic, which as we have said has an internal necessity driving its triadic structure, eternal return back to the same moment, the same beginning, ensures that the beginning is never a beginning of something whole. The circularity of the movement requires always a *new* beginning, but since that newness never develops into any identity, or unity, or truth, it remains the same newness of an always beginning reality. The "same" here is not the sameness of singularity or unity but the sameness of gesture, of repeating again and again the moment of origin, but always a *new* origin. The paradoxical "again" of the new is what characterizes becoming. Contra Hegel, it is a multiplicity of the "same" moment, the moment of a "new" beginning, which as a repeatedly new moment allows continual origination to overpower any stabilities we might try to arrest. As Nietzsche says, "That *everything recurs* is the closest *approximation of a world of becoming to a world of being:*—high point of the meditation."[21]

Nietzsche's specialized understanding of nihilism accords with this high point. Although there are many different kinds of nihilism, even as

Nietzsche sees it, the nihilism that leads us to becoming is that which operates in the overcoming gesture of eternal return. If by eternally returning
to the same all-unifying wholeness or totality is lost, it is lost to a negation
that is *willed*. Eternal return is part of a self-willing to re-will one's own self
and thereby to undo that very self in the re-willing. Such is the negative
empowerment that Zarathustra continually preaches. And such is the will to
power that becomes such a trademark of Nietzsche's thought, though now
predicated on a nihilism that is an activating nihilism, a willing to negate
or overpower that which wants to stabilize itself into a unity or wholeness.
And this will to power, as nihilism, is the becoming of continual origination.
It is not an empowerment of the ego to impose itself over that which is
outside of it; on the contrary, it is the empowerment of the will to re-will
itself anew "within'" or to *de-will* itself asunder, in order to maintain the
multiplicity of its creating gesture. This kind of nihilism is thus a creative
nihilism, a bringing into existence, even if this requires continually destroying the creator in her or his capacity as a self-subsisting subject. "Becoming
as invention, willing, self-denial, overcoming of oneself: no subject but an
action, a positing, creative . . ."[22]

Together, eternal return and an overpowering nihilism allow for an
ongoing reinvention of world. Unlike the necessary trajectory of development in Hegelian dialectics, where the *Geist* makes itself progressively
known to itself in its phenomenological concretion, the appearance of the
world for Nietzsche will always be a fabular, "made up" appearance: "The
world with which we are concerned is false, i.e., is not a fact but a fable
and approximation on the basis of a meager sum of observations; it is 'in
flux,' *as something in a state of becoming*, as a falsehood always changing but
never getting near the truth: for—there is no 'truth.' "[23] The will to power
is not a will to power in or toward truth (a will to truth), even the truth
of an appearance; it is a will to power in active becoming, in an ongoing
generating of things into appearance.

It was Heidegger who saw most astutely that Nietzsche's eternal return
and will to power were to be viewed in light of this self-overcoming, activating nihilism. In the 1936–1940 lectures on Nietzsche at Freiburg, Heidegger
thus links the will to power inextricably with art—the "will to power as
art"[24]—and eternal return with becoming:

> Now, because all being as will to power—that is, as incessant self-
> overcoming—must be a *continual* "becoming," and because such
> "becoming" cannot move "toward an end" *outside* its own "farther
> and farther," but is ceaselessly caught up in the cyclical increase
> in power to which it reverts, then being as a whole too, as this

power-confirming becoming, must itself always recur again and bring back the same.[25]

Heidegger's own project of rethinking Being relies integrally upon these Nietzschean notions of nihilism, art, and becoming. In the first of these, *das Nichts* became a central feature of the Dasein in its being toward its own death (in *Sein and Zeit*), as well as of the whole question of metaphysics (in "What is Metaphysics?" of 1929—"Human Dasein can comport itself towards beings only if it holds itself out into the nothing. Going beyond beings occurs in the essence of Dasein. But this going beyond is metaphysics itself"[26]). But in concert with Nietzsche's nothing as a productive power, Heidegger came to see that nothing stands at the center of *coming into being*, of the power to generate into being. And this is why he will turn increasingly to the question of art in his later thought, as the work of art allows Being to be presenced in the abyssal opening that is Being's coming to be. Yet even in the earlier Nietzschean phase, Art is important as the enabling motive force of the nothing out of which Dasein comports itself. In *The Will to Power as Art*, he will say that "[a]rt is the distinctive counter-movement to nihilism," but by nihilism here he will mean one that will "vitiate life to the point of a general debility and ultimate collapse."[27] The nihilism of the will to power, on the other hand, is one that precisely activates life, energizes affirmation. It is an "ideal of *the supreme powerfulness* of spirit, of superabundant life," the "supreme form" of "thinking *Becoming* as the *Being* of the totality of beings, thinking 'will to power' in terms of the 'eternal recurrence of the same.'"[28]

It is important then in thinking about Heidegger's notion of becoming not to isolate it in the Dasein of *Sein und Zeit* as living toward its ownmost possibility in the care of death, significant though it be as a starting point. We must also take into account the generative function of negation as it leads toward the making possible of Being through creative empowerment, the "will to power as art." But of course for Heidegger this empowerment of the will is not the same as it was for Nietzsche (will as "affect, passion, or feeling,"[29] or as impulse, intensity, tonality [*Stimmung*]). It is the empowerment of Being that brings Being to light out of the nothing that constitutes it. This empowerment is a knowledge that wills—it is not a knowledge *of* something, but, as Heidegger says in the later "The Origin of the Work of Art" (1950)—it is a knowing what Being "wills to do in the midst of what is." And this willing is a willingness, or resoluteness, to present oneself, one's being, in the openness that is Being's true domain. "Willing is the sober resolution of that existential self-transcendence which exposes itself to the openness of beings as it is set in the work."[30] The vestiges of Nietzsche are still here ("self-transcendence," "set in the work") but now toward a truth that unconceals Being's proper disposition before all beings in general and before the world in which it is situated. Art reveals this truth. "*Art then is the becoming and happening of truth,*"[31] the originating of truth, even the opening of that truth, which encircles all that is, and is tantamount to "the Nothing that we scarcely know."[32]

An abrupt shift to Whitehead's cosmology represents, *prima facie*, a radical departure from these existential concerns of Nietzsche and Heidegger, neither of whom he references in his major text *Process and Reality* (though Heidegger's *Sein und Zeit* only appeared in German in 1927, the same year as Whitehead's Edinburgh Gifford Lectures on which *Process and Reality* is based). But such a departure should not surprise us, if we consider that Whitehead's center of intellectual gravity began in the sciences, and that the Gifford Lectures were responding to a certain view of the world dominated by science—the factual world of empirical, mechanical reality. Hence his somewhat antiquated term "cosmology": his philosophy is a philosophy of organism, a return to thinking about the harmonization of reality not as an aggregation of facts ("stubborn facts," as he calls them) into an objective or objectivized whole ("universe") but as an internally coherent reality of wholly integrated parts. His "speculative philosophy" thus tries to elaborate upon the exact nature of this cosmological coherence. The difference with his cosmology from premodern versions, however, is that the reality, the stubborn facts, are in fact not fixed but are in an ongoing state of creative development. They are *in process*. This returns Whitehead to the fundamental questions of the state of reality as first pursued by the Presocratics. The starting point is less the question of transcendence versus immanence (with which none of the Presocratics really concerned themselves) but more the question of permanence versus flux. Whereas we might say Hegel, Nietzsche, and Heidegger are first motivated by a desire to overcome the former polarity through a reconception of metaphysics, Whitehead is first motivated by a desire to overcome the latter polarity through the notion of process.[33] But all four thinkers will converge upon the notion of becoming.

Whitehead says of his philosophy:

> The notion of "organism" is combined with that of "process" in a twofold manner. The community of actual things is an organism; but it is not a static organism. It is an incompletion in process of production. Thus the expansion of the universe in respect to actual things is the first meaning of "process"; and the universe in any stage of its expansion is the first meaning of "organism."[34]

To "expand" here is not in the sense of what astrophysics might understand of an expanding universe. Rather, it is in the sense of what Whitehead calls a "concrescence," a term that embraces both the concreteness of the actual world in immanence and the cellular coalescing of actuality's individual parts into a whole that is itself in a state of ongoing productive development toward something transcendent to itself. That immanent present state he will call "actuality," while the transcendent future state he will distinguish as "reality." Both terms are worked out on micro- and macrocosmic levels: the individual actual entities are in process toward their own reality, but that process involves a full integration of each part with respect to other parts to form a whole, and that whole is also moving from its actuality to reality. So the two terms in the title, process and reality, are connected by way of a becoming—the *process* of moving toward and realizing *reality* becomes, in fact, *becoming*. This is what Whitehead calls a "production of novel togetherness" or a "unison of becoming," where past, present, and future or the old and the new, converge into a single "immediacy," in such a way "that *experience* involves a *becoming*, that *becoming* means that *something becomes*, and that *what becomes* involves *repetition* transformed into *novel immediacy*."[35] There are unacknowledged shades of Nietzsche's eternal return here, except that the "immediacy" manifests itself in a wholeness, and the process of becoming, as an organicism, always strives toward this wholeness.

There is little in *Process and Reality* to link this becoming to art *per se*, as we see in Nietzsche and Heidegger, though there is continual reference to creativity, or "creative origination," as an ultimate phenomenon, synonymous, Whitehead says in one place, with "'thing,' 'being' and 'entity,'"[36] or in another, with macrocosmic activity: "The universe is thus a creative advance into novelty."[37] Many others have since made the connection to art and aesthetics, and I myself have written elsewhere on combining Whitehead with Iser's and Heidegger's notion of becoming for a hermeneutics of reading.[38] But process thought has gained its most systematic following with theologians, and "process theology" has now become a well-established and important body of theological thought (with leading authors included in this volume). And for good reason, since *Process and Reality* ends with a "final interpretation" of God and the world. It is here where the question with which we began returns in connection to becoming: the possible overcoming of the polarities of transcendence and immanence.

For Whitehead, God, who is the very "principle of concretion," is "dipolar": "He has a primordial nature and a consequent nature."[39] This is to say more than he is simply the Alpha and the Omega. It is to say that he is in movement between the poles, from the conceptual ideas we associate with primordial and eternal being to the physical experience we associate with consequent conditions. This is not far off from Hegel, except that it is not self-consciousness that realizes God in the world but organic concrescence. In fact, it is God who supplies the creativity, the "lure of creativity," to advance in concrescence. We might even say it is God who *is* that creativity, "in unison of becoming with every other creative act." This means two things: that God, as creative process, is hardly a static entity but a power itself always and already in flux; and that God is organic, a God "composed of a multiplicity of elements with individual self-realization . . . a multiplicity of actual components in process of creation."[40]

Thus, in a famous passage in a concluding section of his book, Whitehead offers a series of axioms:

> It is as true to say that God is permanent and the World fluent, as that the World is permanent and God is fluent.

> It is as true to say that God is one and the World many, as that the World is many and God is one.

> . . . .

> It is as true to say that the World is immanent in God, as that God is immanent in the World.

> It is as true to say that God transcends the World, as that the World transcends God.

> It is as true to say that God creates the World, as that the World creates God.[41]

Whitehead was not trying to overcome metaphysics in these axioms but rather to develop a "metaphysics in flux." Here we thus have not just a dipolarity but the confluence of polarities, where the one becomes indistinguishable in the other through the process of becoming.[42] If we might still speak of a "beyond," it is a beyond itself always becoming.

Now, in these all-too-brief sketches of modernity's becoming in action, there are obvious differences between the representative positions. And yet we can also see some striking similarities. Hegel's third term of becoming between Being and Non-Being, despite itself sublating into a wholeness, does share the same generative impulse that Nietzsche tried to figure in his notion of will (to power). And the self-overcoming nature of this Nietzschean will bears much similarity to Hegel's self-overcoming that motivates the dialectical rhythm, even if the self-overcoming overcomes the dialectic itself. (And yet it is precisely here that Hegel remains significant in contemporary thinking about negation—the negating power that overcomes every system including its own dialectical system, or Hegel out-Hegel-ing Hegel.)

Moreover, Whitehead's vision of a God coming to self-concretization in the World is indeed all too close to the Hegelian *Geist* and its movement, with some adjustment to nomenclature and without the Idealism that later overwhelms the Hegelian system. Indeed Whitehead himself, despite drawing sparsely on Hegel throughout *Process and Reality*, acknowledges in the preface that his "final interpretation" about God and World might be justifiably considered as a "transformation of some main doctrines of Absolute Idealism onto a realistic basis."[43] It seems, then, that becoming, however construed by modern thought, has a peculiar tendency to pull disparate positions into a common current, much as the process of becoming in each respective thought reshapes multiplicity and individuality into a shared conception or realization.

But what now of transcendence and immanence? Can the specific or shared features of becoming in these various nodes of its own becoming in any way help us to rethink this perduring polarity in the wake of the death of God? Or in Taylor's schema will the vacillation between the two poles—the "altaration"—go on indefinitely, the death of God being resurrected in some reconstituted notion of transcendence, which then falls prey to a reassertion of divine collapse in all-encompassing immanence? Or might process theology become the only available way through this teeter-tottering effect, whether in its more systematic forms put forward by the likes of David Ray Griffin, John Cobb, or Marjorie Suchocki, or in the more mystical and open-ended form of a "theology of becoming" more recently put forward by Catherine Keller?[44]

If Žižek is right, that the problems inherent within immanence—the inconsistencies, the limitations, the ruptures that keep raising themselves in our attempts to define truth or reality—are precisely the conditions which in fact constitute that reality, so that rather than true reality being one side or the other, transcendent to us or immanent with us, we are always actualizing reality by struggling within its very ruptures, might then the becoming we have just briefly outlined, and in some sense fused together, offer itself as a possible way forward? For if in Hegel's becoming we saw that immanence is always being broken up by its own antithesis, and if in Nietzsche's becoming the will's overpowering is never sublated into a wholeness or unity but continually and nihilistically fractures itself, then immanence, contra Spinoza, or Deleuze and Guattari, is not the least troubled plane of existence[45] but the most troubled. And if after the death of God transcendence is no longer available to rescue those troubles, because it has proven only to add more, and if all the alternative models for transcendence (those that do not resort to an out-and-out theism) only result in re-transcribing immanence and reinvoking its troubles and ruptures, then might we think of becoming as the "site" (the constantly moving site) that allows us to begin again?

"Beginning again" would be the operative term here and, in light of Nietzsche and Heidegger, this would necessitate a certain "will to art." Creative origination that is always ongoing, eternally recurring, is the generative becoming that would bring our being—and reality—into its proper existence. The "beginning again," as art, neither is wholly immanent, since, in Whitehead's terms, its consequent reality is yet to come, but nor can it be wholly transcendent, since it must begin here and now in the material stuff or in the stubborn facts we gather (for art). In fact, becoming, as ongoing creative origination, would allow us to see beyond the immanent/transcendent polarity, though with the "beyond" here acting in more of a metaphorical capacity: it is not the beyond within the diode of immanence and transcendence but the *beyond inherent within* becoming and its potentiality, the beyond involved in the connection between two disparate elements (not yet/will be) in the process of creation. To see beyond metaphorically would be to see, in Whitehead's terms, two (or more) contrasting actualities conflated within a relation that becomes something wholly new, as in metaphor. The "will to art" would be such a movement in and to this beyond, a process whereby origination calls together what could be and what will be—the "could" and the "will" in a unison of becoming—but without ever losing sight of its originating mode and function.

What we are not talking about here yet is an aesthetics. Reflection upon art once it is made comes after origination. Nor are we talking about yet the individual doing of art by any one artist as such. This is not a will to art of an *Übermensch*, the self-imposed will of one who dares to create beyond him- or herself. Here Whitehead counterbalances: the will would be organically rendered, so that in each of our creative originations we move together in an overall becoming, though one that never reaches the whole, since the never reaching is precisely the "beyond" that allows us to keep reaching.

What ultimately we may be talking about here, after the death of God, is *making our way back to God*. God is there, at the beginning, and we must make our way there, through a will to art that keeps us returning, always, back to that beginning. But in becoming, which is our making, this "back" is forward, and the movement will always be circular, and God is, as process theology has told us in variously rich ways, part of that circular becoming. Yet as the "death of God" theology has taught us in equally rich ways, that circularity represents a nothing (0), and we must be willing to embrace the movement of that nothing.[46] And this means, in the tradition of Hegel, Nietzsche, and Heidegger, that ultimately, under the guidance of that nothing, we must engage the art of becoming, and this is no easy discipline to master. It means we must engage with art and artists, yes. It may even mean we must become artists ourselves. (We remember Nietzsche's early claim that art is "the properly metaphysical activity of man."[47]) But above all it means we must assume ourselves in the restlessness of becoming, to alter Nancy's phrase—Nancy who reminds us, in writing of Hegel's "restlessness of the negative," that "becoming is not a process that leads to another thing, because it is the condition of every thing."[48] The restlessness does not allow us to rest on any one side of a pole. It keeps us in movement, perhaps between, perhaps amid, perhaps beyond, but always in creative origination.

Our greatest death of God philosophy (Nietzsche, and then, in its way, Heidegger) and our greatest death of God theology (Altizer) have always known this movement through thinking and willing art. There is not a page in Altizer's corpus, for example, that does not allude to the great literary enactments of the death of God. Nor are any of these enactments finalities but ongoing recreations of that event, which constitute the becoming that Altizer will acknowledge as an advent. And of course any reenactment, of an advent, or even of death, is a beginning again, and any beginning again, in the "broken spirit" of a will to art, is a becoming. Others have since been trying to work out this "spirit," inside and outside theology, each in their own way (Derrida, Mark Taylor, Nancy, Žižek, et al.).[49] As for the artists, have they not always known this? The narrator in *Zorba the Greek* looks at his friend Zorba and says, "This, I thought, is how great visionaries and poets see everything—as if for the first time. Each morning they see a new world before their eyes; they do not really see it, they create it."[50] We may never dispense wholly with transcendence and immanence as discretionary categories, but might we, as a different center of gravity, a different default, learn to become anew? Perhaps we might say with the poet:

> inexhaustible creation, enduring
> beyond the earth so long . . .

> still, one with the darkening
> earth, I dare in you to be.[51]

Notes

1. Gilles Deleuze and Félix Guattari, *What Is Philosophy?*, trans. Graham Burchell and Hugh Tomlinson (London: Verso, 1994), 45.

2. Ibid., 35–60.

3. Theodor W. Adorno, *Critical Models: Interventions and Catchwords*, trans. Henry W. Pickford (New York: Columbia University Press, 1998), 142.

4. Jean-Luc Nancy, *Des Lieux Divins* (Mauvezin: Editions Trans-Euro-Repress, 1987), 10, as quoted by Thomas A. Carlson, "Unlikely Shadows: Transcendence in Image and Immanence," in *Transcendence: Philosophy, Literature and Theology Approach the Beyond*, ed. Regina Schwartz (New York: Routledge, 2004), 113.

5. This is evident especially within the Indiana Series in Philosophy of Religion. See, for example, *Transcendence in Philosophy and Religion*, ed. James E. Faulconer (Bloomington: Indiana University Press, 2003); Merold Westphal, *Transcendence and Self-Transcendence* (Bloomington: Indiana University Press, 2004); John D. Caputo and Michael J. Scanlon, eds., *Transcendence and Beyond: A Postmodern Inquiry* (Bloomington: Indiana University Press, 2007); Martin J. De Nys, *Considering Transcendence: Elements of a Philosophical Theology* (Bloomington: Indiana University Press, 2009). Elsewhere, see also Regina Schwartz, ed., *Transcendence: Philosophy, Literature and Theology Approach the Beyond* (New York: Routledge, 2004); Mayra Rivera, *The Touch of Transcendence: A Postcolonial Theology of God* (Louisville: Westminster John Knox, 2007); Thomas J. Csordas, ed., *Transnational Transcendence: Essays in Religion and Globalization* (Berkeley: University of California Press, 2009).

6. Mark C. Taylor, *After God* (Chicago: University of Chicago Press, 2007), 133–134.

7. In this last case, I am thinking of John Caputo's charge in *After the Death of God*, ed. Jeffrey W. Robbins (New York: Columbia University Press, 2007), that the death of God theologies are "thinly disguised *grand récits*." He refers, for example, to "the metaphysical residue that clings to Altizer's patently metaphysical version of the death of God" (68–69).

8. Slavoj Žižek, "The Descent of Transcendence into Immanence, or, Deleuze as a Hegelian," in Schwartz, *Transcendence*, 240.

9. Ibid., 244.

10. These can hardly be the only nodes, however. One might begin, in modernity, with Schelling, or might add, after Hegel, Kierkegaard, as Clare Carlisle suggests in *Kierkegaard's Philosophy of Becoming: Movements and Positions* (Albany: State University of New York Press, 2005). And there are plenty of "postmodern" versions, including Derrida and Deleuze. But I mark these three nodes because they lay the most comprehensive and influential ground for becoming, and, as I will argue, in fact enact a certain becoming between themselves.

11. Jürgen Habermas, *The Philosophical Discourse of Modernity*, trans. Frederick Lawrence (Cambridge: Polity Press, 1987), 58.

12. G. W. F. Hegel, *Phenomenology of Spirit*, trans. A. V. Miller (Oxford: Oxford University Press, 1977), 492.

13. G. W. F. Hegel, *Science of Logic*, trans. A. V. Miller (Amherst, NY: Humanity Books, 1969), 92.

14. Ibid., 129.

15. Ibid., 92.

16. Ibid., 106.

17. Ibid., 105–106. Or as Gadamer has said in examining Hegel's *Logic*: "It lies in the very meaning of Becoming itself that it reaches determinacy in that which finally has become." In *Hegel's Dialectic: Five Hermeneutical Studies*, trans. P. Christopher Smith (New Haven: Yale University Press, 1976), 87.

18. Ibid., 400.

19. In the latter case, negation of nothing, the impetus is placed back upon negation, the very negation inherent in the sublating activity. This is where so much of the resurgent interest in Hegel presently resides, at the originating power of negation.

20. Friedrich Nietzsche, *The Will to Power*, ed. Walter Kaufmann, trans. Walter Kaufmann and R. J. Hollingdale (New York: Vintage, 1968), §600, 326.

21. Ibid., §617, 330.

22. Ibid., §617 (B), 331.

23. Ibid., §616, 330; emphasis added.

24. Martin Heidegger, *Nietzsche Vol. I: The Will to Power as Art*, trans. and ed. David Farrell Krell (San Francisco: HarperCollins, 1979).

25. Martin Heidegger, *Nietzsche Vol. IV: Nihilism*, trans. Frank A. Capuzzi, ed. David Farrell Krell (San Francisco: HarperCollins, 1982), 7.

26. Martin Heidegger, "What Is Metaphysics?" in *Pathmarks*, ed. William McNeill (Cambridge: Cambridge University Press, 1998), 96.

27. Heidegger, *Nietzsche Vol. I: The Will to Power as Art*, 75.

28. Heidegger, *Nietzsche Vol. IV: Nihilism*, 202. Heidegger says earlier: "When Nietzsche himself insists that Being, as 'life,' is in essence 'becoming,' he does not intend the roughly defined concept of 'becoming' to mean either an endless, continual progression to some unknown goal, nor is he thinking about the confused turmoil and tumult of unrestrained drives. The vague and hackneyed term becoming signifies the overpowering of power, as the essence of power, which powerfully and continually returns to itself in its own way" (8).

29. Heidegger, *Nietzsche Vol. I: The Will to Power as Art*, 44–53.

30. Martin Heidegger, "The Origin of the Work of Art," in *Poetry, Language, Thought*, trans. Albert Hofstadter (New York: Harper and Row, 1971), 67.

31. Ibid., 71. This will be a modification of Nietzsche's notion that "truth is an illusion" within a world not of being but of becoming. Heidegger here rehabilitates the notions of truth and Being within a becoming, even if his later work on art will privilege the term "presencing." See Martin Heidegger, *Nietzsche Vol. III: The Will to Power as Knowledge and as Metaphysics*, trans. Joan Stambaugh et al., ed. David Farrell Krell (San Francisco: HarperCollins, 1982), 64–67.

32. Ibid., 53.

33. Of course, he is hardly the first to think this: theologians, especially within Eastern Orthodoxy, have long considered the doctrine of *creatio continua*, while Boehme, Schelling, and Teilhard de Chardin have explored the idea of a self-evolving or self-realizing Godhead. See, for example, Lewis Owen, "Jacob Boehme and the Romantic Roots of Process Thought," in *God, Literature and Process Thought*, ed. Darren Middleton (Aldershot: Ashgate, 2002), 191–205. Whitehead, however, under the influence of Samuel Alexander, is one of the first to think of process within the context of modern, post-Einsteinian science, in opposition to the objectivity of "neutral stuff" within post-Cartesian science. For his role in helping us to rethink our relation to the natural world, through a philosophy of process rooted in both Nietzschean and, later, Heideggerian thought, see Arran E. Gare, *Postmodernism and the Environmental Crisis* (London: Routledge, 1995), 114–128. I am indebted to the editors of this volume for making me aware of Gare's insightful text.

34. Alfred North Whitehead, *Process and Reality*, ed. David Ray Griffin and Donald W. Sherburne (New York: Free Press, 1978), 214–215.

35. Ibid., 136–137.

36. Ibid., 21. Whitehead does, of course, occasionally refer to art in *Process and Reality*; and he certainly speaks directly of art elsewhere, as in his *Adventures of Ideas*, where art is one of the five principle qualities or "aims" of a civilized society, and where "[a]rt at its highest exemplifies the metaphysical doctrine of the interweaving of absoluteness upon relativity" (New York: Free Press, 1967), 264.

37. Ibid., 222.

38. See my "Reading in the Modern Wake" in *God, Literature and Process Thought*, 13–28, a volume that concentrates on process thought in relation to literature in particular.

39. Whitehead, *Process and Reality*, 345.

40. Ibid., 350.

41. Ibid., 348.

42. Whitehead will distinguish between "opposites" and "contrasts." Opposites are truly in opposition, in the Hegelian sense that requires sublation; contrasts are two poles that in fact are related and unite in a whole, a "mode of synthesis" (ibid., 22), or a "conjoint unity which arises from the realized togetherness of eternal objects" (ibid., 229). The axiomatic polarities stated here of course would be contrasts, which are transformed into "concrescent unity" (ibid., 348).

43. Ibid., xiii. For further comparison between Hegel and Whitehead, see Thomas J. J. Altizer, "Dialectical vs. Di-Polar Theology," *Process Studies* 1, 1 (Spring 1971): 29–37.

44. In Keller's case, see especially *The Face of the Deep: A Theology of Becoming* (London: Routledge, 2003) and also the more recent *On the Mystery* (Minneapolis: Augsburg Fortress, 2008). In the former Keller impressively explores the creative power in the depth of chaos (the *tehom*) as a fluid power, as opposed to creation *ex nihilo*, which she argues yields a coercive power. God becomes a co-creator with this *tehom* and therefore a God herself in flux.

45. See Deleuze and Guattari, *What Is Philosophy?*, 60.

46. Thomas Altizer reflects on this movement in his *The Genesis of God: A Theological Genealogy* (Louisville: Westminster/John Knox Press, 1993), saying that we, in our scientific present, have no capacity for thinking backward, or thinking forward and backward at once, and thus no capacity for thinking an eternal cycle of return. Of Nietzsche, he writes: "Zarathustra identifies 'it was' as the will's most secret melancholy . . . the brute fact that we cannot will backwards" (54). And from Hegel's *Logic* we are estranged, "a logic that can only know a beginning which is an eternal beginning, and an eternal beginning releasing and eternally releasing an eternal circle of time" (55). But Altizer insists on the absolute necessity of beginning, a unique event of genesis, a genesis of the will, which is also "the genesis of an actual nothingness" (159).

47. Friedrich Nietzsche, *The Birth of Tragedy*, ed. Michael Tanner, trans. Shaun Whiteside (London: Penguin, 1993), 7.

48. Jean-Luc Nancy, *Hegel: The Restlessness of the Negative*, trans. Jason Smith and Steven Miller (Minneapolis: Minnesota University Press, 2002), 12.

49. Taylor, who has always engaged with art, has more recently been trying to work this out through the dynamisms and complexities of network systems and

cultures. See, for example, his chapter 7, "Religion Without God," in *After God* (313–347). It is arguable whether he remains an immanentist here.

50. Nikos Kazantzakis, *Zorba the Greek*, trans. Carl Wildman (New York: Simon and Schuster, 1952, 1981), 136.

51. Rainer Maria Rilke, "From the Cycle: Nights," in *Rilke on Love and Other Difficulties*, trans. John J. L. Mood (New York: W.W. Norton, 1975), 77.

10

Twilight of an Axial God

·•·————·•·

LISSA McCULLOUGH

God's woe is deeper, you strange world! Reach for God's woe, not for me! What am I? A drunken sweet lyre—a midnight lyre.

—Zarathustra, in Friedrich Nietzsche,
Thus Spoke Zarathustra: A Book for All and None

When Max Weber coined the term "disenchantment of the world" in 1919, he located his observations in the technologically advanced culture of the modern West in express contrast with "primitive" cultures. In writing of disenchantment (*Entzauberung*) he meant to evoke a technical-scientific outlook in which "one need no longer have recourse to magical means in order to master or implore the spirits, as did the savage [*Wilde*], for whom such mysterious powers existed."[1] He characterized the process of disenchantment as one that has been underway in occidental culture not merely for a few centuries—say, since the modern scientific revolution—but for millennia. Following suit with Weber's extended historical time frame, our understanding of the "death of God" in modern Western religious evolution can benefit immensely from taking an especially long, multi-millennial perspective.

Such a wide-angle lens is provided by Marcel Gauchet's speculative theory of religion in *The Disenchantment of the World: A Political History of Religion* (1985).[2] This text makes us mindful of a fundamental change in the status of religion historically that should not be occluded when we study the complex religious transformations of the modern period, limiting our lens to a brief—however decisive and unprecedented—five-hundred-year span. When we become myopically absorbed in analyzing transformations of the religious scene within the last few decades or even centuries, we lose the big picture, which is the millennial one. Tracing back only as far as ancient Greece—as do our primary death of God thinkers Hegel, Nietzsche, and Heidegger, for example—is to begin already too near the end of the story to get sufficient perspective; though certainly, in naming his own prophet Zarathustra, Nietzsche was quite intentionally evoking such an epochal time frame.[3] For Gauchet, no truly fundamental shift or transformation in the structure of reality has occurred within Western civilization since the axial age, ranging from approximately 800 to 200 BCE.[4] Though in making this claim he does not mean that there were not extremely significant transformative developments within this underlying fundamental structure; to the contrary, his book traces these with elaborate attention.

According to Gauchet's principal theses, the demise of religion is not to be ascertained by declining "belief" but by the extent of the restructuring of the human-social universe (3). Religion's most complete and systematic form is its initial one; later transformations, which many have thought corresponded to more advanced stages, progressively call the religious into question (23). Religion's origins lay in a radical dispossession, wherein the foundation of the human universe was considered to be wholly other (25) in precisely the manner described by Mircea Eliade's analysis of mythic religion as eternal return.[5] The essential motive of religion is to gain self-possession by consenting to dispossession, "securing an identity defined and controlled at every step" (7, 22). Despite differences in customs, ways of being, mythologies, and modes of subsistence, he argues, we can indeed reconstruct a coherent system of societies, prior to the advent of the State, where religion plays the central role, and this system entails the radical anteriority of every ordering principle and is thus a system of dispossession, inheritance, and immutability (12). These societies are called "primitive," however, strictly on the grounds of being prior to the State, and in no other sense, for "the most archaic human remains we possess come from fully civilized societies that clearly share a common history with us" (8). Indeed, the universality of this religious structure for thousands of years among the "infinitely fragmented groups and cultures throughout the world" makes it one of those features that "strongly confirms the unity of the human race and its history" (24).

Radical ethnocentricity is an integral part of the religious system: that is, believing that *ours* is the only proper way to exist and *we* are the only ones worthy of being called human (42). The underlying belief is that we owe everything we have, our way of living, our rules, our customs, and what we know, to beings of a different nature: to sacred ancestors, heroes, or gods. All we can do is follow, imitate, and repeat what they have taught us, as everything governing our works and days was *handed down to us*. The essence of the religious act lies wholly in this antihistorical frame of mind, reflecting a "systematic denial" of freedom and a "systematic bias toward immobility" (23–25)—one that employs repetition methodically to repress the obviousness of daily change, of human transforming activity. This *a priori* conceptual framework of primitive society, which cannot be attributed to any external determinism, can only be explored through an internal analysis of human motives (25–26).

Thus Gauchet characterizes the logic of religion in its full integrity, its most systematic structural embodiment, as a "well-defined type of society" (27). The religious is "the principle of mobility placed in the service of inertia" (22); it is the principle of transformation mobilized to protect the inviolability of things. Humankind began by denying precisely this unsettling truth about itself, Gauchet writes, this uncertainty about its place in the world. Hence he characterizes religion as grounded in a "choice for the absolute past" (11): everything that happens in the social universe flows from that past as its absolutely authoritative source. The repetition of origin at the heart of the religious system ensures a "radical conservatism" (25): we always arrive on the scene *after* things have been determined (11).

This is a *political* history of religion in that Gauchet's theory argues that the historical birth and dominance of the State (that is, of empire) in the period 3000–1000 BCE is the watershed era of history: it severs history in two and ushers human societies into a new age (9–10). This era, so crucial to Gauchet, will remain unexplored here; for our purposes it is sufficient to understand that the advent of imperial domination and expansion was the indispensable precondition, in his judgment (seemingly also in Weber's), for the axial transformation (34–37).[6] The emergence of the State, the "main event in human history," brings about a "massive revision of the articulation of the human situation" (10) and as such catalyzes the advent of "superstructural" religion. According to Gauchet, "There is a 'superstructural' religion capable of outliving 'infrastructural' religion. This occurs to such an extent that we could plausibly imagine a society whose members would all be driven by a sincere faith and whose material, political, and intellectual axes would still originate from the dynamic reversal of traditional religious subjugation" (164)

Formulations of the divine in the axial period that *seem* to maintain and reinforce its power, as well as human dependence on the divine, actually correspond to a reduction of the religious other as the world's ultimate organizing principle in favor of agents here below. This is effected through the "*metamorphosis of otherness*" that constitutes the very basis of the axial age, the axial turning point (46, 48; emphasis added). Counterintuitively, perhaps, immanence presupposes severance from the aboriginal foundation, whereas transcendence brings it nearer and makes it accessible; the more transcendent the gods, the freer humans are. Transformations of religion during the axial age manifest this *corrosion* of religion by divine transcendence, making a transition from "a system of cohabitation with several minor deities to one of being separated from a single all-pervasive divine principle" (51).

In Gauchet's perspective, then, the so-called major religions or universal religions, including the latecomer Christianity, far from being the quintessential embodiment of religion, are so many stages of its abatement and disintegration (9). They are major stages in challenging the religious, if not indeed departing from religion, since the more God is thought of as wholly other, the less his creatures' existence is perceived by them as being controlled by something other (34). Meaning is no longer given by a destiny allocated from the origin but can now be found here below in a voyage of inner discovery. It is no longer to be located within the human and cosmic hierarchical chain but lies transcendently beyond it (47). Or as anthropologist Lewis Mumford characterizes this axial change: "Civilization now became a vehicle, not the goal toward which the vehicle traveled."[7]

Benjamin Schwartz articulates what the axial religions have in common, while cautioning us that not all were world-renouncing or world-negating, as early Christianity would later be:

> If there is some common underlying impulse in all these "axial" movements, it might be called the strain toward transcendence . . . a kind of standing back and looking beyond—a kind of critical, reflective questioning of the actual and a new vision of what lies beyond. . . . All of these transcendental movements involve negations but not necessarily of the "whole." . . . The melding of Greek, Jewish, Roman (and perhaps Persian) elements in late Western antiquity seems to have produced a much more radically "world renouncing" orientation than anything we find in the original separate strands of this "triangle" during the age of breakthrough.[8]

The axial prophets, Mumford points out, were in possession of a "new law" governing human relations, which detached them from their past and from corporate limitations; as a result they generally left society as they found it: "they might mightily rebuke its institutions, but they left them alone" (67). They explored new methods of association that transcended both the chaos of the metropolis and the tyranny of empire (69).

Consistent with this trend, Gauchet underscores the point that the resistance Jesus proposed to his followers was of a wholly different order than any involving an uprising against occupying power, for "his god was so far removed from this world's ties that it would not have made any sense to confront terrestrial thrones and principalities" (118). He acted as a second Moses to free his people from Caesar's grasp by "removing them from the world while remaining in it" (117).

> The problem [i.e., Judaism's internal contradiction] was how a god meant for all humans was worshipped by only one people. Jesus' genius was to resolve the problem by using the memory of the chosen people, of Moses and his founding actions, as the source for a new god, by breaking free from terrestrial domination. Jesus urged an even more radical repudiation since his was no longer a removal from the world's empire, but from the world itself. His god thus became the truly universal god, directly accessible to all. (123)

At this point, Jan Assmann's argument, published a decade after Gauchet's book, that "monotheism always appears as a counter-religion," marking off all older and other religions as paganism or idolatry, dovetails with and also forces readjustment of Gauchet's theory in fascinating ways worthy of careful consideration.[9] What Assmann identifies as Judaic "counter-religious" monotheism was the implicit background universalism conditioning Jesus's radicalized apocalyptic universalism, even if Gauchet emphasizes the discontinuity.

It follows that the profound disenchantment of the world—even as Weber employs that term—occurred with the rise in Western religion of a radically transcendent God, the God of the ancient Hebrews, the God who was later absorbed and transformed by early Christianity. The religious history of this disenchantment over the last two millennia manifests, for Gauchet, a fuller and fuller working out of the logic imbedded in the Christian theological worldview—though not, he insists, in any deterministic sense. Gauchet offers a structural analysis of Christianity as that religion whose emphasis on human freedom and autonomy vis-à-vis God permitted and encouraged a full emancipation from religion: it was *a religion for departing from religion* (4). While recognizing its commonalities with other axial religions, Gauchet argues for the singularity of Western Christianity's trajectory as a "highly individualized branching off": it was the beginning of a movement that took the questioning of religion's very principle to its conclusion (104).[10]

Absolute divine transcendence effected a reunification of two dimensions that were previously separate: the *original* and the *actual* (52, 54). In the human quest for renewal and regeneration, we do not have to return to the original founding of the world but only look "above" here and now. The supernatural power of the one God is *both* our world's origin and its driving force. For instead of having acted definitively at the beginning of time, the God of revelation operates in the present; he is the all-embracing subject of a world distinct from him (55). "The deity culminates in absolute self-unity signaling its ultimate separation from us, and leaves the world to us to understand, to penetrate and change in every way" (63).

According to Gauchet, it was precisely the dissolution of *religion* that opened the space for *theology*, which is a speculation on the absent, on what previously had managed to evade both mythical status and human understanding (39). The new role of theology inaugurated by the logic of otherness was speculative: that of "structuring our thought processes from the One's viewpoint" (146). Thus reason, in the West, progresses through God (62).[11] While "this world" was gradually—over the course of a millennium—objectified, de-paganized, and converted into a realm governed by physical laws (54), the divine realm became increasingly subjectivized through metaphysical rationality and speculation, with theology the reigning queen of this domain: "The trend toward specifying the One, both internally and externally, both by distancing it from the sensory and by purifying its intrinsic essence, led to assimilating it to absolute self-identity, thus giving it a subjective form. Hence, the drift toward an ontotheology" (147).

The "death of God" is the final theological culmination of the long process of *abatement* or *dissolution* of religion, per Gauchet, or the multi-millennial transvaluation of religion from fate to freedom. The historical transformation that ultimately "killed God," to cite Nietzsche's phrase, commenced when deity was universalized, suddenly elevated out of time and place, rendered perfectly transcendent to the engagements of human life in the world. In that process the God of Christendom became "God as spirit," "God degenerated to the *contradiction of life*," per the well-known Nietzschean diatribe, thereby achieving the "low-water mark in the descending development of the God type." "Even the palest of the pale have been able to master him, *messieurs* the metaphysicians, the conceptual albinos. These have spun their web around him so long that, hypnotized by their movements, he himself became a spider, a metaphysician."[12]

The axial transformation caused God's claim on human affairs to be pushed back, out of the world, devitalized, "spiritualized" to the point that the deity was condemned gradually to evaporate, as the ascetic vocation directed toward an otherworldly *telos* gave way with time to the secular vocation, "blessed" by an absent God and teleologically imbedded in this world. As we can only relate to a God who is purely other by recognizing what separates us from him, Gauchet observes, "the specific otherness of God took shape as an unavoidable obligation to the world" and a "deepening engagement in the autonomous substantiality of our own terrestrial sphere" (85). In the wake of the Reformation's restructuring of society, what remained of the old God's this-worldly apparatus could be expiated "under our knives," as Nietzsche's madman puts it, a *coup de grace* epitomized in the violence of the French Revolution against both the holy Roman Catholic Church and the anointed monarch's crown.[13]

For Gauchet, the death of God does not mean that humanity becomes God by "reappropriating the conscious that absolute self-disposition once attributed to god"—a reappropriation pursued by absolute idealism, and even by Nietzsche in his own fashion through the Will to Power. "On the contrary, it means that man is categorically obliged to renounce the dream of his own divinity. Only when the gods have disappeared does it become obvious that men are not gods" (199). Hence the meteoric epiphany of the *nothing* (*nihil, das Nichts*) in thinking, art, and literature that is consciously post-Christian, "a Nothing which is surely," writes Thomas J. J. Altizer, "the opposite of everything which we once knew as God."[14] Gauchet accounts for the void or nothing as an experience for our thought deriving from the axial bifurcation of God and world.[15]

The death of God theology of Altizer centers on this atheological Nothing, exploring the post-Christian "depths for us beyond what we can know as God" (23). With the advent of a uniquely modern nihilism, "the Nihil as Nihil and Nihil alone fully stands forth"—a pure and absolute negativity that cannot for a moment be confused with the absolute nothingness that mystics such as Eckhart discovered in the primordial Godhead. This is a nothing that negates the Godhead of God in an absolute and final annihilation. "Nietzsche could understand," Altizer writes, "that we are finally called upon to sacrifice God to the Nothing"; only thereby does the purely negative pole or potency of the Godhead become fully actual and real (153). God becomes fully God only with self-annihilation, an absolute kenosis that enacts an absolute otherness in place of primordial identity. The revelation of God for Altizer is the historical process by which Alpha actually transfigures itself into Omega: once the will of God is thus fully effected, God is no more. "Then bad faith would be simply belief in 'God,' a belief in God refusing the Passion of God" (139).

> It is not until the advent of modernity that a genuine totality of evil or nothingness is truly called forth in consciousness, not until then that an abyss can appear which is a total abyss, one comprehending Godhead itself, and comprehending the deepest depths of Godhead, as for the first time these appear and are real as a totally negative abyss, and an abyss apart from which Godhead itself can no longer be known or envisioned. (73)[16]

So we find ourselves having to assess, while participating in, the strange history of a self-evacuating God: a God who eventually becomes too transcendent, too metaphysical to matter, yet who in death and dissolution nonetheless leaves a comprehensive void. The legacy of this axial God in the final throes of modernity has been a mysticism of the nothing, a mysticism of the "mind of winter," the mind of a "listener, who listens in the snow, / And, nothing himself, beholds / Nothing that is not there and the nothing that is" (Wallace Stevens).[17] Two nothings penetrate each other in this winter mysticism: God, the nothing that is not there, and the death of God, the nothing that is.

So, Altizer claims, tragedy has not disappeared in full modernity but has "become more deeply interiorized, finally culminating in the dissolution of self-consciousness itself," which can be understood as an ultimate sacrificial dissolution (23). Absolute death brings forth a darkness that "shines" in us as the purest possible darkness, as we serve as the midnight lyre accompanying the final woe of God. The absolute sacrifice of God in death generates an overwhelming abyss of dark night, visible as such. Its very visibility implies a light that shines in this deep darkness, a light that can perhaps be carried forward in hope, into new life, for "midnight too is noon; pain too is a joy; curses too are a blessing; night too is a sun."[18] This twilight that *is* the darkness, that allows the darkness to be visible as such, may be quite real to the twilight visionary, but it is as abstract as the transcendent God. How can such a sacrificial light, such a shining darkness, become a principle or power or energy in support of creative work, building a world, living a life, reinventing and reenergizing a process of civilization through which we might pursue the bottomless task of being human? Will this divine twilight prove to be pregnant or sterile?

In the course of characterizing axial religion's massive importance in human history, Mumford sets forth keen criticisms of its shortcomings as well. To wit, the otherworldly orientation of the axial religions counted on the spur of disaster and suffering: "They prospered in adversity, when the pomps and vanities of the world became shadows, but by the same token they suffered in prosperity." The great achievements of axial religion "rested in some degree on illusion," as their overemphasis of the cerebral and spiritual tended toward "isolated perfection," hence they did not offer a sufficiently representative ideal of human potentiality. The spiritual conversion and alteration that the axial prophet seeks cannot become operative on a collective level until it has remolded social institutions, Mumford writes, and this happens to be a weak point due to axial religion's turn away from the world.[19] "The radical division between community and individual soul, between earthly attachments and heavenly aspirations, between 'this world' and 'the other world,' was one of the great flaws of most axial theologies." For the axial way, which leaves all to the individual soul, "even success brings a certain alienation and loneliness" (75, 77).

With the death of God, Gauchet's thesis implies, the system of religion has self-declared the end of its dominion, as we Westerners are now "inhabitants of a world that at a certain point completely turned its back on the reign of the gods" (199)—not at the level of personal belief but at the level of effective social organization. This has become possible because religion has reached the end of its power as a system built on a collective *denial* or *refusal* (25, 22), a response to something "unbearable" (26), precisely because this dread has been gradually mitigated in the course of history by the axial transformation.

> If we no longer need to exorcize becoming by clutching to tradition or origin, it is because we are situated within a frame of reference assuring us that we will retain our identity. Permanence used to be affirmed by repetition; now it is experienced through change. It used to demand that time be frozen; now it presupposes being immersed in its flow and systematically turning it to our use. (91)

Inherent to Gauchet's argument is the contention that religion in its purest form is inherently not a freedom. To speak of "religious freedom" is already to speak of a radical disenchantment vis-à-vis the divine order—a disenchantment that more or less puts the option for secularization on a par with the option for fundamentalism. When religion becomes an option, that is, a decision of personal faith and/or elective communal allegiance, it is no longer religion in its original sense (164). Gauchet's hypothesis would suggest, then, that the secularization thesis has not been in error full stop, but has been too shortsighted in its scope and too undialectical in its predictions of human response.[20] The new inventions and neo-affirmations of religious identity witnessed around the globe in the third millennium confirm that the secularist, even the nihilist "temptation," is alive and potent, provoking reactive response. It need not be the case that religious belief is destined to fade away—Gauchet doubts it ever will (4, 200)—but religious faiths *are* destined to bear a new burden of asserting themselves in the face of cultural forces—science, technocracy, rationalization, radical pluralism, skepticism, nihilism—that ignore, compromise, or threaten them, thus compelling them to persist, if they persist, deliberately, insistently, sometimes aggressively or militantly.

This mode of religious persistence is not a product of fate and social-structural inertia but of active election, of personal or communal decision—or what Peter L. Berger has termed the "heretical imperative."[21] Socioculturally one has ever within reach the intellectual possibility to question, change position, and at least "interiorly" opt into or out of a religious faith to varying degrees. Gauchet calls this the "to-ing and fro-ing" of our age's specific religiosity (205). While we are unable to subscribe wholeheartedly to any of these earlier belief systems, we occupy an unstable compromise between belonging and withdrawal. For in our "dreadful uncertainty," we "are uncomfortably experiencing as *problematic* what spiritual systems [in the distant past] had presented to us as *resolved*"; and "although we desire the soothing effects of a resolution, we are not entirely ready to renounce the freedom to question" (205).

From Gauchet's viewpoint, the original "enchantment" of religion is the deeper enigma of human history because it reflects a choice by *homo religiosus* to submit to an immutable order received *in toto* (11, 26, 29); in other words, it is a choice made not to quest searchingly toward an identity or destiny presently undefined, but through collective "self-negation" and "desubjectivation" (22, 26, 206) to embrace one qua *received* and *immutable*. It is not surprising, he thinks, that we humans have discovered our freedom to critique and reject sacerdotal traditions, question hierarchical religious-political institutions, and believe what our hearts and minds independently lead us to accept. What is surprising and mysterious—the "seminal mystery of the religious outlook"—is that religion once existed as an organized collective system for repressing and denying that freedom as systematically as possible (6, 25).

If there is validity to Gauchet's historical theory, a validity whose possibility we are entertaining here, it has the deepest implications for understanding religion as a system of alienation that has gradually been empowered by internal transformations to overcome itself—to bring itself to an end.[22] Religion began as a social system of radical self-dispossession, an aboriginal alienation through which *homo religiosus* bartered the terrors of freedom for the security of self-possession and fixed identity. To this negation of freedom, in turn, the axial transvaluation was an alienated reaction that increasingly mitigated this alienation of the human from itself—by putting the divine at bay. Transcendence embodied a meta-alienation that permitted liberation from the immanent, self-binding, self-dispossessing immutabilities of religion. Can it be that the death of God inaugurates the final axial moment, the apotheosis of negation, in the wake of which a more generative, less reactive and reactionary basis for human thinking and acting may potentially commence? Placed in this light, the depth of Altizer's question concerning the pathologies of our past resounds more profoundly: "Is nihilism itself only truly real within the horizon of a consciousness and a society that is deeply bound to the past, a past that has now truly ended, thereby issuing in a new world which is liberated from the deep pathologies of our past?"[23]

Nietzsche could assert that *fear* is "the original and basic feeling of man; from fear everything is explicable, original sin and original virtue."[24] Perhaps, though, an epochal maturation is afoot in human history that can challenge this aboriginal primacy of fear. Perhaps human beings, in the process of universalizing their consciousness not only to levels of the species and the biosphere but also more comprehensively to the diametric infinities of quantum physics and physical cosmology, are developing an unprecedented tolerance for an existence that is actual, not alienated; an identity that is not occult, not mythical or mystical but created in the immediate, local, real particularity of the actual world, where the most sacred challenges—challenges evaded or deflected by religion as we have known it—still await our attention. Might our supreme task be to redeem the holy of holies under our feet and everywhere within our reach?

In such a mood Zarathustra characterizes the post-axial return to earth of his soul—a soul that is "only a word for something about the body."[25]

> Like a ship that has sailed into its stillest cove—now it leans against the earth, tired of the long voyages and the uncertain seas. Is not the earth more fruitful? The way such a ship lies close to, nestles to the land—it is enough if a spider spins its thread to it from the land: no stronger ropes are needed now. Like such a tired ship in the stillest cove, I too rest now near the earth, faithful, trusting, waiting, tied to it with the softest of threads.[26]

Here is a "soul" no longer in bondage to immanent powers on earth, having experienced transcendental flight; but also a soul no longer "beating [its] wings against eternal walls," now delivered back to the earth in freedom.[27]

The great gain of axial faith has been its invention and potentiation of a de-hierarchizing universalism that brings freedom in multiple forms. That universalism has too often proved vacuous or abusive because it entailed a neglect, devaluation, condemnation, or destruction of particular existence. The third millennium calls its denizens to a universality achieved not—absolutely not—at the expense of particular existence but rather through recognition that actual existence of absolute particularity is the only universal. In their different ways Spinoza, Hegel, Kierkegaard, Nietzsche, Whitehead, the American pragmatists, Deleuze, and the contemporary D. G. Leahy have posited philosophies that inform this universalism of absolute particularity.[28] But as Mumford points out, philosophy works by a different process than religion, relying on "studious exercises and rationally validated customs, rather than on conversion and faith" (71). Whether a sea-change of global consciousness—an epochal *metanoia*—can occur without neo-religious prophets, gods, or charismatic teachers remains to be seen. After "religion," must we each become a saint or holy Word to prove worthy of sending the divine away? How will we proceed from where we are now—a world of radical divisions, demoralizing disparities, and massive powers of needless destruction—to the next age of absolutely inclusive particularity that is infinitely cherished as such?

The first creature in Genesis 1: 3 is Light. Transcendence is life itself, made possible by Light, its center everywhere, and everywhere absolutely particular.

Notes

1. Max Weber, "Science as a Vocation," in *From Max Weber: Essays in Sociology*, ed. and trans. H. H. Gerth and C. Wright Mills (New York: Oxford University Press, 1946), 139.

2. First published in France by Gallimard in 1985, an English translation appeared twelve years later: Marcel Gauchet, *The Disenchantment of the World: A Political History of Religion*, trans. Oscar Burge, with a foreword by Charles Taylor (Princeton: Princeton University Press, 1997). Though my heavy citation of page numbers in Gauchet's work may be an irritation, I do this because the argument is so groundbreaking, risky, and deserving of scholarly attention—and still little cited to date.

3. Zarathustra bears the Persian name for the sage Zoroaster, one of the earliest "axial" figures; see Friedrich Nietzsche, *Ecce Homo*, trans. Walter Kaufmann (New York: Random House, 1967), part 4, "Schicksal," sec. 3.

4. The heuristic notion of an "axial age" is introduced by Karl Jaspers in *The Origin and Goal of History*, trans. Michael Bulock (New Haven: Yale University Press, 1953) and developed further by Shmuel N. Eisenstadt. Eric Voegelin scrupulously reviews the dangers of the "axial" designation in *The Ecumenic Age*, volume 4 of his *Order and History* (Baton Rouge: Louisiana State University Press, 1974), 2–6, but does not outright reject the term when it is used fully critically as a heuristic (5).

5. Mircea Eliade, *The Myth of the Eternal Return: Or, Cosmos and History*, trans. Willard R. Trask (Princeton: Princeton University Press, 1954). It is extraordinarily puzzling that Eliade is not cited anywhere in Gauchet's work, as the former would seem to be the principal source for his understanding of religion as eternal return *ab illo tempore*.

6. Although Weber surprisingly never attempted to account for the axial transformation, according to Robert N. Bellah, he had an intimation that empire was important. Bellah cites an unexplored "throw-away line" in Weber's *Economy and Society*: "Perhaps prophecy in all its forms arose, especially in the Near East, in connection with the reconstitution of the great world empires in Asia, and the resumption and intensification of international commerce after a long interruption." Robert N. Bellah, "Max Weber and World-Denying Love: A Look at the Historical Sociology of Religion," *Journal of the American Academy of Religion* 67, 2 (June 1999): 277–304, quotation on 288 n. 16.

7. Lewis Mumford explores "Axial Man" in *The Transformations of Man* (New York: Harper & Row, 1956), chap. 4, quote on 74.

8. Benjamin Schwartz, "The Age of Transcendence," *Daedalus* 104, 2, Wisdom, Revelation, and Doubt: Perspectives on the First Millennium BC (Spring 1975): 3, 5.

9. Jan Assmann, *Moses the Egyptian: The Memory of Egypt in Western Monotheism* (Cambridge: Harvard University Press, 1997), 7.

10. Adam B. Seligman, in his review of Gauchet, points out one of the book's most serious shortcomings: that "the analytic boundaries between what is unique to Christianity and what was expressed in all Axial religions is blurred," with the consequence that "general components of the Axial revolution are presented as specifically Christian while specifically Christian innovations are presented as concomitant with the very idea of transcendence" (961). In independent book reviews both Seligman and Martin Riesebrodt express surprise that Gauchet does not cite or engage the work of Eric Voegelin, who was dedicated to analyzing Western religious-political structures in their relation to perceptions of historical temporality, an undertaking profoundly parallel to Gauchet's. See Adam B. Seligman, *The American Political Science Review* 92, 4 (December 1998): 960–961; Martin Riesebrodt, *The American Journal of Sociology* 104, 5 (March 1999): 1525–1526. Voegelin deconstructs the "unilinear construction of history" (*historiogenesis*) that Gauchet rather uncritically practices, seeing it as a symbolic form developed by the end of the third millennium BC in the empires of the ancient Near East (Voegelin, *The Ecumenic Age* [Baton Rouge: Louisiana State University Press, 1974], 7); in other words, this occurred during the very period of State domination and expansion that Gauchet identifies as the watershed of human history (cf. 10, 34–37).

11. This claim that processes of reasoning in the West have been structured from the viewpoint of God is given powerful support, in different ways, by Amos Funkenstein, *Theology and the Scientific Imagination from the Middle Ages to the Seventeenth Century* (Princeton: Princeton University Press, 1986), and Rémi Brague, *The Law of God: The Philosophical History of an Idea* (Chicago: University of Chicago Press, 2008).

12. Nietzsche, *The Anti-Christ*, in *Twilight of the Idols* and *The Anti-Christ*, trans. R. J. Hollingdale (New York: Penguin, 1968), 140.

13. Cf. Gauchet, 61. It is surely no accident that Gauchet is French; see his fascinating analysis of the intrinsic metaphysical superfluity of the Roman Catholic Church (132–142), the "first bureaucracy to give history meaning, the first administration of ultimate meaning," yet whose claims to mediation were to prove an "absurd hoax" and whose "existence signified the breakdown of any possible organic connection between administering the world and concern with heaven" (133, 137).

14. Thomas J. J. Altizer, *Godhead and the Nothing* (Albany: State University of New York Press, 2003), x.

15. Gauchet insists, "The real question is not that of being, but that of the internal constraints forcing us to present the question in this way." So the deeper question for the post-religious mind is not, Why is there something rather than nothing? but rather, "Why is there this structural division presenting all reality in two antagonistic aspects?" (202). Useful for drawing forth the profound

historical-theological background here is Emilie Zum Brunn, *St. Augustine: Being and Nothingness*, trans. Ruth Namad (New York: Paragon House, 1988).

16. Later Altizer remarks: "This is the context in which we can most deeply know ours as a truly theological age, one that for the first time calls forth a truly and fully negative theology, and an absolutely negative theology, and one that is most clearly so in ultimately embodying an absolute abyss" (135).

17. Excerpt from "The Snow Man," in *Wallace Stevens: Collected Poetry and Prose*, ed. Frank Kermode and Joan Richardson (New York: Library of America, 1997), 8.

18. Friedrich Nietzsche, *Thus Spoke Zarathustra: A Book for All and None*, trans. Walter Kaufmann (New York: Penguin, 1954), "The Drunken Song," sec. 10, 323.

19. Benjamin Schwartz reminds us that the axial turn away from the world need not imply a full-blown world negation but simply a diverting emphasis on the transcendent or the inward. Schwartz, "Age of Transcendence," 2, 3.

20. Here I employ the term secularization with due caution, recognizing, with Mark Cauchi, that "there is nothing purely and simply religious or purely and simply secular" and that "all acts of secularization are structurally incomplete or structurally deferred, which . . . is precisely the possibility of ongoing secularization." Mark Cauchi, "The Secular to Come: Interrogating the Derridean 'Secular,'" *Journal for Cultural and Religious Theory* 10, 1 (Winter 2009): 1–25, quotes on 11, 12. Certainly one of Gauchet's core theses is that Western secularization is a process specially preconditioned and enabled by—therefore inside the fold of—the structural dynamics of Western religion (61).

21. Peter L. Berger, *The Heretical Imperative: Contemporary Possibilities of Religious Affirmation* (Garden City, NY: Anchor, 1979).

22. Here Gauchet is careful to qualify what he means by the end of religion: "Even if we assume that the age of religions has been definitively closed, we should not doubt that, between private religious practices and substitutes for religious experience, we will probably never completely finish with the religious" (200; see also 163).

23. Thomas J. J. Altizer, "The Challenge of Nihilism," *Journal of the American Academy of Religion* 62, 4 (Winter 1994): 1013–1022, quotation on 1017.

24. Nietzsche, *Zarathustra*, 302 ("On Science").

25. Ibid., 34 ("On the Despisers of the Body").

26. Ibid., 277 ("At Noon").

27. Ibid., 76 ("On the Gift-Giving Virtue," sec. 2).

28. For the latter, see D. G. Leahy, *Novitas Mundi* and *Foundation: Matter the Body Itself*, published by the State University of New York Press in 1994 and 1996, respectively.

Afterword

Thomas J. J. Altizer

While this volume is an extraordinarily diverse theological work, it is nonetheless genuinely theological, even if it inevitably poses the question of just what is theology, and what could theology be in our time? Remarkably enough, here the very centering upon the death of God truly opens up theology, making possible new theological investigations and truly challenging theological questions, and if the purest theology is a deep and ultimate questioning, perhaps that most decisively occurs in thinking the death of God. Certainly the deepest modern philosophical theology is the thinking of the death of God, and if this occurs in radically divergent expressions, as in Hegel and Nietzsche, each of these realizes a philosophical revolution, and a philosophical revolution creating new worlds. Not until the full advent of modernity does an actual thinking of the death of God occur, nor until then do imaginative enactments of the death of God fully occur, and both conceptually and imaginatively these enactments are truly positive and truly negative at once, each brings a final end to its original ground, and yet even thereby each realizes the absolutely new. For there is a profound dichotomy at the very center of the enactment of the death of God, a dichotomy between an absolute No and an absolute Yes, or an absolute negation and an absolute affirmation, and each is wholly unreal apart from the other.

Thus a genuine enactment of the death of God is inevitably a dialectical movement, and just as the philosophical enactment of the death of God has given us our most profoundly dialectical thinking, the imaginative enactment of the death of God is purely dialectical, too, and the deeper the imaginative enactment the purer its dialectical ground and movement. Indeed, it is the uniquely modern realization of the death of God that has given us our most profoundly dialectical movements, movements that have exploded in late modernity with an ultimate and devastating power, wholly transforming everything in their wake. Yes, late modernity is the age of the death of God and also the age in which a birth occurs of the absolutely new, and an absolutely new only made possible by the death of God. The dawning of classical Greece was an age of the absolutely new, just as was the advent of the depths of the Renaissance, and each was only made possible by an absolute negation of its given and established ground, an absolute negation essential and necessary to the birth of the absolutely new.

Only in the prophetic revolution of Israel does an absolute negation occur in the ancient world, a negation that is truly renewed in the advent of Christianity, a Christianity effecting an absolute negation of an old aeon or old creation, and only that negation realizes apocalypse. Now apocalyptic fantasy or apocalyptic illusion can exist only apart from an absolute negation, a negation realizing actuality itself or realizing the world as a fully actual world. So far from being a fantasy world, a genuine apocalypse is actuality itself, and if apocalypticism was born in the later expressions of the prophetic revolution, these became a revolutionary power in the Hellenistic world, and all of the great historical revolutions are apocalyptic revolutions. The English, French, Russian, and Chinese revolutions are all enactments of apocalypse, and this is true even of the scientific revolution of the seventeenth century, which created an absolutely new world only by bringing an old world to an end. Thus despite all sectarian expressions of apocalypticism, genuine or full expressions of apocalypticism are the very opposite of fantasy and illusion and are more overwhelmingly real than anything else that we can imagine.

It is in genuine apocalypticism that the power of an absolute negation is fully manifest, and if an absolute negation is enacted in every actual enactment of the death of God, that enactment can illuminate absolute negation itself, a negation that thereby can be understood as self-negation and as the self-negation of Godhead itself. Now even if such understanding is purely Hegelian, Hegel himself resisted this language, as do virtually all Hegelians, and although the Crucifixion can be understood as the self-negation of God, this language too is resisted by virtually everyone. Apparently an openly theological language of an absolute self-negation is deeply if not absolutely offensive, but as Kierkegaard so profoundly realized, it is faith itself that is absolutely offensive, and the paucity of faith is the absence of offense. Is it in faith itself that we know the self-negation of God and know it in knowing the Crucifixion, a crucifixion that is an absolute self-negation and an absolute self-negation of Godhead itself?

The Crucified God is that primal name of God evoking the self-negation of God, but this name is not spoken or realized until the advent of modernity, then decisively occurring in the Lutheran Reformation, and Hegel could know Luther as the original enactor of an absolute freedom. Indeed, Hegel knows absolute freedom as a consequence of the Crucifixion and thus as a consequence of the death of God, a self-negation or self-emptying of God realizing the most ultimate grace. However, Luther's one full treatise, *The Bondage of the Will*, is a violent assault upon freedom in the name of an absolute predestination, a predestination apart from which all and everyone would be eternally damned, and a predestination realizing a justification in the Crucifixion that is an absolutely free grace and the sole source of an absolute freedom. This is the free gift of the Crucified God, but it perishes when we attempt to realize it as our own, a perishing of freedom that is the consequence of an evasion or refusal of the Crucified God.

There are two discordant poles of the Reformation in Lutheranism and Calvinism, and dogmatically they only share an ultimate faith in an absolute predestination, and while this is a Catholic doctrine created by Augustine and sustained by Aquinas, after Augustine and apart from the Nominalists it is never central in Catholicism, whereas it is primal in classical Protestantism, and as Weber discovered, it is a Calvinistic predestination that gives birth to Capitalism and an absolutely new pragmatic praxis. As opposed to a Lutheran iconography in which the Crucifixion is primal, Calvinism is deeply iconoclastic, just as the Calvinistic God defies all imagery, until Melville gave us *Moby-Dick*. Moby-Dick is that absolutely alien God who is a consequence of the death of God, or the Calvinistic God when grace is no longer actual or real; this had always been a possibility for the purely Calvinistic God, whose absolute sovereignty is inseparable from an absolutely free grace. But Moby-Dick does usher in that world that has now so fully become our own, a world certainly embodying the death of God, yet with the advent of postmodernity theological thinking or perhaps genuine thinking itself has come to an end, and despite the proliferation of religion, theological expressions of religion have simply become impossible, and religious depth or subtlety has disappeared.

Thus the death of God has released a vast number of worlds, but overwhelmingly at hand is a truly new emptiness, a new vacuity so empty as to be free of all signs, an absolutely new anonymity now becoming all in all. Many can rejoice in this anonymity as a new freedom, a new peace dissolving all *Angst*, and even a new joy that can be celebrated in our megachurches; and serious political dissent has seemingly come to an end with the ending of all ultimate conflict. Can a world of such tranquility be a consequence of the death of God? Is absolute negation inseparable from God so that the death of God brings all such negation to an end? Is a Luther or a Calvin no longer possible in our world, to say nothing of an Augustine or an Aquinas? Such questions are now becoming inescapable, but does that demand a rebirth or renewal of theology? Is it even possible that the death of God itself could make possible a renewal of theology? The truth is that the death of God impelled both Hegel and Nietzsche into profound and revolutionary theological thinking, just as it impelled Blake into the most revolutionary of all imaginative visions and gave us in Kafka and Beckett irresistible enactments in which the deepest darkness is apocalypse itself.

Perhaps the death of God has ended the impossibility of theology, so that as a consequence of the death of God it is impossible not to think theologically and impossible not to exercise a theological imagination. True, our professional or open theology has seemingly ended, but theology has returned to our philosophical world, and our fiction and drama is apparently more theological than ever before, which could well be a result of the death of God. Already Kierkegaard could understand his world as a post-Christian world and know all modern philosophy as an atheistic philosophy, but Kierkegaard became our greatest modern religious thinker and perhaps the most revolutionary of all theological thinkers. Is it just the most radical profane that induces the purest call to the radical sacred, a radical sacred wholly unmanifest apart from the radical profane. And what could be more radically profane than a realization of the death of God? But as we know all too well, such realization is sacred and profane simultaneously, and its most profane expressions are inseparable from its sacred expressions.

It may well be Hegel himself who most decisively makes manifest this truly dialectical condition, a Hegel whom many if not most of our theologians know as our most atheistic thinker, and yet a Hegel who alone among thinkers has fully incorporated into his purest thinking each of our primal theological categories, and above all so, the crucifixion and the resurrection. Not until Hegel does a pure thinking of the crucifixion occur, and that realization of the death of God revolutionized philosophy, even making possible a Kierkegaard and a Marx. Despite many of Hegel's own remarks, and even judgments, philosophy and theology are deeply united in his purer thinking, as most decisively manifest in the penultimate section of the *Phenomenology*, and although this is the point at which he most deeply thinks the death of God, it is also the point at which he most deeply thinks the resurrection. Indeed, in this thinking crucifixion and resurrection are one event, and it was not until the twentieth century that New Testament scholarship could recognize that crucifixion and resurrection are one event in Paul and the Fourth Gospel.

Now if the death of God is the resurrection of God, a deeply Hegelian motif, it is deeply paralleled in Nietzsche's finally knowing the death of God as Eternal Recurrence, an Eternal Recurrence that is Nietzsche's enactment of the resurrection, and an Eternal Recurrence that is the very opposite of a pagan eternal return. Both Nietzsche and Hegel are profoundly theological thinkers, and revolutionary theological thinkers, each of whom turned the world of theology upside down. And the death of God can be understood as the center of the theological thinking of each, their most original and radical thinking was given to realizing that death, and that is precisely the movement that must be renewed in any genuine theological thinking today.

Contributors

THOMAS J. J. ALTIZER is Emeritus Professor of Religious Studies at the State University of New York at Stony Brook. He is the author of nearly twenty books, including *The New Gospel of Christian Atheism* and more recently *Revisiting Radical Theology*.

JOHN B. COBB JR. is Emeritus Professor of Religion at the Claremont Graduate University, emeritus holder of the Ingraham Chair of Theology at the Claremont School of Theology, and the emeritus holder of the Avery Chair in Religion at the Claremont Graduate University. He is the founder of the Center for Process Studies and the author or editor of many books in process theology, ecological theology, and economics and theology.

CLAYTON CROCKETT is Associate Professor and Director of Religious Studies at the University of Central Arkansas. He is a coeditor of the book series Insurrections: Critical Studies in Religion, Politics and Culture for Columbia University Press. His most recent works are *Deleuze Beyond Badiou: Ontology, Multiplicity, and Event* and *Religion, Politics, and the Earth: The New Materialism* (with Jeffrey W. Robbins).

ANDREW W. HASS is Lecturer in Religion at the University of Stirling (United Kingdom). He is the General Executive Editor of *Literature and Theology: An International Journal of Religion, Theory, and Culture* and the author of *The Poetics of Critique: The Interdisciplinarity of Textuality*.

LISSA MCCULLOUGH is the editor of many important texts in radical theology, including *Thinking through the Death of God* (with Brian Schroeder) and, most recently, *The Call to Radical Theology*, by Thomas J. J. Altizer. She is an independent scholar, living in Los Angeles, California.

DANIEL J. PETERSON teaches humanities for Matteo Ricci College at Seattle University. He is the author of *Tillich: A Brief Overview of the Life and Writings of Paul Tillich* and an ordained minister in the Evangelical Lutheran Church in America.

SARAH K. PINNOCK is Associate Professor of contemporary religious thought at Trinity University (San Antonio, TX). She is the author of *Beyond Theodicy: Jewish and Christian Continental Reponses to the Holocaust* and the editor of *The Theology of Dorothee Soelle*.

JEFFREY W. ROBBINS is Professor of Religion, Chair of the Department of Religion and Philosophy, and Director of American Studies at Lebanon Valley College (Annville, PA). He is the coeditor of the Columbia University Press book series Insurrections: Critical Studies in Religion, Politics, and Culture and the author of several books, most recently *Radical Democracy and Political Theology* and *Religion, Politics and the Earth: The New Materialism* (with Clayton Crockett).

CHRISTOPHER DEMUTH RODKEY teaches at Lancaster Theological Seminary and Lebanon Valley College. He is the pastor of St. Paul's United Church of Christ in Dallastown, Pennsylvania, and is the author of *The Synaptic Gospel*.

JOHN K. ROTH is the Edward J. Sexton Professor Emeritus of Philosophy at Claremont McKenna College and the founding director of The Center for the Study of the Holocaust, Genocide, and Human Rights at Claremont McKenna College. He is the author or editor of more than forty books, including *Genocide and Human Rights: A Philosophical Guide*, *Gray Zones: Ambiguity and Compromise in the Holocaust and Its Aftermath*, and *Ethics During and After the Holocaust: In the Shadow of Birkenau*.

ROSEMARY RADFORD RUETHER is the Carpenter Emerita Professor of Feminist Theology at Pacific School of Religion and the Graduate Theological Union, as well as the Georgia Harkness Emerita Professor of Applied Theology at Garrett Evangelical Theological Seminary and currently Visiting Professor of Religion at the Claremont Graduate University and the Claremont School of Theology. She is the author of more than thirty books and over six hundred articles on various topics in religion, history, and theology.

G. MICHAEL ZBARASCHUK is Visiting Assistant Professor of Religion at Pacific Lutheran University and Lecturer in Interdisciplinary Arts and Sciences at the University of Washington Tacoma. He is the author of *The Purposes of God: Providence as Process-Historical Liberation* and is one of the editors of the book series Radical Theologies from Palgrave Macmillan.

Index

Printed in Great Britain
by Amazon